Machine Learning Approaches for Convergence of IoT and Blockchain

Scrivener Publishing
100 Cummings Center, Suite 541J
Beverly, MA 01915-6106

Publishers at Scrivener
Martin Scrivener (martin@scrivenerpublishing.com)
Phillip Carmical (pcarmical@scrivenerpublishing.com)

Machine Learning Approaches for Convergence of IoT and Blockchain

Edited by

Krishna Kant Singh

*Faculty of Engineering & Technology, Jain (Deemed-to-be University),
Bengaluru, India*

Akansha Singh

Amity University Uttar Pradesh, Noida, India

and

Sanjay Sharma

KIET Group of Institutions, Delhi-NCR, Ghaziabad, India

Scrivener
Publishing

This edition first published 2021 by John Wiley & Sons, Inc., 111 River Street, Hoboken, NJ 07030, USA and Scrivener Publishing LLC, 100 Cummings Center, Suite 541J, Beverly, MA 01915, USA
© 2021 Scrivener Publishing LLC
For more information about Scrivener publications please visit www.scrivenerpublishing.com.

Wiley Global Headquarters
111 River Street, Hoboken, NJ 07030, USA

For details of our global editorial offices, customer services, and more information about Wiley products visit us at www.wiley.com.

Limit of Liability/Disclaimer of Warranty
While the publisher and authors have used their best efforts in preparing this work, they make no representations or warranties with respect to the accuracy or completeness of the contents of this work and specifically disclaim all warranties, including without limitation any implied warranties of merchantability or fitness for a particular purpose. No warranty may be created or extended by sales representatives, written sales materials, or promotional statements for this work. The fact that an organization, website, or product is referred to in this work as a citation and/or potential source of further information does not mean that the publisher and authors endorse the information or services the organization, website, or product may provide or recommendations it may make. This work is sold with the understanding that the publisher is not engaged in rendering professional services. The advice and strategies contained herein may not be suitable for your situation. You should consult with a specialist where appropriate. Neither the publisher nor authors shall be liable for any loss of profit or any other commercial damages, including but not limited to special, incidental, consequential, or other damages. Further, readers should be aware that websites listed in this work may have changed or disappeared between when this work was written and when it is read.

Library of Congress Cataloging-in-Publication Data

ISBN 978-1-119-76174-7

Cover image: Pixabay.Com
Cover design Russell Richardson

Contents

Preface

Blockchain technology and the Internet of Things (IoT) are two of the most impactful trends to have emerged in the field of machine learning. And although there are a number of books available solely on the subjects of machine learning, IoT and blockchain technology, no such book has been available which focuses on machine learning techniques for IoT and blockchain convergence until now. Thus, this book is unique in terms of the topics it covers. Designed as an essential guide for all academicians, researchers and those in industry who are working in related fields, this book will provide insights into the convergence of blockchain technology and the IoT with machine learning.

A rapidly advancing fourth industrial revolution, brought about by a digital revolution characterized by the convergence of technologies, is blurring the lines between physical, digital and biological objects. The speed of the fourth revolution, which is evolving at an exponential rate, certainly cannot be compared with that of any previous technologies. Some of these technologies include the artificial intelligence (AI) and IoT currently being used in interactions and operations in various fields such as home appliances, autonomous vehicles, nanotechnology, robotics, cognitive systems and wearable devices; and nowadays the potential of blockchain technology is also being realized in many sectors as well, since security is a crucial factor everywhere.

Readers in many domains will be interested in this book as it covers two major areas of the field of machine learning—blockchain technology and the IoT. Also, it will be appealing for those who want to further their research in this area, as the latest topics are covered. Therefore, the target audience of this book is composed of professionals and researchers working in the field of machine learning with IoT and blockchain technology. Moreover, the book will provide insights and support from practitioners and academia in order to highlight the most debated aspects in the field. A detailed description of each topic relevant to machine learning technologies is presented along with the concepts involved in their convergence.

In addition, research problems are included to facilitate further research based on the concepts described in the book.

First and foremost, we express heartfelt appreciation to all contributing authors for their hard work and patience. I would like to thank them for contributing chapters in this book. Thanks to the Scrivener Publishing team who helped us so much. Special thanks to Martin Scrivener for all his support, suggestions, and patience.

The Editors
June 2021

Blockchain and Internet of Things Across Industries

Ananya Rakhra*, Raghav Gupta and Akansha Singh

Department of CSE, ASET, Amity University, Noida, Uttar Pradesh, India

Abstract

In this chapter, we will come across different kinds of industries and how Internet of Things and blockchain technologies are applied to them. We commence with an overview about what an industry is and the nature of various industries, followed by knowledge about the technologies of IoT and blockchain. These technologies have facilitated advancement and ease in one's day-to-day life, the industrial sector being one among many where its impact is prevalent notably. Further, incorporation of these technologies across various sectors of industry and their scope has been focused upon. The advancements brought about, especially in fields such as that of healthcare sector, have revolutionized the previously existing methods, helping us attain better care and improved life expectancy. Also, the scope of these technologies beyond the industrial sector has been discussed. These technologies have facilitated specialization, so much so that its positive imprint can clearly be seen onto the nation's economy. This text on the whole allows the readers to attain a clear understanding and also unveils the great scope for further research and development offered by this sphere.

Keywords: IoT, Internet of Things, blockchain, technology, industry, smart devices

1.1 Introduction

Through the course of this chapter, we will come across various types of industries and how implementing IoT and blockchain through these industries

---

Corresponding author: ananyarakhra@gmail.com

Krishna Kant Singh, Akansha Singh and Sanjay Sharma (eds.) Machine Learning Approaches for Convergence of IoT and Blockchain, (1–34) © 2021 Scrivener Publishing LLC

will help facilitate the achievement of enormous endeavors beyond the scope one could think of a few years ago. These technologies have widened prospective and enhanced scope across varied fields; we will attempt to obtain an in-depth understanding of the same. Industries form the backbone of a country's economy. Any organization that is involved in large-scale production or providing services to a lot of customers is categorized as an industry. According to the purpose of the industry, they are classified as the primary, secondary, and tertiary sectors. Classification based on the organisational framework of an industry is done as organized and unorganized sectors of industry. Categorization may also be done according to the ownership of the firm as either public or private sector industry. Each industry has varying demands and requirements based on the nature of production or service that they intend to provide. We will explore this phenomenon through the domains of various industries, for example, the agriculture industry, manufacturing industry, food production units, healthcare, military, it sector, and banking. We will see what the goals and functions of these industries are and how the efficiency and output can be highly improved, along with reducing human effort and also increasing accuracy. Then, we will move on to learn about the blockchain technology, its mechanism, requirements, advantages, and disadvantages. Blockchain technology is basically the practice of storing data into blocks that are connected to each other in the form of a chain. The distinctive feature of this technology is that once the data is entered into this chain it is immutable, which provides a very strong system to prevent any sort of tampering with the stored data, hence ensuring high level security. The chains are also encrypted and decentralized which further enhance its security. Next, we will look into what IoT is, how it works, and how it is beneficial to us. IoT is the acronym for Internet of Things, wherein we basically connect the physical devices to each other over a network enabling them to communicate and share information among each other. Here, devices are able to gain knowledge about their surroundings with the help of sensors. Common examples of IoT that have been incorporated in daily life are smart watches, smart lighting for households, surveillance cameras, etc. After understanding the functioning and applications of these, we will further see their combined applications of these two technologies in the industry. Incorporating these technologies in the industry opens up a very broad perspective to achieve new levels of specialization. Human tasks have been eased and accuracy and precision has spiked because of these. Profits made by companies have also seen increment; hence, it has proved beneficial to industries in a lot many ways. Further through the course of this chapter, after looking into the non-industrial applications of these technologies in depth, exploring various domains of implementation we will next see the applications and scope of these technologies beyond industries as well. In particular, we will be looking into how they have helped enhance life in different possible ways. First, we will get to know what smart homes are and study the involvement of these technologies in its creation and implementation. This advancement has brought about a lot of ease and pace into one's day-to-day household tasks and also evolved one's lifestyle. Then, we will read about how security via surveillance has been technologically boosted with the coming of IoT and blockchain into this sphere. The ways of monitoring have been specialized and the security of the data thus obtained is also highly increased due the usage of blockchain. Life and property are now being better guarded with the help of these. Smart solutions such as automated street lighting have also come up which contribute toward saving energy and resources, and incorporation of security mechanisms such as surveillance along with the street lights making the equipment multi-purpose and more useful. Let us begin with introducing what an industry is and how it functions.

1.2   Insight About Industry

In today's time, the types and scope of industries are massive. Industries have met with a lot of varied applications and requirements and are serving to facilitate the same. These industries provide to serve needs of mankind, ranging from the most basic necessities to comfort and exotic offerings. Industry can be referred to as any large-scale productive activity. It is these industries that strengthen a nation's economy, fulfils its needs, and provide safety, security, etc. Most spheres around us are industries in themselves. Some sectors of industry are depicted in Figure 1.1. The main features of any industry are large-scale production, specialization, research and development, mechanization, standardization, and management. We will now look into types or classification of industries and get to know about each one of them individually [1]. Industries can broadly be classified into the sectors: primary, secondary, and tertiary. The primary sector comprises of industries that are mainly involved in the extraction of raw materials, for examples, industries extracting metals from their ore, mining, and farming.

The secondary sector is where industries perform manufacturing and packaging of goods and commodities, examples of this sector of industries include food processing industries, car part manufacturing, and other such industries. The tertiary sector is also known as the service sector; industries such as IT, defence services, judicial workforce, banking, and teaching come under this category. Other bases of classification are either as organized and unorganized sector industry or as public sector or private sector industry.

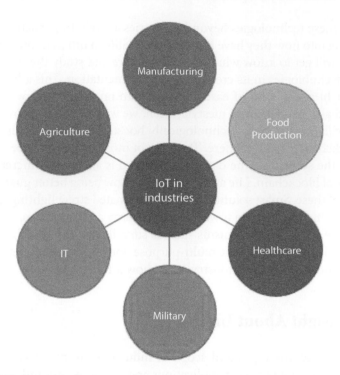

Figure 1.1 Industries in focus.

Organized industry sector is such that all its employees are assured work throughout their employment and there terms for the same are fixed and regular. In contrast, the unorganized sector provides flexible employment at the discretion of the employer and there exist no regularity or guarantee of the employment term, also such institutions may not necessarily be registered with the government. Public sector industries are those which are owned, funded, and managed by the government and like most other government jobs provide benefits to its workers such as pension. Private sector industries are owned by individual or partnerships between individuals.

The main motive of the individual running the company is to earn profit and these are not state controlled. The terms of employment may vary from company to company based on the interests of the owner. In India, most of the private sector industries are known to be paying higher salaries to its employees as compared to government industries but government jobs are seen to offer more job security benefits while under employment and even after it. All these are interdependent, we may say that primary sector industries are responsible for production of raw materials, the secondary sector process these raw materials to transform them into useful goods, and the tertiary sector utilizes and makes these products available to the consumers. Let us now focus on some industries and understand their requirements and production mechanisms.

In this part, we will be discussing about all the various industries, their functioning, and the importance that they hold. Let us understand the working of a few industries.

1.2.1   Agriculture Industry

This is one of the most important sectors as it caters to resolve the hunger of the country's entire population. This industry is the source of livelihood to about 58% of India's population. Most of the agricultural plots happen to be in the rural areas where development is far behind that in the bigger towns and cities. In India, particularly, agriculture is very widely practiced and it serves as the source of income to a considerably large section of India's working population, both men and women. Especially the residents of suburbs, villages and small towns have taken to agriculture as their means of employment and livelihood. Industrial agriculture is the practice of monoculture of a particular crop to be sold commercially, i.e., not only for the purpose of one's own usage. Cultivation of any crop requires resources such as land, soil, water, and fertilizers along with knowledge, dedicated, constant attention, and care. It is one sphere that requires physically intensive efforts especially if there is an absence of machinery. In earlier times, when technology was not what we know it as today, agriculture was practiced with the help of animals to facilitate various tasks. In present times, with the ever increasing size of the population the demand for food crops is also going up, the scope of agricultural produce is local, national as well as international as there is a massive trade prevalent between various countries over the exchange of these commodities, which, in turn, adds to the economy of the country. The crop needs constant care and treatment from the time the seeds are sown up until its harvest. The produce from this industry serves as raw material for certain other industries therefore the need to ensure good product quality is further heightened as it will directly impact the other sectors as well. Incorporation of advanced technologies has benefitted this sector extensively, which we shall look into later in the course of this chapter.

1.2.2   Manufacturing Industry

Manufacturing industry is a broad term used to refer to any industry that is involved in the task of production of any particular commodity. Considering the example of a car manufacturing company, there exist various stages of manufacturing and assembling different components. Precision remains a key necessity to ensure proper product quality as even if a single part deviates from its correct dimensions, the end result would be faulty leading to wastage of resources, money, and time. The other key requirement is to ensure maximum utilization of available machinery to increase production and thus profit. The quality of a raw material chosen also plays a major role in determining the finished product and hence needs to be kept under check. Keeping track of quantities of each part that is produced and sent down the assembly line is a cumbersome yet essential task. Record of date of production and assembly of parts need be kept as in case a fault in equipment is seen later, it will be necessary to trace down the articles that went through it as there may be risk of faulty products having been produced. Also, to provide good after sales care to the users and to ensure timely renewal or maintenance is carried out as per requirement. Lastly, demand of any particular product should be kept under consideration so as to increase or decrease the quantity to maintain the demand supply chain.

1.2.3   Food Production Industry

The major difficulty for this industry is the perishable nature of food items. Storage and processing need to be carried out at suitable temperature so as to keep the commodity intact. The accuracy of the date of manufacture and date of expiry that are mentioned on the packaging needs to be maintained. Like any other manufacturing, a proper record needs to be maintained as to which product is processed with which equipment and at what time so that in case a fault is found in any equipment, the products requiring a review can be tracked. Since food items are meant for consumption by the customers, certain standards pertaining to the quality and handling of these commodities need to be kept under consideration. It is also recommended that a complete record of where the raw material was obtained from, how was has been transported, processed, packed, and delivered should be kept and should also be made available to any customer who may want to know the same. The ingredients must also be mentioned correctly as a considerable chunk of population beholds allergies; therefore, the correct composition of the product should be mentioned. Another key factor is to maintain hygienic conditions at all levels of handling food stuff, any contamination to edible products may make the consumer ill, which would, in turn, invoke legal response against the manufacturing unit depending upon the severity of harm caused. This industry also needs to keep a close watch at the demand and supply chain because of the perishable nature; some items may not have a very long shelf life.

1.2.4 Healthcare Industry

This industry has become one of India's biggest sectors in term of both economy as well as employment. It is also a primary determinant factor for the GDP of a country. This is one such critical industry that encompasses great responsibility and attention. Even the minute details sometimes end up putting a patient's life at stake. Specialization and accuracy form its foundation. In any condition ranging from minor discomfort, fever to emergencies such as a fracture or heart attack are all taken care of by this sector. The composition of the services it provides covers prevention, diagnosis, treatment, and medical rehabilitation. Herein, it is essential to keep accurate and updated records of the available drugs as in case a patient requires its administration it must be available and should be well within its shelf life. Hospitals need to maintain proper records of the patient who have been treated and store case history along with the treatment provided to any individual. For patients suffering from a chronic disease, case history must be available in case the patient is brought in emergency. This industry also performs surgeries and transplants in keeping with procedures to cure or lengthen the life span of the patients. In this process, certain highly specialized surgeries are sometimes conducted which require sophisticated equipment and knowledge.

1.2.5 Military

This industry comes under the tertiary sector as it is a form a service to a nation and its citizens. The Indian Armed Force is under the Government of India and is managed by the Ministry of Defence (MoD). India possesses the world's second largest military after China. The military service in India serves in three three wings each for a different landform. The three arms are the Army, the Air Force, and the Navy. The Army is the ground force that battles any threat that prevails in their country on land. The Air force is the unit that takes charge of all the aerial operations and security. The naval force maintains the safety of the waters that come under the jurisdiction of the country. All these forces have officers that are allotted various ranks and positions according to their specialization; the highest rank is that of the chief who also holds the responsibility of making all the crucial decisions. Each officer has to qualify for the National Defence Academy (NDA) where they undergo rigorous training and are toughened to withstand extreme conditions. This indeed is one of the most disciplined industries of all. This industry's peculiar feature is the intelligence service, who serves to keep a close watch on the activities in and around the country, they also keep a close watch on the happenings of their rival countries to ensure that if there happens to be any threat to their country, they're sufficiently prepared to counteract. India has the world's third largest defence budget which enables it to equip itself with aircrafts and other machinery that are par above other countries.

1.2.6   IT Industry

IT industry stands for Information and technology industry [2]. IT sector has been majorly responsible for transforming India into a global economy since we have received multiple outsourced and mediated technology-based work contracts. These are the companies that provide us with computing solutions as well as other hardware and software applications such as Intel, Hcl, and Apple. Utilization of computers for storage, transmission, manipulation and retrieval of data or information is the basis of this type of industry. This sector has gained advancement and has enlarged considerably in our country over the last few years, generating employment for a huge chunk of the population and also contributing to the country's overall economy. The major IT hubs in India are Bangalore, Chennai, Noida, and Hyderabad. The initial wave of the IT industry that we see today was first established when the government set up the Software Technology Parks of India (STPI) in the early 90s. Let us consider a day-to-day life scenario as an example to understand the services and features of the IT industry. So, consider that a person is facing trouble with the signal strength on his mobile device. He will convey his problem to the customer care service that the network company offers. They will then work toward tracing the cause of inconvenience, if it is a faulty sim card or a trouble with the signal tower of that area and then work for providing a solution at the earliest possible. Network provider is one type of industry that comes under the IT sector; many such companies exist under this sector functioning under the umbrella of information and technology.

1.3   What is Blockchain?

In layman's language we may understand it as a chain of blocks containing information as illustrated in Figure 1.2. The original purpose of blockchain was to time stamp documents however it did not find much application [3]. The blockchain majorly picked up popularity when it was adapted to create a digital cryptocurrency—Bitcoin, by Satoshi Nakamoto in 2009. The most prominent feature of blockchain is that once any information is entered, it

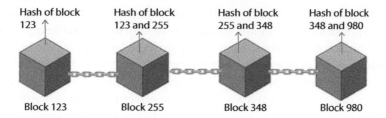

Figure 1.2 Illustration of blockchain technology.

is nearly impossible to edit or delete it. Each block in a blockchain has three components associated to it, which are data, hash, and hash of the previous block. The data of a block contains information relevant to the purpose which the chain is utilized for. The next component, i.e., hash is like the finger print of the block and is thus unique to every block. The hash of a block is calculated after the data in entered. Therefore, if the content of any block is tampered with, it, in turn, changes the hash, and hence, it is no longer the same block, and this feature particularly allows us to ensure that any information once entered in a blockchain cannot be modified or deleted. The third component of a block is the hash of the previous block. Each block contains the hash of the previous block which enables the chain formation. If any block in this chain is modified, its hash changes, hence breaking the linkage through the entire length of the chain, disrupting the entire chain formation. This is how the safety and integrity of any blockchain is ensured. The first block of a blockchain is referred to as genesis block.

Let us now understand how blockchain ensures a high level of security. Firstly, since each block contains the hash of the previous block, it is not possible to modify the content of any block without disrupting the chain henceforth. Secondly, this technology follows a practice called proof of work. Hashes are insufficient to ensure protection because computers these days are fast enough to recalculate all the hashes of the blocks within seconds; this is where proof of work comes into the picture. Through this method, we considerably increase the time required to calculate the hash of a single block. These two features when put together enhance the security mechanism. Thirdly, the entire blockchain in available to all its users; in other words, we may say that a blockchain is distributed. This peer-to-peer network enables all members to receive any new block that is formed; it is then verified by each node and is given consensus, only then it is incorporated into the chain. So, in case a block comes up that is tampered with it will be rejected be the other nodes [4]. The benefits of this architecture as observed are tamper-proof nature and better traceability along with resolving trust issues that may otherwise interrupt the supply chain [5]. Blockchain can fall under two categories private and public. A public blockchain is a completely transparent ledger and is decentralized. The information in this platform is encrypted and can be accessed on multiple devices. A public blockchain is nearly impossible to hack, as that will require acceptance from at least 51% of the nodes which is very difficult to attain for a malicious task, as the total number of nodes connected to this chain is very large. In contrast, a private blockchain has a limited audience that can access the content stored on the blockchain. It is an invitation only blockchain and is under the control of a single entity, hence not decentralized. A public blockchain is comparatively more secure than a private one.

Although every user in the network has access to all the blocks, not complete knowledge of any transaction or activity may be gained by all users. The details of all transactions are encrypted. For examples, if user A buys apples from user B via this network, the other users can know that there has been a transaction but would not attain all details, i.e., they may know that there has been a transaction but may not know that is was held for the exchange of apples. Most of the platforms or services that we use today be it Facebook or Google are centralized in nature and they have a lot of control in terms of privacy, and you may not be willing to give any one entity access to all your data. So, blockchain technology overcomes this concern where no one node or entity can have monotonous control or access to any piece of information.

The most common application of blockchain is seen in the cryptographic currency of Bitcoin. Cryptocurrency is a completely digital form of money. A distinctive feature of transaction with Bitcoins is that there is no requirement for a mediating institution. A conventional electronic payment involves third party other than the buyer and seller, usually a bank that facilitates the transfer of money. This technology of Bitcoin eliminates the need of any such mediation. Also, the Bitcoins are decentralized which implies that their distribution and circulation globally can be monitored by a government or any similar organisation. Whenever a bitcoin transaction occurs, the blockchain records the sender's and receiver's Bitcoin addresses along with the amount. Each transaction is encrypted with public key cryptography and verified by multiple nodes; these transactions cannot be tampered with. The computers than individuals connect onto this network are referred to as bitcoin miners. The cost of entering into the Bitcoin network is fairly high and bitcoins can only be profitably mined using specialized devices. As the number of nodes in the network increases the difficulty of mining generally increases. What attracts people to bitcoins is to keep their money safe in a bitcoin network as compared to any bank. Some people see it as an investment but there happens to be lot of risk but it is claimed that by 2040 this network will be very well established. Even though we presently seem to observe bitcoins as the only major application of blockchain, a lot of scope beholds for this technology some aspects of which we will be coming across through the course of this chapter [6].

Another growing application of blockchain is the Smart contract. The purpose of smart contract resembles just what a usual contract does i.e., beholds conditions, clauses and agreements. The only difference is that here they are stored as a few lines of code that is kept safe inside a blockchain. Also, this technology allows two parties to bind a contract without the requirement of any third party mediation. These are beneficial and binding as once the details of a smart contract are put in to a blockchain they cannot be modified. We specify the terms and condition of the contact along with the fulfilment condition, this is an efficient means to seal a contract because once made it cannot be manipulated or breached. For example, person A promises to deliver a commodity to person B after exactly 1 year from signing the contract. In this case a smart contract may be brought to effect specifying that the payment made by person B shall only be received by person A on the fulfilment of the contract, till then it may be held as cryptocurrency within the smart contract.

The drawback associated with the bitcoin application of blockchain technology is that the value of a bit coin is highly variable and thus faces a lot of risk. Also this technology demands for very high energy consumption. The data stored in a blockchain is immutable which particularly serves as an advantage and a disadvantage at the same time. Along with these, blockchain technology possesses a high implementation cost. Finally, this technology is not yet standardized or practiced regularly creating an air of ambiguity about it.

1.4   What is IoT?

IoT stands for Internet of Things. The motive of using IoT is to connect the physical devices present across the globe to each other via a wireless network and to allow them to communicate without any human interference as depicted in Figure 1.3. In today's world, we witnesses the impact of IoT in our daily lives ranging from the way we drive to how we attain energy in our homes. Some simple examples of IoT that we come across nowadays are say a light bulb that can be switched on using a mobile application. Here, the mobile and the light bulb are allowed to communicate without any human interruption to perform a task, which in this case is to switch the bulb on

Figure 1.3 Illustration of IoT.

or off. We witness IoT through various complexities ranging from maybe a child's stuff toy to much more complex applications such as highly specialized healthcare. A brief insight into the history of IoT tells us that the term "Internet of Things" was coined by Kevin Ashton; however, the concept of connected devices came into existence long back dating to 1830s when the first electronic telegraph was developed. This field has gained a lot of sophistication since then and stands at the levels we see it at today and there yet lies more scope to unveil its advanced applications further.

But firstly let us see how IoT works. Four basic contents for IoT are sensors, connectivity, data processing, and finally a user interface. The first key requirement for any device connected to IoT is to first be able to gather the information that it wants to process and communicate to other devices over the network. This is possible with the help of sensors, since they can detect an event or change in the environment of the device that they are attached to. The sensors may be in the form of cameras, microphones, motion sensors, accelerometers, temperature sensors, etc., allowing any device to know its surroundings without requiring any human interventions. The information or data through these sensors is continuously sent to a cloud or server that the device is connected to from where other devices which have access to that server may attain the information. The information from the cloud is utilized for performing certain tasks without the need of any human to machine or human to human interaction. This technology allows us to refer to devices as smart devices since they are capable to perform some activities on their own when required to do so. Let us consider a common example, smart watches have seen a surge in the number of people using it. These watches gather and present data such as, lets the user know about the number of steps that he took throughout the day, the distance covered, their pulse rate, their body temperatures, some also notify when they sense a surge in heart rate or suspect a medical condition, in case a call or text message notification is received. All this has been made possible with the use of sensors and the technology of IoT. Another example that we all have heard about is Amazon's Alexa or Google home, these function on voice commands given by the user with the help of sensors that convert verbal instructions into commands understandable by the device's software and then converts the device's output into speech to be delivered back to the user, such appliance is also referred to as a chat bot. These may also be configured with smart lighting system or may regulate ac controls with the help of IoT [7]. One widely applicable benefit of IoT is prognostics and advanced system health management (PHM). Herein, we are able to keep a check on the reliability of a device; reliability implies how the asset would perform under the expected set of conditions. This is done by *in situ* sensing. *In situ* sensing implies accommodating sensors in various parts under the same environment as the particular area that this sensor is responsible for providing details about. Four dimensions of prognostics and systems health management are sensing, diagnosis, prognosis, and management. Sensors are embedded across different machine parts, and these sensors provide data regarding time-based degradation of the particular part and notify if any anomaly arises. Diagnosis implies extraction of complete fault related information from the signals received by the sensors and lets us know about the amount of damage and provides warning regarding need for replacement or repair in advance. Prognostics help us figure out the remaining life of the equipment and calculate when it would require replacement so that it can be done as per need and sudden disruption can be avoided. Finally, management implies deciding how to tackle the requirements of the machine and performing the procedures accordingly [8]. However, with the advancement and automation that is brought about by this technology, accompanying it are concerns regarding the security issues that may arise due to this technology. Threats such as unauthorized access, phishing, or hacking surround, since it is a digitally augmented space. It is essential to have solutions to such problems or else it would not be possible to benefit from this technology. One solution suggested to tackle this is to combine the technology of IoT with the support of blockchain technology. How we benefit from this will be seen in better detail in the following section.

1.5   Combining IoT and Blockchain

As we have already seen, IoT connects and facilitates communication for devices connected to each other via the internet and provides storage space over a cloud, thus enabling devices to establish communication between one another and interact to successfully perform certain tasks without the requirement of any human intervention. But we see the need to ensure that this transfer mechanism as well as storage of any shared signals or information should be made secure and attack proof. This is taken care of by incorporating blockchain along with IoT. The combination of both these technologies helps fulfil the necessary security mechanism requirement to IoT which it otherwise lacked. The information that is received by a cloud can be accommodated in a tamperproof and permanent storage in a blockchain thus ensuring that the functioning of the machines, task communication, and messages to each other cannot be manipulated and reach completion in their intended manner. With incrementing the safety standards that the technology offers we will be able to attract a larger chunk of users to adopt and utilize this, and explore more vivid application throughout various spheres. No matter how huge the advancements any technique offers, without it being secure and trustworthy it cannot be brought in usage as the customer world will not accept it and might lead to theft of information or any such crime.

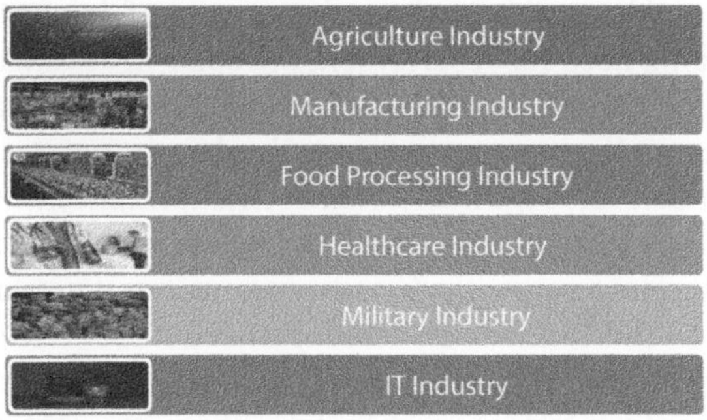

Figure 1.4 IoT and blockchain across industries.

Let us now look into the enhancement that these have brought about through various spheres as mentioned in Figure 1.4.

1.5.1   Agriculture Industry

As we already know, this is the industry that provides employment and income to a very large section of India's population particularly. Not just in India but almost all countries across the globe practice some form of agriculture or the other to meet the needs of their countrymen and often also from the trading perspective be it within the country's boundaries or beyond it. In earlier times, this industry was mainly dependent upon natural factors and human labor, whereas now technologies like IoT and blockchain have found implementation in this sector in not just one but many beneficial ways. There are a number of difficulties that this industry has to tackle with. Some of them can be seen as, once the farm produce is obtained only about 50% of the total quantity produced is actually delivered to the end users the rest of it undergoes wastage due to multiple reasons. Another one being the natural degradation of the land resources, with continuous exploitation of the land and soil in order to yield crops for commercial purposes, the maximum capacity and quality of the produce is deteriorating with the passage of time. There are occasions where there has been loss of crop due to either unexpected weather patterns or pest outbreak or even instances of wild animals that happen to enter the field, ruining large portions of the produce. At times, variables such as fluctuation in demand drop in prices or excessive presence of middlemen that may hamper the growth of this industry. Let us know explore what solutions are offered by the technologies of IoT and blockchain and how they are beneficial for this industry [9]. Before the farmers sow the seeds of any crop, they must be aware about the demand that the crop has. It is possible to have an estimate of the same by analysing the trends in the sale of the crop over the previous years. This ensures that demand and supply can be kept proportional hence avoiding wastage and loss.

Crops are best sold fresh therefore incorporation of IoT with the logistics responsible for delivering the product to the market would allow the producer as well as the consumer to be sure of the food being fresh and also to keep a check that no wastage occurs during the transportation of the same. IoT can also serve to improve the quality of the crop. Sensors such as air temperature and humidity sensors, soil pH sensors, sensors to check the water content of the soil, and sensors to evaluate the nutrient content of the soil. All these when connected to each other and onto a server will deliver wholesome information and allow the farmer to cater to the needs of the crop in a better manner. Since every crop has varying requirements of all these factors the farmer can set the parameter in keeping with those that best suit the crop thus allowing him to achieve the optimum conditions for plant growth. In case there is any deviation that is either lack or excess of any factor the farmer will get to know though his smart mobile connected onto the server where signals from all the sensors are stored, this mechanism will ensure better care to the to the target crop and thus provide better quantity and quality.

A suggested application in this field is to use surveillance cameras along with motion sensors. These motion sensors would be equipped to sense the movement of a body that would resemble that of pests which are dangerous to the crop. If any such motion is detected, the farmer will immediately be alerted through this mobile device and he can also access the cameras output at the time and therefore will be able to keep the produce safe [10]. The problems that faced while trying to implement these technologies in the agricultural industry are the high investment required for installation of required equipment and the technologies ought to bring about sea change in the functioning of this industry and due to lack of any technical knowledge the farmers will face difficulty adapting to this new system. However, once these are successfully integrated these techniques they will serve to regain the vibrancy and attain higher crop yields and better quality

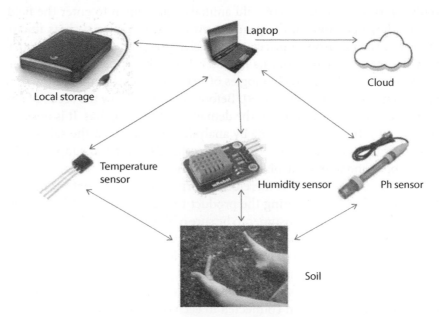

Figure 1.5 IoT and Blockchain in agriculture industry.

final products overall application in the field of agriculture can be seen in Figure 1.5.

1.5.2   Manufacturing Industry

Manufacturing industry particularly is embracing these potential technologies. Many are already using supervised systems with connectivity, these production units are able to deliver almost 100% efficiency as they are able to pre-plan and also predict any possible problems before they actually happen and cause delays. All the equipment that is connected via IoT to one another continuously receive and transmit information and maintain coordination helping yield the maximum product from the available raw material in minimum time. The intelligent objects are capable to sense, behave and act in the smart environment to ease the task, reduce human intervention, and increase precision and efficiency. Let us consider an example to see how there technologies are applicable in the manufacturing industry. As in Figure 1.6, consider a car manufacturing company; here, a large number of jobs are conducted ranging from manufacturing various car parts to assembling them together to attain the final product. A key necessity throughout the process is that of accuracy and machines cater to this need which is further enhanced with the incorporation of IoT. Apart from applying IoT to operate the equipment of this industry, its scope can be extended further.

Sensors can be attached to the parts that when put together make the car functional. Followed by connecting all these entities onto a network and establish communication between. It is because of this concept that a user is able to control certain features of the vehicle through an app or with voice commands. Along with this, these sensors will send signals to alert the user about any defect that may arise in the vehicle during the course of

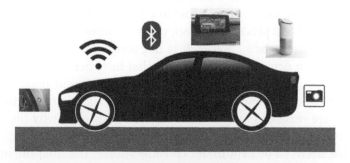

Figure 1.6 IoT and blockchain in manufacturing industry.

its usage. The manufacturing company may also keep access to the cloud that stores the sensor's output. They may foresee any part failure and warn the user for the need of service for the vehicle as when required. In case an accident occurs, the company will be able to trace the cause down. Also, say, if multiple complaints are received regarding products manufactured in a particular batch, other vehicles that house products from the same batch may be tracked down and taken care of. This will, in turn, improve the after sale service quality and ensure more convenience and enhanced safety to the customers [11]. Involving IoT also lets manufacturing companies better analyse the sale pattern of various commodities and the can manage production according in a manner such that the quantity produced is proportional to the demand, this will ensure that not huge amounts of surplus of a particular commodity might remain unused, whereas there may be shortage of another product. There we observe that these technologies serve varying purposes all for the betterment of this industry, to meet customer demands and requirements and also to maintain the company's profit at a high level.

1.5.3   Food Processing Industry

Under the sphere of the food processing industry, certain advancements have been brought about with the introduction of technologies such as IoT and blockchain [12]. One major feature is the better traceability of all the commodities throughout the farm-to-plate chain. The quality of the raw material that any such industry uses is of key importance and can be kept track of by linking all aspects and platforms where the material is passed through. It helps to ensure that the raw material has been treated properly and stored under sanitary and suitable conditions according to its nature. For example, any milk-based product requires to be stored under a cool temperature at all times and any carelessness in this regard would lead to spoiled food which if in any case is served to humans may lead to condition of illness. The same is applicable to all perishable items; they require careful handling and processing. Also, when it comes to food, most people are very picky with their choices. It is important for these companies to provide accurate details about the things that have been put into any particular product. Some individuals also bear allergies and need to ensure that they do not consume anything that they are allergic to or else it may lead to severe reactions and discomfort. This adds onto why the content details provided by the manufacturer need to precise. Another important aspect that needs to be kept under consideration is the shelf life of edible commodities, once manufactured it is advised that it should be consumed within a specified period of time to ensure that it is good and healthy condition at the time of usage.

These particulars can be kept track of with the help of the technologies of IoT and blockchain. The farm where the raw material is produced and transported may accommodate intelligent equipment (that has sensors installed and connected to a cloud or network) which would upload precise details about the date and method of handling onto the cloud where all information is to be stored onto a blockchain to ensure decentralization and access to the processing units, stores as well as the consumers, hence offering transparency. Inclusion of these technologies also ensure the absence of counterfeiting of harmful ingredients into food substances, since the manufacturer is obliged to provide complete details regarding ingredients and processing used, it minimizes the possibility of such frauds. Apart from this, at processing units utilising equipment that incorporate *in situ* sensing allows to maximize production yielding better profit and foreseeing any machine related faults and cater to the needs to avoid abrupt machine part failure or other such disruptions to the work flow. Hence, the technologies have helped achieve better standards of food quality along with having eased the very task of production because of a better organized and well equipped industry as illustrated by Figure 1.7.

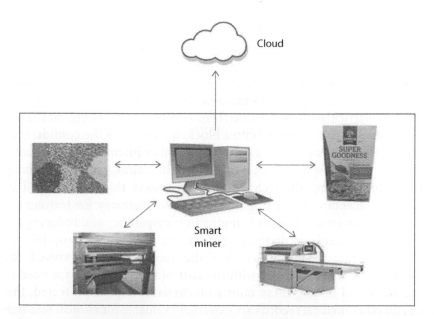

Figure 1.7 IoT and blockchain in food processing industry.

In the above figure, we can see that there are various machinery used in manufacturing of goods such as seeds and rice, we can monitor the progress of our manufacturing with the help of IoT. So, there are various machineries which are used to clean the product and then o process it and package it. So, what we can do is create an IoT of all this machinery and create a system with constant monitoring. We can also integrate AI to this system to optimize our production rate. This system is much better than existing one as it streamlines all the necessary machinery and monitors it, thereby increasing the production rate. All this data can then be uploaded to the cloud and have all the details of your manufacturing and can help in accounting of all this data.

1.5.4   Healthcare Industry

Ever since embodying technological advancements such as IoT and block-chain technology into the healthcare sector, we see scope to be able to reach unforeseen endeavors [13]. Application varies from medical record access to highly specialized patient's health activity monitoring and performing surgeries. It is a fact that machines sometime engulf more precision that is not humanly possible. Let us consider that a patient has just been discharged from a hospital or has an underlying medical condition which requires continues monitoring over a span of time, in such cases, certain wearable sensors or any other convenient sensors may be attached to the person. This allows the person to perform his day-to-day actives keeping his health under observation continuously. These sensors then upload the data onto a cloud service. The doctor is also connected to the same cloud via his device and keeps himself updated about the condition of any patient. In case any abnormalities are observed, the doctor may call upon that particular person to perform proper examination. Storage of an individual's health records onto a blockchain ensures the confidentiality and permanent storage of all details. Another hitch that is frequently observed in the hospitals is that of fraudulent claims and discrepancies in the billing system, the technologies can resolve this as there will be automated workflow and a single decentralized pathway for transaction and contact information hence bringing in transparency and reducing the probability of frauds or disagreement among parties. The hospitals are responsible for maintaining details of the people who have visited, the treatment administered along with the cost of the service. These need to be accurate and storing these onto a blockchain keeps it protected, this data and other medical records are extremely valuable for clinical research as they are first hand details and can help observe disease patterns or the most effective remedy for a particular disorder or to figure out the prominence of any syndrome among the target population. Another application under this sector is the drug supply chain management. Here, we use the technologies to keep track of drugs from their manufacture until they are given to patient. Its pros are that we can have accurate track of how, when, and where the medicine has been manufactured, its means of transportation, and it ensures that proper storage has been done in accordance with the nature of the drug. This also makes sure that no drug ends up being given to a person that any have any allergies or intolerance against the components of the medicine and that no medicine that has crossed its expiry date is used under any circumstances. We can also track the approximate quantity of a particular drug that is needed over a fixed time period and order them according so as to minimize wastage. Apart from the techniques that are currently being used, we are proposing a theoretical concept that has not yet being utilized, but holds future potential to provide better care to patients who are under critical conditions. Herein, we can link a ventilator and say a temperature measuring device to record the condition. We them connect the ventilator and all other related equipment through IoT, in case there happens to be an abnormality in the condition of the patient, the concerned medical staff will be notified immediately, and hence, care can be provided immediately. Hence, we see how these technological improvements have served for the betterment of this industry and have also assured better facilities to the people as seen in Figure 1.8.

As we can see in the above figure, we have created a hub or a network of all the necessary healthcare utility and connected then to each other to have a better and a more efficient monitoring system than the existing one. As we can see, we have a smart miner which is connected to carious other appliances such as a ventilator, an ambulance, and an oxygen meter to have an in depth knowledge of the patient.

1.5.5   Military

Military is an organization that is extremely important and integral to any country. Figure 1.9 shows some of its roles. Any state is marked by its border and the military holds the responsibility to guards the terrain against anyone who tries to hamper it. The complexities of military operations have considerably increased with the evolution of modes and methods, warfare has become more sophisticated that it ever was, and hence defence schemes and counter strategies should be at par. Incorporation of IoT and blockchain technologies has facilitated certain beneficial applications, and

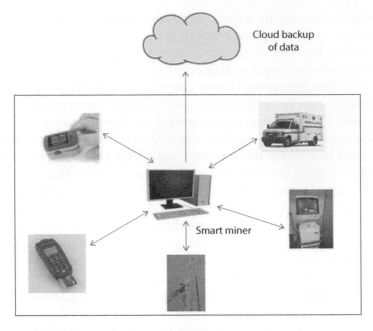

Figure 1.8 IoT and blockchain in healthcare industry.

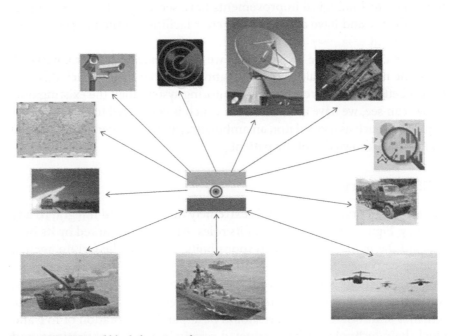

Figure 1.9 IoT and blockchain in military.

we shall consider them one by one [14]. In terms of logistics, the technologies have made it possible to be able to track the equipment supply from its place of production up until the battlefield where they are required. In case of an emergency, they can calculate the amount of equipment available and track future supply that is expected and accordingly plan out their usage.

This planning is critical especially in times of an emergency. Another application is creation of smart bases; this is extensively helping in reducing man power and enhancing security. Here, sensors can be accommodated with everyday operation for better analysis and efficiency. Storing the sensor signals is a challenging task, since most of the military operations are highly confidential and the information, if leaked, may lead to extensive misuse and might become a threat to a nation. If we try to resolve the security issue with the use of blockchain technology, a public blockchain would not be recommended as it is decentralized and can be accessed by multiple nodes, so a private blockchain is the alternative that we turn to, but the security offered by it is not fool proof and thus cannot be 100% relied on [15]. Another application is that of data warfare, this comprises of any data that will be useful to the military ranging from tracking food supplies to keeping track of weather forecast at all times to make sure no operation or mission is planned during an unfavorable weather condition, for example, air defence practice or performance would be scheduled keeping the expected weather under consideration. The military is also required to maintain proper records of data pertaining to equipment availability, training of employed personnel, track of the enemy's activity allowing them to observe any suspicious activity that may be performed, knowledge about the strength and equipment possessed by the enemy forces, thus on the whole boosting the intelligence and field forces of the military to be prepared and equipped for any possible threat well in advance.

A suggested application is to attach a sensor onto the solider similar to a RFID (radio frequency identification) which will be extremely beneficial especially during times such as that of war. Even if any solider is martyred or abducted, there will be a better chance to tracking and retrieving the person. It will also allow to monitor the actions undertaking by any solider and to be able to cover all scopes of improvement. However, this is a sphere where deploying IoT will be very money intensive, the scope is very large and so is the required investment. While implementing any such model, budgetary constraints play a major role as a determinant factor. Looking at the changes that have been brought about, we may say that the military sector has undergone considerable advancement and specialization due to the incorporation of these technologies in this sphere. They can now be better equipped and prepared to face various adverse circumstances.

1.5.6   Information Technology Industry

In this part, we will be discussing about the IT sector. The information technology industry is also commonly known as the IT industry. It sector is one of the fastest growing sectors in India. It provides employment to major chunk of people in India. The main hubs of IT sector in India are Bangalore, Hyderabad, Gurugram, and Noida. In a cooperate office, the work flow needs to be efficient, fast, and secure. This can be obtained with the combination of blockchain, AI, and IoT, in this mode what we can do is we connect various sensors to make our work more efficient. We will be creating a network of sensors such as light sensors, motion sensor, Bluetooth, and projectors. To make an efficient work flow, we need all these variables under one umbrella. There are various programs that use Bluetooth to share data such as ShareIt and Airdrop. By interconnecting all these networks/nodes, we are creating a data sharing platform. All this data needs to be secure from a third party; this can be achieved using blockchain. For an information technology workspace, we will be using a private blockchain to secure our data from a third party. All the relevant data can only be accessed by the person authorized to. As the private blockchain is governed by a single entity, it is centralized which thereby ensures no access of data is taking place which is unnecessary. In the office environment, since we are adding various sensors such as motion sensors we are ensuring that the lights are automatically switch off when not in use, thus saving a valuable resource. At its very core, we are creating a system that is more secure efficient and user friendly than the existing one.

This model can be extremely helpful when incorporated with the banking sector. Since banks nowadays have undergone digitalization it is highly essential for such critical institutions to maintain highly secure servers. Blockchain can be an example of one such technology which can be used to securely log records in the database. All this can/cannot be encrypted as per the discretion of the bank. This technology has already been utilized in bitcoins and various other crypto currencies. The blockchain can be private or public depending upon the bank and the scope of its usage. The advantage of using public blockchain is that it is decentralized and anyone can view the transaction history creating a transparent platform for banking. Whereas the advantage of using a private block is that we can create a hub of users of only the ones who need to access the data base. The banking sector can incorporate both a public blockchain and private blockchain. The private blockchain can be used internal organization of the bank where as the public blockchain can be used in the customer interface to make the system transparent and make it easier for the customers to trust the bank.

1.6   Observing Economic Growth and Technology's Impact

An economy can be understood as a system of exchanging goods and services for monetary value. All countries maintain records of the overall economic activity throughout the course of each financial year. A parameter called as gross domestic product (GDP) is calculated based on certain criterion and formulation carried out by financial experts, this factor is used to determine the development of any country. The developed countries tend to have a higher GDP than that of developing ones. The more the active and working population, the better it is for the economy of that country. Low dependency ratio and a larger portion of the population in the working sector that is between the age of 15 and 64 years that are seen as the active section of population are known as the asset of the country, as the facilitate all productive activities provide goods and services and spend money according to their preferences and needs and thus keep the flow of capital active. Factors that play a role in shaping an economy are population, natural resource, physical capital, human capital, technology, etc [16]. As obtained from critical observation of the economy between 19660 and 1990 points toward several other critical determining factors, some of them are maintenance of law, higher initial schooling, and better life expectancy. Another major sphere that the economy depends upon is the utilization of resources and the flow of money. Industries hold a considerable contribution toward the economy because it is these industries that transform raw materials into useful products and thus add value to them and cater to the needs and demands of the population. Industries at all levels be it product manufacturing or those from the service sector contribute toward the net values.

IoT's adoption across industries promises economic returns as it facilitates waste management, both of time and resources. Since it will reduce manpower and upscale production with increased accuracy, the transformation of the product will, in turn, positively impact the monetary flow of the company. The better the quantity and quality, the more flourished will be overseas trade bringing in currencies from across the globe, thus acting as another boost to the economy.

Year	GDP	Per capita	Growth rate
2005	$820.38B	$715	7.92%
2006	$940.26B	$807	8.06%
2007	$1216.74B	$1028	7.66%
2008	$1198.90B	$999	3.09%
2009	$1341.89B	$1102	7.86%
2010	$1675.62B	$1358	8.50%
2011	$1823.05B	$1458	5.24%
2012	$1827.64B	$1444	5.46%
2013	$1856.72B	$1450	6.39%
2014	$2039.13B	$1574	7.41%
2015	$2103.59B	$1606	8.00%
2016	$2290.43B	$1729	8.17%
2017	$2652.24B	$1981	7.17%
2018	$2718.73B	$2010	6.81%
			[17]

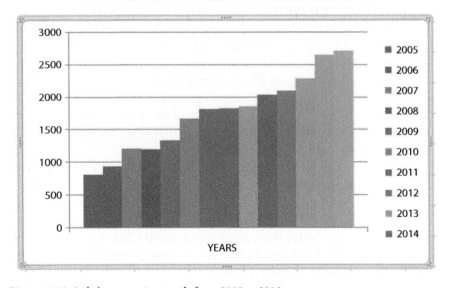

Figure 1.10 India's economic growth from 2005 to 2018.

The above data and graph, i.e. Figure 1.10 depict the economic growth observed in India staring from 2005 up until 2018. The value has been progressively increasing through the passage of these years. The amounts here are mentioned in Billion Dollars. Now, to observe the technological growth, let us observe the increase in number of internet user in the past 5 years. The data for the same is as follows.

Using the number of internet users as a parameter to estimate the rate of spread of technology, we can conclude that both technology and development go hand in hand with advancement in technology and we can create a much more efficient workflow in our industries, thereby increasing our GDP significantly as shown in Figure 1.11.

Year	Number of users	% World population
2015	3270M	45%
2016	3631M	49.5%
2017	3885M	51.75%
2018	4208M	55.1%
2019	4383M	58.8%
2020	4648M	59.6%
		[18]

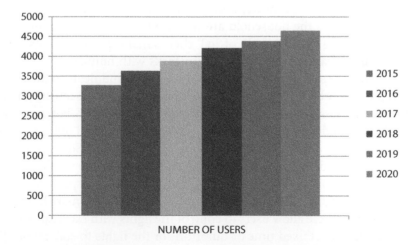

Figure 1.11 Internet users.

1.7   Applications of IoT and Blockchain Beyond Industries

There are basically three models suggested in this part of the discussion which are not only limited to the industry. These models use combinations of different technologies to make a better system than an existing one. The models shown over here can be much safer and efficient; the three models suggested over here are as follows:

- Smart homes
- Intelligent CCTV monitoring
- Smart street lights

Apart from finding applications in the industrial sphere, the technologies of IoT and blockchain find scope beyond it as well. We will look into some such aspects where we are widely exploiting these technologies in our day-to-day life. We will see how smart homes and security via surveillance devices such as cameras have been improved depicted in Figure 1.12 is. Smart home is a living space wherein human effort required for basic activities is minimized giving superior comfort to the inhabitants. IoT and blockchain are enhancing the everyday living experience and making chores a lot easier and fun. They enhance the quality of life basically by providing automated appliance control and assistive services [19]. Feature exhibited by smart homes are major due to sensors, actuators, etc., being embedded in the structural fabric. Smart homes have evolved sustainability, comfort, healthcare, and security at one's residence. Various components across the household are made intelligent by being aware of their surrounding with the help of IoT that is making components eligible to communicate and perform certain tasks with human interference. Any data that the sensors across various devices communicate to the cloud should preferably be stored onto a blockchain to ensure the security and to minimize the possibility of any information being misused. For a remote are such as a residential plot, private blockchain a preferred option as not many nodes are required to be given access or control to it. So, the centralized control would remain with the owner of the house who would be able to access the data as per his wish. Let is focus onto certain aspects of smart home particularly and discuss the same. One element of smart homes is smart lighting. These allow users to control the lights with the help of their mobile device or set fixed time or duration for the lights to stay on or off. Some smart lights are also linked to motion sensors, when these motion

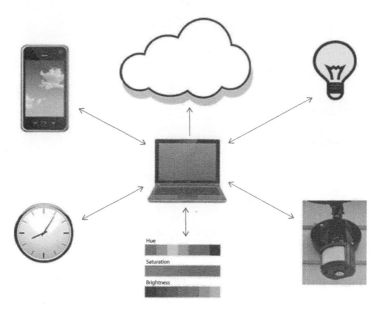

Figure 1.12 Smart homes technology.

sensors do not sense any activity or commotion in a room for some fixed duration of time say 5 minutes, the intelligent system automatically turns the lights out. This feature extensively helps in minimising energy consumption and prevents any wastage of this resource. Apart from just controlling the power, the user may even be able to control the brightness or the shade and tone of the lighting according one's own taste and preference. Another element is automated facial recognition of frequent visitors.

The owner of the house may add details of certain individuals who happen to visit regularly. Upon their arrival, the facial recognition system installed will automatically inform the residents about their presence, either through mobile device notification or voice assistance already existing in the house and access to enter may be granted accordingly. This will reduce human effort required and will increase convenience. Another element that is presently under the future scope for being included into the smart home technology is that of inclusive health monitoring.

Let us all see how IoT and blockchain can be used for physical security at any location as in Figure 1.13. Safety and security have met new heights with the help of these techniques for example, surveillance cameras. CCTV cameras (closed circuit television cameras) have been in use for quite some time now, but its functioning has largely been impacted by these technologies [20]. With the help of IoT, smart cameras have come up. What makes

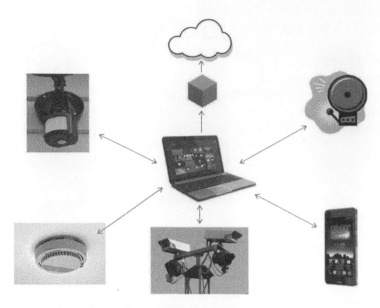

Figure 1.13 Specialized surveillance using IoT and blockchain.

these unique and useful is that along with cameras that deliver live footage and some also save recent recording, we have installed other sensors to it [21]. A microphone accompanying the camera allows the user to communicate via means of voice to the person or event that they witness on the camera. Cameras come with vision both during day and night time. Motion sensitive sensors are attached to the camera to the camera, now what happens if we can program the device for if it is in the night mode or the user does not expect any motion at any particular time; these motions sensors may be activated. In case any movement is present in the range of the camera, it will capture multiple images for those instances along with the video footage so that the cause of the happening can be recorded. This is a great feature from the security point of view as if it happens to be a trespasser or maybe even a thief there is high probability that the suspect would be captured. Along with this alarm can also be incorporated within this device so that in case motion sensors are evoked or someone tries to damage the equipment, the alarm is set off [22]. Additionally, fire or smoke detectors can also be attached with this device making the equipment multipurpose. With the help of IoT, the camera along with all the sensors can be connected to the user's mobile phone and all information gather by the camera and the sensors can be directly received by the user. To enhance this further, all the data that is generated by the device and all its attached sensors can directly be linked to a server or cloud storage and should be stored using a blockchain.

This will ensure that once the camera captures any particular event it cannot be erased or tampered with [23]. Another feature that can be combined with the surveillance technology mentioned so far is that once the images captured by the camera are sent out to the cloud, it can be put under two step processing. First step is face detecting and extraction wherein if there happens to be face in the pictures or videos captured by the camera, it would be recognized and an image of the face would be extracted as clear as possible. The second step is face matching, which will give details about the anonymous defaulter to be traced. However, only authorized personal will be able to access the required database resource for face matching in order to ensure that it cannot by misused. The surveillance cameras mentioned thus far can be used for residential areas as well as public spaces. The cameras with the face detection involved particularly can be used to track down drivers who do not abide by the traffic rules through the data delivered by the camera. Thus, IoT and blockchain together have set new standards for ensuring specialized safety [24].

Another application of IoT and blockchain is smart and adaptive street lighting system depicted in Figure 1.14. Under this concept, a sunlight

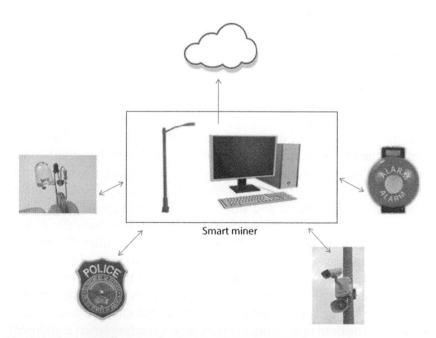

Smart miner

Figure 1.14 Smart street lighting enabled with IoT and blockchain.

sensor is attached to the street light which automatically switches the street light on or off detecting whether it is day or night time. In case as some instance due to weather or any such cause there happens to be darkness, these street lights will sense it and illuminate. Alongside, a camera should be put on the top of the pole to monitor the activities of the vehicles or people surrounding it. The input from the camera and sensor is to be stored onto a cloud server. Storage of the content of this cloud server onto a blockchain will help ensure the safety of the data transferred by the sensors and the cameras. Another feature that can additionally be present is to create a panic button on the street light poles, at a height reachable by humans. In case of an emergency or mishappening this button can be pressed which will set of an alarm in the nearest police station. The concerned police station will also be able to access the live footage of the place of incident via the cloud server. This will immediately inform the police regarding the requirement of their presence and also help them keep proof against the culprit that will later help while seeking judicial remedy.

In Indian scenario, cases like robbery, assault, and kidnapping can be tracked down and prevented. The problems that this technique solves are conserving energy by preventing wastage and turning the street light on or off as and when required; it also contributes to making streets safer by helping police trace defaulters and prevent many crimes. This also eliminates the need of man power required to regulate the power of street lights. Since this technique involves sensors and storage over cloud using blockchain, we refer to this as a "smart" street lighting system.

1.8   Conclusion

Let us now summarize all that we read throughout the chapter. First of all, we understood the concept of what an industry is, how it functions and its features and responsibilities. We particularly read about the functioning of the agriculture industry, the manufacturing industry, food processing units, healthcare, military, and information technology industry. Next, we discussed about the technology of blockchain. It is basically storage of information into blocks that are connected to each other; the benefits that this technology offers are security and decentralization of control over all information. Another technology mentioned in this chapter is that of Internet of Things, also called as IoT. This facilitates to establish communication among devices, enabling them to share information and perform task without the need of any human intervention creating smart equipment.

Further, we observe how IoT and blockchain when put together find multitude of applications throughout various industries. We see how these technologies have brought about betterment in industries such as agriculture, manufacturing, food processing, healthcare, military, and IT. The scope of these technologies lies beyond industries also. We discussed some everyday applications such as smart homes, improved surveillance cameras, and smart street lighting systems. So, to conclude with, we may say that with the evolution of these technologies and their incorporation throughout various aspects of life, it has brought convenience and specialization into everyday affairs. Tasks and tools that were not even imaginable few years ago have now been made possible with the help of advanced technologies such as IoT and blockchain. A lot of applications have been explored and implemented, and yet, there remains huge scope for further research and development to ease and facilitate our being.

References

1. Kenessey, Z., The primary, secondary, tertiary and quaternary sectors of the economy, in: *Review of Income and Wealth*, vol. 33, no. 4, pp. 359–385, 1987.
2. Upadhya, C. and Aninhalli, R.V. (Eds.), *In an outpost of the global economy: Work and workers in India's information technology industry*, Routledge: Taylor and Francis Group, 2012.
3. Crosby, M., Pradan, P., Sanjeev, V., Vignesh, K., Blockchain technology: Beyond bitcoin. *Appl. Innovation*, 2, 6–10, 71, 2016.
4. Kamble, S., Gunasekaran, A., Arha, H., Understanding the Blockchain technology adoption in supply chains-Indian context. *Int. J. Prod. Res.*, 57, 7, 2009–2033, 2019.
5. Guegan, D., Public blockchain versus private blockhain, halshs-01524440, version 1, 2017.
6. Buterin, V., A next-generation smart contract and decentralized application platform, in: *White Paper*, vol. 3, no. 37, 2014.
7. Kwon, D. *et al.*, IoT-based prognostics and systems health management for industrial applications. *IEEE Access*, 4, 3659–36705, 2016.
8. Celik, Z.B. *et al.*, Program analysis of commodity IoT applications for security and privacy: Challenges and opportunities. *ACM Computing Surveys (CSUR)*, vol. 52, no. 4, pp. 1–30, 2019.
9. Dagar, R., Subhranil, S., Kumar Khatri, S., Smart farming–IoT in agriculture. *2018 International Conference on Inventive Research in Computing Applications (ICIRCA)*, IEEE, pp. 1052–1056, 2018.
10. Ruan, J., Wang, Y., Sun Chan, F.T., Hu, X., Zhao, M., Zhu, F., Shi, B., Shi, Y., Lin, F., A life cycle framework of green IoT-based agriculture and its finance, operation, and management issues. *IEEE Commun. Mag.*, 57, 3, 90–96, 2019.

11. Zhong, R.Y., Xu, X., Klotz, E., Newman, S.T., Intelligent manufacturing in the context of industry 4.0: a review. *Engineering*, 3, 5, 616–630, 2017.
12. Tsang, Y.P., King, L.C., Chun, H.W., Sum Ho, G.T., Lam, H.Y., Blockchain-driven IoT for food traceability with an integrated consensus mechanism. *IEEE Access*, 7, 129000–129017, 2019.
13. Ray, P.P. *et al.*, Blockchain for IoT-Based Healthcare: Background, Consensus, Platforms, and Use Cases. *IEEE Syst. J.*, Volume 15, 2020.
14. Ren, J., Wang, Q., Jun, W.Z., Study on the application of the technology of IoT in military logistics [j]. *Logistics Sci-Tech*, 11, 029, 2011.
15. Yushi, L., Fei, J., Hui, Y., Study on application modes of military Internet of Things (MIOT). *2012 IEEE International Conference on Computer Science and Automation Engineering (CSAE)*, vol. 3, IEEE, pp. 630–634, 2012.
16. Barro, R.J., *Determinants of economic growth: A cross-country empirical study.* No. w5698, National Bureau of Economic Research, Massachusetts, 1996.
17. https://www.macrotrends.net/countries/IND/india/economic-growth-rate
18. https://www.internetworldstats.com/emarketing.htm
19. Chan, M., Campo, E., Estève, D., Fourniols, J.-Y., Smart homes—current features and future perspectives. *Maturitas*, 64, 2, 90–97, 2009.
20. Ahn, E.-M. and Kim, D.-H., Implementation of Integrated Platform of Face Recognition CCTV and Home IOT. *J. Digital Contents Soc.*, 19, 2, 393–399, 2018.
21. Park, W.-H. and Cheong, Y.-G., IoT smart bell notification system: design and implementation. *2017 19th International Conference on Advanced Communication Technology (ICACT)*, IEEE, 2017.
22. Cho, J.-R. *et al.*, Smart CCTV Security Service in IoT (Internet of Things) Environment. *J. Digital Contents Soc.*, 18, 6, 1135–1142, 2017.
23. Amin, A.H.M., Ahmad, N.M., Ali, A.M., Decentralized face recognition scheme for distributed video surveillance in IoT-cloud infrastructure. *2016 IEEE Region 10 Symposium (TENSYMP)*, IEEE, 2016.
24. Abinaya, B., Gurupriya, S., Pooja, M., IoT based smart and adaptive lighting in street lights. *2017 2nd International Conference on Computing and Communications Technologies (ICCCT)*, IEEE, 2017.

2

Layered Safety Model for IoT Services Through Blockchain

Anju Malik[1] and Bharti Sharma[2]*

[1]College of Engineering Roorkee, Uttarakhand, India
[2]DIT University, Dehradun, India

Abstract

The IoT or Internet of Things is gaining a set of interest due to its prevailing in our daily life. Its use is not only defined to commercial application but also in domestic use such as electric equipment, AC, washing machine, sensors, and safety locker. The Internet connectivity and easily available computing facilities provide a strong foundation for IoT services. The main idea behind this concept is the combination of network connectivity, efficient use of sensors, and optimized computing infrastructure. The communication model supported by IoT is as follows:

    i.   Physical Device Communication
    ii. Devices to Online Communication (Cloud Services)
    iii. Device to Network Devices (Gateway, Hub, and Internet)
    iv. Data sharing (Back End Data Analysis)

The main hurdle in adoption of these kinds of services is security and privacy issues. Blockchain provides the solution to this problem because the use of cryptography is not constrained to an explicit field. The combination of network data usage, combination of public and private keys, and latest computing technologies makes the services safe.

Keywords: Blockchain (BC), IoT (Internet of Things), Lightweight Scalable Blockchain (LSB), Distributed Digital Ledger (DDL), Confidentiality, Integrity, Availability (CIA)

*Corresponding author: bharti.sharma@dituniversity.edu.in

Krishna Kant Singh, Akansha Singh and Sanjay Sharma (eds.) Machine Learning Approaches for Convergence of IoT and Blockchain, (35–56) © 2021 Scrivener Publishing LLC

2.1   Introduction

Definition by IT experts is "IoT or *The Internet of Things shows the inter connection of multiple type of devices and the internet, i.e., it can be using inbuilt software and physical devices in the form of sensors to communicate, collect and exchange data with one another.*"

The following figure depicts the interconnection of all kind of IoT services that is related to devices and less human interaction control. It can be IoE (Internet of Everything), P2P (People to People), P2M (People to Machine), and M2M (Machine to Machine).

IoT or we can say Internet of Everything services are entering into our day-to-day life as a basic necessity just like food, water, and shelter (Figure 2.1). This framework facilitates millions of devices to gather and communicates with Internet and builds them intelligent and efficient. The modern competitive edge of analyzed data is also growing in the same way. The handling of enormous volume of current and projected data is also very daunting. This data is produced through multiple devices and provides a foundation of interaction and communication to IoT services. The extraction of raw-sensory data which is captured by machine-dependent devices is very interesting to understand [1]. The derivation of abstracted data needs to be processed by machine interpretable sensors and Internet.

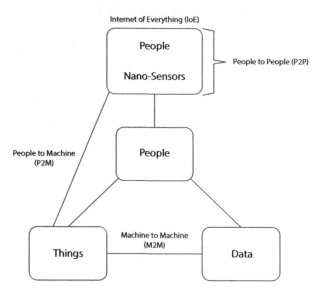

Figure 2.1 Interconnection of IoT services.

The inclination of modern computing means is toward the real-world objects by the help of Internet. The environment that connects billions of objects and interacting software is processed through middleware; this layer integrates data from devices, communicates with software, and finally takes decisions from the collected data [1–3]. IoT allows all these infrastructure and software services that are processed remotely in the presence of network capabilities.

General architecture for IoT services is as follows:

In the adoption of any new technology, many issues come in the way, i.e., reliability, robustness, adoptability, safety, and privacy. In the case of IoT, Blockchain may be the solution due to its well-defined immutable nature and the benefits of its security and privacy [4]. Blockchain in merge with cryptography provides the solution to all security and privacy problems. In the terms of computation and calculation, Blockchain is expensive, limited, and scalable in nature, and the overheads of bandwidth are also very high. In some context, it is not suited for IoT applications [5]. In some particular cases, we can adopt one of its variations called as Lightweight Scalable Blockchain known as LSB. It can be used for optimized IoT requirements. In the smart home setting, LSB can be worked as broader IoT applications. In a smart home architecture, the main hurdle is very limited devices that can be controlled by centralized manager with a combined set of shared keys (both public as well as private) for communication and then processes all requests (incoming as well as outgoing requests) [6]. An overlay network is established for LSB decentralization which connects highly resources devices with a public Blockchain and ensures end-to-end security and privacy. The architecture of IoT services is illustrated in Figure 2.2. The overlay network is organized as distinct clusters; it will reduce overheads. The scattered

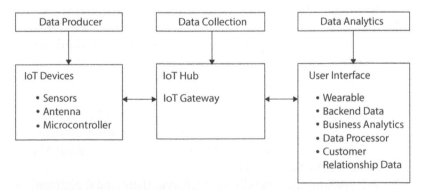

Figure 2.2 Architecture of IoT services.

cluster heads are combined together for managing the overall public Blockchain heads. This technique provides multiple optimizations such as procedure and mechanisms for lightweight nodes, disseminated trust and the management of its total throughput values. The arguments of qualitative values state that least significant bit method is flexible to several security attacks. Many simulations represents that it decreases packet overhead, delay, and also increases Blockchain scalability as compared to other appropriate baselines [8–10].

2.1.1   IoT Factors Impacting Security

The rising pervasiveness of surrounded smart systems in practically all types of shopper devices and the undertaking the criticality of some applications (such as observation, e-health, and network organize) utter the need for consistent security.

There are many factors which are directly coupled with trustworthy security in IoT applications. Some of them are as follows:

1. IoT services and technology are comparatively new, and these services are less understood than other traditional systems.
2. IoT services are habitually distributed over scattered regional and geographical environments which are generally uncontrolled in nature.
3. IoT systems are generally organizationally federated, in the reference of much heterogeneous architecture, their environments, technologies, and the security mechanism among them.
4. IoT systems are installed with insulary across all application to vendor neutral or specific services; these are created as fragmented technology and their administrative positions.
5. IoT services are comprehensive for architecture standards, network devices, and security protocols. These standards are adopted, stabilized, and implemented with integration and consisted with vendors.
6. IoT applications in multiple straight down applications generally address parametric models, their formats, and complexity.
7. IoT supports specific supporting OS (operating systems) may typically modernized feature sets that will limit the capabilities and its simplicity.
8. IoT systems are generally inexpensive, their nodal platform has low complexity, and also, it has limited power, memory,

and supply. The firewall feature and limited use of heavy-duty security mechanism.

9. IoT-enabled devices have a limited electricity power because that is battery driven devices [17–22].

2.2   IoT Applications

The Internet of Things (IoT) provides the ideal combination of interrelated multiple computing devices, any object, mechanical, electric devices, any real-world entity, animal, and any human being. The data produced by any means is classified by their unique identifier or UID. Lack of human interaction is the pivot point that works behind this whole concept. The application areas of IoT are shown in Figure 2.3. So, the data collected and

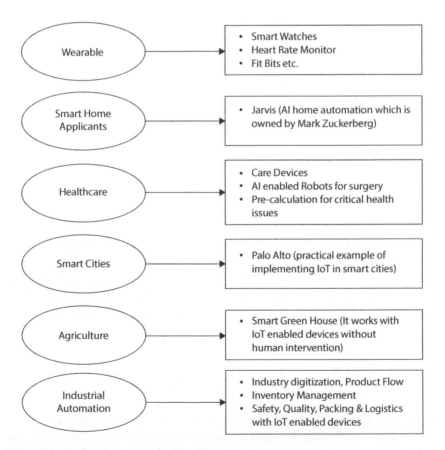

Figure 2.3 Application areas of IoT services.

produced by such sensors are accurate and consistent to their original mean.

As far as the commercialization concerns, everyday a new company announces a wide range of some IoT-enabled products. Various domains are equipped with these new frameworks usages.

2.3   IoT Model With Communication Parameters

The success of IoT model depends on its supporting technology that is responsible for its successful deployment. These factors are as follows:

2.3.1 RFID (Radio Frequency Identification)
2.3.2 WSH (Wireless Sensor Network)
2.3.3 Middleware (Software and Hardware)
2.3.4 Computing Service (Cloud)
2.3.5 IoT Software

2.3.1   RFID (Radio Frequency Identification)

Data capturing, tag values, reader, and its identification are performed by RFID and its referenced Internet connection. The tag used in IoT is different from traditional bar code scheme because its value is treated as global tag value.

2.3.2   WSH (Wireless Sensor Network)

WSN is the ideal combination of multiple topologies and multihop. This system is generally used for the maintenance and tracking systems. One of its examples is GE (General Electric) that is deployed in jet engines, wind shield, and its turbines. On analyzing the data in real-time applications, GE saves money and time with less maintenance. In the same way, American Airlines also uses sensor-enabled flight services with data capturing of 30 terabytes and its preventive maintenance. IoT-based devices and services used that data consistently monitored the flow of data.

2.3.3   Middleware (Software and Hardware)

The intermediate software layer that is interposed between software applications and communicating devices works as a middleware that helps the high language programmer to perform communication and input-output.

This feature hides the details of different technologies which is the basic of IoT developers. The architecture of distributed infrastructure is complex and it also requires multiple heterogeneous devices that simplify the expansion of new services and applications. So, this is the middleware that is the best fit with IoT application development. One of its examples is GSN (Global Sensor Network). It is a type of open source technology that is a platform that enables development and installation of sensor services without any programming effort. Generally, middleware for IoT services is a service-oriented approach for unknown and active system topology.

2.3.4   Computing Service (Cloud)

Computing is the framework that provides infrastructure, platform, architecture, and software in the form of services. It is basically categorized into software services, infrastructure services, and platform services. Any user can access any service with a simple internet connection and any machine. One of the best features of the IoT is vast enormous data that is captured by sensor devices. Apart from this many IoT middleware require very large data storage and the high processing speed enables the online application and devices time decision analyzer to take appropriate decisions. The high speed broadband networks streams data, audio, and video. Cloud computing provides a platform for this data capturing and data handling and is also process that gathered data.

2.3.5   IoT Software

IoT nurtures the enlargement of multitude corporate-slanting and particular customer-detailed IoT applications. The procedure and network connection provides interconnection, IoT services multiple devices to physical components, and human being to physical device interactions in a robust and reliable mode. The application layer on the physical devices make certain that data have been received and decision taking on them must be processed on time. For example, any inventory house may capture the status of good received, delivered and status of short material.

2.4   Security and Privacy in IoT Services

The adoption of IoT services depends on the safety and privacy concerns because any user does not have in hand, all information are either online or with the cloud. Just as in the case of smart health equipment that takes all records of patient and Smart car services include its GPS location, movements, and their purchasing preferences. All these data are analyzed and processed in any controlled environment. All these data can be used to improve daily life of customers and decreasing dependency on service providers. According to a survey in 2014, IoT services improve the quality index by 22% [24]. IoT gains the thrust through smart cities, smart houses, and other wearable devices. The acceptance of IoT services comes from the confidence of IoT devices and reliable network connection.

There is always a requirement of application support in insightful framework and other premeditated services just like elegant grid application and other competence protection. Some IoT applications increase large amount of individual statistics about domestic things, and their monetary status about the enterprises that will be proficient to influence for their business. The lack of proper privacy and security creates resistance in implementation of the IoT industry and persons. Many safety measures challenge get determined by sharpening the developers to integrate sanctuary solutions into the devices and also support user to use IoT safety features for their devices [27–30]. Some examples are firewalls and intrusion systems.

Every consumer's product has an innovation cycle that will works according to their usage but in case of IoT technologies, all devices are accelerated with innovation cycle which is faster than typical devices. If devices are not designed properly, then it may create hurdles in our life. The main competing factors are as follows:

- Standards and protocols
- Complex communications
- Security issues
- Privacy issues
- Proliferation

In a non-connected world, any error may not generate any hazardous result, but in IoT environment, any single error may generate very critical results that may affect multiple further studies and unexpected safety problems. The Internet speed and data speed can get soaked with speed limit with devices and system wide performance problems [34]. Smart home devices and health observing systems consist of many interconnected sensors and their communicating devices. A single device in the whole system may be some insignificant problem but as a whole it may disturbs the whole cycle. So, to stamp out the disarray in the hyper connected world, enterprises require making every probable effort to reduce the complexity of all connected devices that will increase the security

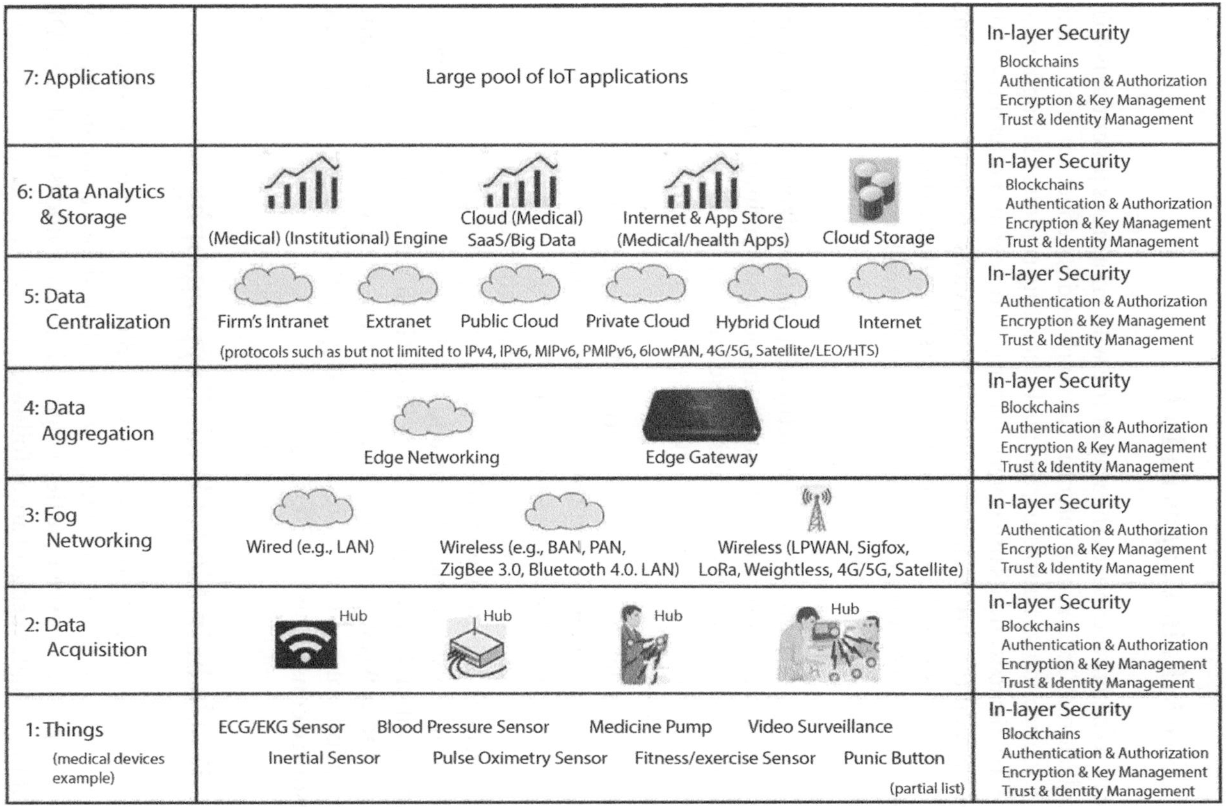

		In-layer Security
7: Applications	Large pool of IoT applications	Blockchains Authentication & Authorization Encryption & Key Management Trust & Identity Management
6: Data Analytics & Storage	(Medical) (Institutional) Engine Cloud (Medical) SaaS/Big Data Internet & App Store (Medical/health Apps) Cloud Storage	Blockchains Authentication & Authorization Encryption & Key Management Trust & Identity Management
5: Data Centralization	Firm's Intranet Extranet Public Cloud Private Cloud Hybrid Cloud Internet (protocols such as but not limited to IPv4, IPv6, MIPv6, PMIPv6, 6lowPAN, 4G/5G, Satellite/LEO/HTS)	Blockchains Authentication & Authorization Encryption & Key Management Trust & Identity Management
4: Data Aggregation	Edge Networking Edge Gateway	Blockchains Authentication & Authorization Encryption & Key Management Trust & Identity Management
3: Fog Networking	Wired (e.g., LAN) Wireless (e.g., BAN, PAN, ZigBee 3.0, Bluetooth 4.0. LAN) Wireless (LPWAN, Sigfox, LoRa, Weightless, 4G/5G, Satellite)	Authentication & Authorization Encryption & Key Management Trust & Identity Management
2: Data Acquisition	Hub Hub Hub Hub	Blockchains Authentication & Authorization Encryption & Key Management Trust & Identity Management
1: Things (medical devices example)	ECG/EKG Sensor Blood Pressure Sensor Medicine Pump Video Surveillance Inertial Sensor Pulse Oximetry Sensor Fitness/exercise Sensor Punic Button (partial list)	Blockchains Authentication & Authorization Encryption & Key Management Trust & Identity Management

Figure 2.4 IoT reference model (Source Minolli [65]).

parameters and standards. It also guarantees the protection and privacy of users all time [37–39]. The IoT reference model is shown in Figure 2.4.

2.5   Blockchain Usages in IoT

The technology that changes the way of life with enormous potential is IoT. The collision of IoT on the Internet network and its effect on the overall worldwide economy is inspiring, and its forecasting exploits the augmentation of IoT devices and its use is very exciting and new in modern era [40].

The structure and complexity of IoT services is bottom-up and organic that ensures the outcome addresses for all existing and current challenges [41–43]. One of its prime potential needs is the involvement of stakeholders and its fluid nature of privacy and security in middleware and software layer [45–47].

In the long-term process, internationally harmonized standards are harmonized, but it is very hard to get at the accurate moment and receive proper time, to enhance the security and privacy at regional, national, and international to collaborate with all other entities to better security layer [44].

It is the main factor to improve safety and reducing the risk of consumer IoT device adoption in the improved framework toward the consumers. It includes educating consumers and start practicing for the adoption of best practices for the development of International standards [48–52].

IoT network brings new hurdle in the security and privacy issues are massive scale, clustered mechanism, and distributed nature of IoT networks [7]. The solution to these problems is Blockchain which gives distributed security and privacy, but it also involves a huge energy impediment and computation overheads with high computing facilities [53–57]. It is typical for resource constrained IoT devices.

2.6   Blockchain Model With Cryptography

The security model in combination with Blockchain and cryptography provides a secured and distributed ledger that allows a secure layer of transferring data between parties (Figure 2.5). The nodes used in DDL (Distributed Digital Ledger) are as follows.

1. Full node
2. Lightweight node

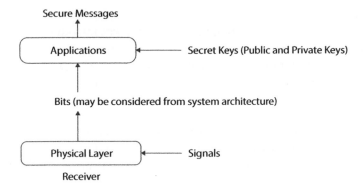

Figure 2.5 Layered architecture of blockchain with cryptography.

In the Blockchain, full node preserves the complete status of each block; it uses SPV (simplified payment verification) and full node takes more memory space. Full node takes full external memory space for heavy node [58]. While lightweight node takes only header part of each block, it is light in nature because memory requirements are taken for uploading process only. A lightweight node only takes part in verification part only and it is consensus in nature [59].

2.6.1 Variations of Blockchain

Data fetching process to read and write accesses are used with permutation and combination that are done with Blockchain. This ecosystem can be divided into three different models. These are as follows:

- Public (permission less)
- Private (permissioned)
- Hybrid (consortium)

The variation of different version of Blockchain is coined with new features and updated versions such as follows.

Blockchain (1.0)
This is the first type of Blockchain that works with cryptocurrency in Bitcoin. It was introduced in 2008 by Shatoshi Nakamoto. The first version is known as 1.0. Internet-based financial transactions are enabled by Internet of Money or cryptocurrencies. This is the basic type works on 16 bit architecture.

Blockchain (2.0)

In the smart contraction of digital contacts that was introduced in 1994 by Nick Szabo, it is a programmable turing-based language. Transactional or contract based system is automatically triggered for the execution of predefined rules and its predefined set of conditions. It was applicable to 1997.

Blockchain (3.0)

This version makes the operation of decentralized operations which is known as DApp; the main feature of this type is that it removes Single Point of Failure which is most common in traditional centralized applications.

Blockchain (4.0)

The foundation of this version is same as its above types but its variants make it more efficient than others such as enabling utilization of the Blockchain technology in solutions design, business models specially in case of cyber physical systems for industry 4.0, the current model brings the revolution in every phase of industry automation system [63].

The architecture of traditional IoT systems is based on central type in which information from the device to the cloud center is processed by using analytics and after that sent back to IoT devices. In modern time, millions of devices are connected together, so the traditional approach has a limited scalability. Firstly, it is very approach to the network security and very expensive also. Secondly, it is very slow for third party because it constantly checks and authenticates each micro transaction between all devices and its origin cloud center.

Blockchain networks is widely use in smart contracts of IoT devices; it allow devices to act securely and autonomously by creating policies that are only expected after the completion of particular requirements. Blockchain restricts those individuals who want to see and protect their data for their own personal benefit. It also allows greater automation, increased scalability, and cheaper transfers without the involvement of intruder transactions.

If any single point failure occurs at any point of time, then it will be easily eradicate by centralized network. This approach provides safety to those million users whose data is processed at individual nodes but later than transferred to center for the smoothly running process [11, 67].

2.7   Solution to IoT Through Blockchain

The foundation of security depends on three basic parameters, which is broadly known as CIA. Security solution to IoT through cryptography are shown in Figure 2.6.

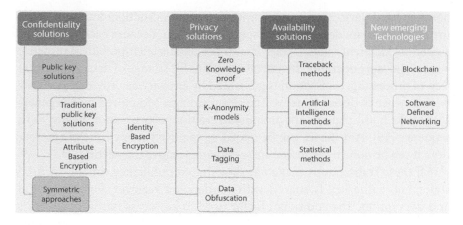

Figure 2.6 Security solution to IoT through cryptography (Source [16] Yang).

These are

> C stands for Confidentiality
> I stands for Integrity
> A stands for Availability

Confidentiality makes sure that only authorized user can read the data. Integrity makes sure that receiver and sender of data is only authorized users. Availability stands for the presence of required data all the time. These security values can be checked with Cooja which is a simulator that can be used for this purpose [13].

Blockchain is used with two key set along with cryptography. The key list has two components part:

1. Requester Key
2. Requested Key

Requester key lists down the set of all overlay users with primary key that makes sure that only allowed users can access data for the smart devices which are associated to the cluster.

Requested key drops the register of primary key of elegant devices which are joined to cluster which are allowable to access. To store the data with devices, cloud is used for storage and processed.

Designed layer of security models includes basics of Blockchain with primary key set of encryption and decryption. Its features are indirectly accessible devices and many transaction structures in the smart devices and middle layer. Symmetric encryption standards are easy to use for smart devices and lightweight security model [14]. Transactions are known as the communications between local devices and middleware data center. Multiple transactions in the Blockchain are designed for a specific function, because each device has a need for different overlay [12]. The stored data is encrypt with symmetric key set and store operation is generate by plans for storage of data. At the next step of processing, transaction is generated by any service provider or it may be the owner of device to access the cloud storage. Monitored deal is generated by the home plans or any provider to continuously monitor the device in sequence [15]. Any device can be added or removed at any time of transaction; it can be done by genesis transaction and remove transaction.

All these transactions make use of a shared public key for the secured statement. Same key is shared with sender and receiver, for encryption and decryption. The additional factor used in key set is hashing, which is employed to observe changes in transactions [8]. These are the contents which are observed in editable contents of transaction. All dealing contents are stored in local confidential center with Blockchain [12]. This local storage is a storage place for backup and recovery, e.g., a constrain is used by physical devices to store the data at local center. It can be further integrates with the miner or it can be a separate device for storage. Although the device has a limited space, and the algorithm FIFO is used to store and fetch data. It stores each devices detains the form of ledger which is chained as a starting point of data fetching process [64, 66]. Figure 2.7 illustrates the use of Blockchain in smart cities.

Blockchain along with symmetric key provides multiple features and secured communication. These benefits are as follows:

1. Decentralization: The central architecture of Blockchain is distributed in nature and its ledger is replicated in its all nodes whether they are full mode or lightweight node. In the central node, it can never be achieved. So, the main advantages are driven by the decentralization nature [42, 55].

2. Transparency: All transactions are recorded and time valued at the different point of time in the decentralized approach, so all are completely transparent. Validation and verification of transactions are done by Merkle Tree set. Data at each node is captured by B-tree method. One another point in transparency is that the ledger can be accessed by chain variable and its authenticity can be accurately done by its origin point. So, transparency is the main feature for security model [67].

3. Security: The proposed approach of Blockchain with cryptography is secured and distributed in nature. The Blockchain network protects the denial of service attacks also. Apart from this main focus is on Immutability, which is almost 51% of total security and privacy attacks. All the records

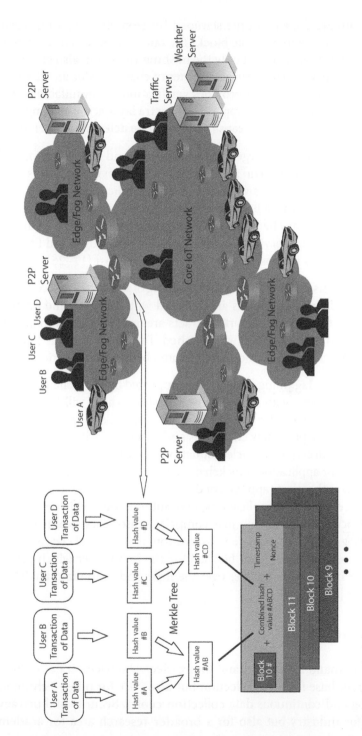

Figure 2.7 Blockchain in smart cities [Reference by Minoli 1-2 (2018)].

of Blockchain are done in a time stamped by geometric functions such as hashing which is use to generate blocks for safety parameters. Altering one transaction may invalidate not only the hashing values but also changes the values in other blocks. The replicated values of chained value are distributed on all nodes of the network. It provides verification on immutable nodes of network. The ledger used here append only extra layer at the existing record which are non-editable that means that cannot be deleted nor altered.

4. Cost: The overall cost of large scale applications and its installation needs less maintenance. For long run it is economical and very affordable solution with less cost. In some cases when the scale of application is small, then it may be expensive because it requires a distributed network. In cloud service distribution, it may be treated as a Blockchain as a service. Many third party vendor or cloud service provider such as Hyperledger and Ethereum can be used for this purpose that sounds a little bit cost [17–26].

4. Smart Contracts: Blockchain requires enabling of smart contract conditions. The set of predefined conditions are matched with contracts and automatically starts the transactions. Smart contracts are implemented with lightning network; it is directly enabled with Hashed Timelock Contract known as HTLC. Bi-directional transactions are initiated between two parties.

5. Micropayment: Lightning network are supported by Blockchain and these are truly comfortable with micropayment system which will be the future technology. It also works for the future business models because it promotes innovation and adapting new challenges and ventures easily [24–31].

In all IoT services, it is an unclear situation that which version will be used for a platform or application. Blockchain may be use for the request requirements and to authenticate app type of dealings, e.g., imbursement of parking fee, insurance data, UBI applications, and autonomous vehicle [32, 33, 35, 36]. The processed information may comprise sensor data, health and medical history, graphical shots, video observation, and medical claims [60, 61]. Blockchain security model can be used for the lower layer which provides integrity for information transfer over the links and centralized analytics of cloud server [62].

2.8   Conclusion

IoT is the demand for present and future electric devices. It not only supports current base for data collection but also base for other technologies such as fog and continuous data collection center. Security and privacy is not only for industry but also for a broader research area for academia.

Existing solutions are not enough for smart devices, because there is a lack of efficient energy consumption and also a lot of overhead. Current solutions are paving around the Bitcoin. Blockchain with cryptographic security model has the following advantages over others:

- Reliable data
- Robustness
- Trusted data collection
- Audit trial of historic actions
- Optimized file sharing
- Decentralized approach for better control
- Cost reduction
- Transactional control
- Better data analysis

Fog architecture is enabled with Cloud platform which can be used with computing, control, communication, and better networking services. A new term Cloud-to-thins can be worked as analyzed and processed area, and it covers both segment hardware and software. The architecture and framework can work for the upcoming trends such as

- Fifth-generation wireless systems
- Embedded application set
- AI-enabled services
- Machine learning with IoT devices

References

1. Ganz, F., Puschmann, D., Barnaghi, P., Carrez, F., A practical evaluation of information processing and abstraction techniques for the Internet of Things. *IEEE Internet Things J.*, 2, 4, 340–354, 2015.
2. da Cruz, M.A., Rodrigues, J.J.P., Al-Muhtadi, J., Korotaev, V.V. and de Albuquerque, V.H.C., A reference model for internet of things middleware. *IEEE Internet of Things J.*, 5, 2, 871–883, 2018.
3. Bera, S., Misra, S. and Vasilakos, A.V., Software-defined networking for internet of things: A survey. *IEEE Internet of Things J.*, 4, 6, 1994–2008, 2017.
4. Chiang, M. and Zhang, T., Fog and IoT: An overview of research opportunities. *IEEE Internet of Things J.*, 3, 6, 854–864, 2016.
5. Lee, I. and Lee, K., The Internet of Things (IoT): Applications, investments, and challenges for enterprises. *Business Horizons*, 58, 4, 431–440, 2015.

6. Books on Internet Society, Enhancing IoT Security: Final Outcomes and Recommendations Report Canadian Multistakeholder Process: Enhancing IoT Security.

7. Dorri, A., Konhare, S., Jurdak, R., Towards an Optimized BlockChain for IoT, Internet-of-Things Design and Implementation (IoTDI). *IEEE International Conference on IoT*, 2017, https://ieeexplore.ieee.org/xpl/conhome/7939940/ proceeding.

8. Ahmad, M. and Salahb, K.K., IoT security: Review, blockchain solutions, and open challenges. *Future Gener. Comput. Syst.*, 82, may 2018.

9. Dorii, A., Kanhare, S., Jurdak, R., Gauravramana, P., LSB: A Lightweight Scalable BlockChain for IoT Security and Privacy. *J. Comput. Sci. Secur.*, Cornell University, December 2017.

10. Banerjee, M., Lee, J. and Choo, K.K.R., A blockchain future for internet of things security: a position paper. *Digit. Commun. Networks*, 4, 3, 149–160, 2018.

11. Dorii, A., Kanhare, S., Jurdak, R., Gauravraman, P., Blockchain for IoT Security and Privacy: The case Study of a Smart Home, Conference on *IEEE PERCOM Workshop On Security Privacy And Trust In The Internet Of Thing*, March 2017.

12. https://www.wired.com/2016/10/internet-outage-ddos-dns-dyn/, [Online; accessed 10-December-2016].

13. Cooja. http://anrg.usc.edu/contiki/index.php/CoojaSimulator/, [Online;accessed 19-November-2016].

14. F.-S. sense. https://sense.f-secure.com/, [Online; accessed 19-November-2016].

15. Miraz, M., Blockchain of Things (BCoT): The Fusion of Blockchain and IoT Technologies. Research paper number 2019-13, https://link.springer.com/ chapter/10.1007%2F978-981-13-8775-3_7.

16. Kouicema, D.E., Bouabdallaha, A., Lakhlefa, H., Internet of Things Security: a top-down survey. https://www.researchgate.net/publication/323912995_ Internet_of_Things_Security_a_top-down_survey.

17. Sadeghi, A.-R., Wachsmann, C., Waidner, M., Security and privacy challenges in industrial internet of things. *2015 52nd ACM/EDAC/IEEE on Design Automation Conference (DAC)*, IEEE, pp. 1– 6, June 2015.

18. Raspotnig, C., Karpati, P., Katta, V., A combined process for elicitation and analysis of safety and security requirements, in: *In Enterprise, business-process and information systems modeling*, pp. 347–361, Springer, 2012.

19. Höller, J., Tsiatsis, V., Mulligan, C., Avesand, S., Karnouskos, S., Boyle, D., *From Machine-to-Machine to the Internet of Things: Introduction to a New Age of Intelligence*, 1st ed, Academic Press Ltd, London, United Kingdom, 10 Apr 2014.

20. Yan, Z., Zhang, P., Vasilakos, A.V., A survey on trust management for internet of things. *J. Network Comput. Appl.*, 42, 120–134, 2014.

21. Neisse, R., Steri, G., Baldini, G., Tragos, E., Fovino, I.N., Botterman, M., Dynamic context-aware scalable and trust-based IoT security, privacy

framework, in: *Chapter in Internet of Things Applications-From Research and Innovation to Market Deployment*, IERC Cluster Book, 2014.

22. Taddeo, A.V., Mura, M., Ferrante, A., Qos and security in energyharvesting wireless sensor networks. *Proceedings of 2010 International Conference on Security and Cryptography (SECRYPT)*, IEEE, pp. 1– 10, 2010.

23. Sahraoui, S. and Bilami, A., Efficient hip-based approach to ensure lightweight end-to-end security in the internet of things, in: *Computer Networks*, vol. 91, pp. 26 – 45, 2015.

24. King, S., Primecoin: Cryptocurrency with prime number proof-of-work. 1, 6, July 7th 2013.

25. Dorri, A., Kanhere, S.S., Jurdak, R., Blockchain in internet of things: Challenges and solutions. *arXiv preprint arXiv*: 1608.05187, 2016.

26. Narayanan, A., Bonneau, J., Felten, E., Miller, A., Goldfeder, S., *Bitcoin and cryptocurrency technologies*, Princeton University Press, 2016.

27. Bogdanov, A., Knezevic, M., Leander, G., Toz, D., Varıcı, K., Verbauwhede, I., *spongent: A Lightweight Hash Function*, pp. 312–325, Springer, Berlin Heidelberg, 2011.

28. Delfs, H., Knebl, H., Knebl, H., *Introduction to cryptography*, vol. 2, Springer, 2002.

29. Komninos, N., Philippou, E., Pitsillides, A., Survey in smart grid and smart home security: Issues, challenges and countermeasures. *IEEE Commun. Surv. Tutorials*, 16, 4, 1933–1954, 2014.

30. Notra, S., Siddiqi, M., Gharakheili, H.H., Sivaraman, V., Boreli, R., An experimental study of security and privacy risks with emerging household appliances. *Communications and Network Security (CNS), 2014 IEEE Conference on IEEE*, pp. 79–84, 2014.

31. Sivaraman, V., Chan, D., Earl, D., Boreli, R., Smart-phones attacking smarthomes. *Proceedings of the 9th ACM Conference on Security & Privacy in Wireless and Mobile Networks*, ACM, pp. 195–200, 2016.

32. Hosenkhan, R. and Pattanayak, B.K., A secured communication model for IoT. In *Information Systems Design and Intelligent Applications*, pp. 187–193, Springer, Singapore, 2019.

33. Burel, B., Barker, L., Divitini, M., Peret, F.A.F., Russell, I., Siever, B., Tudor, L., Courses, content and tools for internet of things in computer science edcuation. *Proceedings of ITICSE Conference on Working Group Reports*, Italy, pp. 125–139, 2017.

34. Kahn, R., Khan, S.V., Zaheer, R., Khan, S., Future internet: the internet of things architecture, possible applications and key challenges, possible applications and key challenges. *Proceedings of 10th International Conference on Frontiers of Information Technology ("FIT")*, pp. 257–260, 2012.

35. Mamatha, G., Overview and Concept for IOT Models. *Int. J. Innovative Res. Comput. Commun. Eng.*, 4, 11, November 2016.

36. Singh, S. and Singh, N., Internet of Things (IoT): Security challenges, business opportunities & reference architecture for E-commerce. *2015 International*

Conference on Green Computing and Internet of Things (ICGCIoT), October 2015.

37. IDC, 30 Billion Autonomous Devices By 2020. https://securityledger.com/2013/10/idc-30-billion-autonomous-devicesby-2020/.

38. THE CONNECTED-HOME, Forecasts And Growth Trends For The Leading 'Internet Of Things' Market. http://www.businessinsider.in/THE CONNECTED-HOME-Forecasts-And-Growth-Trends-For-TheLeading-Internet-Of-Things Market/ articles how /43913798.cms.

39. Researchers show that IoT devices are not designed with security in mind. http://www.pcworld.com/article/2906952/researchers-show-thatiot-devices-are-not-designed-with-security-in-mind.html.

40. Gartner's Internet of Things predictions. http://www.informationage.com/technology/mobile -and networking/123458905/ gartners internet-things-predictions.

41. It's Official, The Internet Of Things Takes Over Big Data As The Most Hyped Technology. http://www.forbes.com/sites/gilpress/2014/08/18/itsofficial-the-internet-of-things-takes-over-big-data-as-the-most-hypedtechnology/.

42. Internet of Things market to hit $7.1 trillion by 2020. IDC, http://www.zdnet.com/article/internet-of-things-market-to-hit-7-1- trillion-by-2020-idc/.

43. Who's Winning The Internet Of Things Developer War? Apple And Google. http://readwrite.com/2015/04/10/internet-of-things-developersapple-google.

44. Virgin Atlantic to Integrate iBeacon Technology Into London's Heathrow Airport. http://www.macrumors.com/2014/05/01/virginatlantic-ibeacons-london-heathrow-airport/.

45. Gartner Says a Thirty-Fold Increase in Internet-Connected Physical Devices by 2020 Will Significantly Alter How the Supply Chain Operates. http://www.gartner.com/newsroom/id/2688717.

46. IBM Connects "Internet of Things" to the Enterprise. http://www03.ibm.com/press/us/en/pressrelease/46453.wss.

47. Minoli, D. and Occhiogrosso, B., Blockchain mechanisms for IoT security. Internet of Things, 1, 1–13, 2018.

48. Magyar, G., Blockchain: solving the privacy and research availability tradeoff for EHR data: a new disruptive technology in health data management. Proceedings of the 2017 IEEE ThirtiethNeumann Colloquium (NC), Budapest, Hungary, NC, Nov. 2017.

49. Samaniego, M. and Deters, R., Blockchain as a service for IoT. Proceedings of the 2016 IEEE International Conference on Internet of Things (iThings) and IEEE Green Computing and Communications (GreenCom) and IEEE Cyber, Physical and Social Computing (CPSCom) and IEEE Smart Data (SmartData), Chengdu, China, Dec. 2016.

50. Zhang, Y. and Wen, J., The IoT electric business model: using blockchain technology for the Internet of Things. Peer-to-Peer Netw. Appl., 10, 4, 983–994, 2017.

51. Huckle, S., Bhattacharya, R., White, M., Beloff, N., Internet of Things, block-chain and shared economy applications. *Procedia Comput. Sci*, 98, 461–466, 2016.

52. Kim, H.M. and Laskowski, M., *Toward an Ontology-driven Blockchain Design for Supply-chain Provenance*, Wiley Online Library, March 2018.

53. Sun, J., Yan, J., Zhang, K.Z.K., Blockchain-based sharing services: what blockchain technology can contribute to smart cities, in: *Proceedings of the Financial Innovation*, Springer, December 2016.

54. Huh, S., Cho, S., Kim, S., Managing IoT devices using blockchain platform. *Proceedings of the 2017 Nineteenth International Conference on Advanced Communication Technology (ICACT)*, Bongpyeong, South Korea, Feb. 2017.

55. Samaniego, M. and Deters, R., Using blockchain to push software-defined IoT components onto edge hosts. *Proceedings of the International Conference on Big Data and Advanced Wireless Technologies BDAW '16*, Blagoevgrad, Bulgaria, November 2016. Article No. 58.

56. Gou, Q., Liu, Y., Yan, L., Li, Y., Construction and Strategies in IoT Security System. *2013 IEEE International Conference on Green Computing and Communications and IEEE Internet of Things and IEEE Cyber, Physical and Social Computing*, https://doi.org/10.1109/GreenCom-iThings-CPSCom.2013.195.

57. de Leusse, P., Periorellis, P., Dimitrakos, T., Nair, S.K., Self Managed Security Cell, a security model for the Internet of Things and Services[C]. *2009 First International Conference on Advances in Future Internet*, pp. 47–52, 2009.

58. Lamba, A., Singh, S., Singh, B., Dutta, N., Muni, S.S.R., Mitigating IoT Security and Privacy Challenges Using Distributed Ledger Based Blockchain (Dl-BC) Technology (April 2017). *Int. J. Technol. Res. Eng.*, 4, 8, April-2017. AvailableSSRN: https://ssrn.com/abstract=3492690 or http://dx.doi.org/10.2139/ssrn.3492690.

59. Samaniego, M. and Deters, R., Blockchain as a Service for IoT. *2016 IEEE International Conference on Internet of Things (iThings) and IEEE Green Computing and Communications (GreenCom) and IEEE Cyber, Physical and Social Computing (CPSCom) and IEEE Smart Data (SmartData)*, Chengdu, pp. 433–436, 2016.

60. Huh, S., Cho, S., Kim, S., Managing IoT devices using blockchain platform. *2017 19th International Conference on Advanced Communication Technology (ICACT)*, Bongpyeong, pp. 464–467, 2017.

61. Conoscenti, M., Vetrò, A., De Martin, J.C., Blockchain for the Internet of Things: A systematic literature review. *2016 IEEE/ACS 13th International Conference of Computer Systems and Applications (AICCSA)*, Agadir, pp. 1–6, 2016.

62. Rose, K., Eldridge, S. and Chapin, L., The internet of things: An overview. *The Internet Society (ISOC)*, 80, 1–50, 2015.

63. Jesus, E.F., Chicarino, V.R.L., de Albuquerque, C.V.N., de A. Rocha, A.A., A Survey of How to Use Blockchain to Secure Internet of Things and the Stalker Attack, in: *Hindawi Security and Communication Networks*, vol. 2018, Article ID 9675050, p. 27.

64. Natoli, C. and Gramoli, V., Te Blockchain Anomaly. *Proceedings of the 15th IEEE International Symposium on Network Computing and Applications, NCA 2016*, IEEE, pp. 310–317, November 2016.

65. Zhang, Y. and Wen, J., An IoT electric business model based on the protocol of bitcoin. *Proceedings of the 2015 18th International Conference on Intelligence in Next Generation Networks, ICIN 2015*, France, IEEE, pp. 184–191, February 2015.

66. Natoli, C. and Gramoli, V., Te Blockchain Anomaly. *Proceedings of the 15th IEEE International Symposium on Network Computing and Applications, NCA 2016*, IEEE, pp. 310–317, November 2016.

67. Dorri, A., Kanhere, S.S., Jurdak, R., Towards an optimized blockchain for IoT. *Proceedings of the 2nd IEEE/ACM International Conference on Internet-of-Tings Design and Implementation, IoTDI 2017*, ACM, Pittsburgh, PA, USA, pp. 173–178, April 2017.

3

Internet of Things Security Using AI and Blockchain

Raghav Gupta*, Ananya Rakhra and Akansha Singh

Department of CSE, ASET, Amity University Uttar Pradesh, Noida, India

Abstract

Internet of Things (IoT) is essentially an interconnection of different registering gadgets to one another. They can speak with one another and divide their information between themselves without the communication of any human. IoT, for the most part, has one principle brilliant gadget which at that point speaks with other registering or computerized gadget with the assistance of different segments, for example, sensors and processors. Man-made brainpower (AI) and square chain are two of the main parts which help this entire entomb associated framework in banking and security. IoT works fundamentally in three segments; part 1 comprises of gadgets which gather your information, for example, reception apparatus and sensors. The subsequent segments comprise of parts that examine this information the instances of this can be an IoT passage or a center. Finally, the third segment investigates this information and makes the right move required. We have likewise presented numerous future models which can be utilized with progressions of innovation toward making a more astute environment of advances. The blockchain innovation gives us a specific measure of secrecy and helps in encoding our information; blockchain additionally guarantees that our information is hard to adjust or eliminate. There are various models presented which can help everyone in creating a much safer and an efficient environment to share and work on their data.

Keywords: IoT, security, AI, blockchain, cyber security, smart devices, IoT security, IoT models

*Corresponding author: raghavgupta1@hotmail.com

Krishna Kant Singh, Akansha Singh and Sanjay Sharma (eds.) Machine Learning Approaches for Convergence of IoT and Blockchain, (57–92) © 2021 Scrivener Publishing LLC

3.1   Introduction

Nowadays, cyber security is one of the major concerns of many people as technology is constantly upgrading and evolving; it has become even more difficult to ensure the safety of your data. With this boom in technological advancement, more and more data leak and hacking is becoming common. Internet of Things (IoT) is a great tool but it needs to be protected as well so IoT is basically an interconnection of various computing devices to each other. They can communicate with each other and share their data among themselves without the interaction of any human. IoT generally has one main smart device which then communicates with other computing or digital device with the help of various other components such as sensors and processors. Artificial intelligence (AI) and blockchain are two of the most important components which aid this whole inter-connected system in banking and security. They reduce human effort to a major extend and help us integrate various different tasks together. There are various applications of IoT and is used in a lot of industries to simplify, for example, the IT sector, farming and security to name a few. Many heavy machines used in manufacture of food also use IoT to communicate with one another. All this helps the devices to communicate with each other and automate them in a much truer sense. Now, coming to AI or machine intelligence is basically ability of a machine to make a decision by them without any human interface and is done to mimic the human decision taking power. AI is constantly improving itself and evolving. There are various artificial intelligent devices which have defeated the world champions in their game such as chess, which proves how efficient these machines are and how easily they can do the same work in less time. One of the most popular applications of AI is chat bots such as Siri and Bixby. AI is also used in marketing and banking as well to ensure smoother and efficient workflow. Self-diving cars are also one such example; it uses AI. AI is also used in answering some standard queries and questions in customer care which, in return, reduce human workflow and makes their work much more efficient. Now, coming to blockchain, blockchain is generally associated with banking sector and is used to store the data, and this technology was behind bitcoins in the sense it helped them in maintain their records. At a very basic level, blockchain is digital information (block) stored in public database (chain). These blocks consist of various data components. There are mainly three components. Component 1 consists of details such as date, time, and currency. Component 2 stores data consisting of your personal information such as username or a digital signature. Component 3 consists of a distinguishing feature which helps in differentiating various records from one another. It is extremely secure as whenever we change the data in a particular block, its unique signature or hash also changes. It is invented earlier in the 90s to act as a time stamp that was later used in bitcoins. All these systems together can work together and help us crate a much more secure network which can help make a much more secure environment and help in prevention of data leak. We will be looking at the security of IoT using AI and blockchain. There are various applications and different types of combination that can be used to make different types of smart devices using the principals of IoT, AI, and blockchain technology.

3.2   IoT and Its Application

IoT is the connection of many devices connected to each other. They have the ability to transfer and share data among themselves and do not require any human interference. IoT is more being used to create smart devices. The IoT helps us in automating things to an extent and reduce human effort. It is used in a lot of industries such as the medical sector and manufacturing of goods.

To understand at a very basic level, we are using the two devices together to form a smarter alternative. So, for example [4], there is a blood pressure monitor and there is a watch so when we combine both of these technologies to make a smarter and a more user friendly device that is a smart watch. This whole process is known as IoT. This has helped in creations of new and much more efficient technology. It is always evolving and improving. Some of the existing applications are as [11] follows.

Smart lock: In this particular application, we combined a camera, a door lock, and a remote which trigs the lock to open. So, when we combine all these, three things together we make IoT which communicate with each other and let the user know with all the gathered data whether they want to unlock it or not. This is just one of many examples of how IoT is used in our day-to-day life. IoT enabled the user to create a much safer alternative to an already existing system.

Smart speakers: Over here, we have a speaker and a chat bot; so by integrating both of these systems, we are creating a smart speaker with the abilities of a chat bot so the speaker can communicate with the user. So, what I mean by this is the need of physically standing up and changing your music is no longer required; you can simply command your chat bot to do that work for you and this is how a simple system can help us reduce human effort to such an extent. Some applications are as seen in Figure 3.1.

Military application: The military often uses the concept of IoT to invent different types of technology for surveillance and data collection by using various different types of sensors and radars. These are often used in drones as well which enables them to gather data from places where a person or a soldier cannot go. These tools often come handy in the detection of missiles as well because that system also uses various combinations of different types of technologies that come under the umbrella of IoT. Smart tags: these tags consist of various QR codes which can be scanned and can help a user to know more about their product. This is an example of IoT as we are basically using a tag and integrating it with a QR code so these types of tags can help in a much better customer acquisition. Over here, IoT is helping in advertisement as well as customer care.

Remote monitoring: We can use IoT for monitoring of people in the hospitals as we can use various sensors and we can combine various technologies such as sensors like pulse calculator and blood monitoring. It can be used to create more personalized kits. It can be used in various parts and can be used in the places where they cannot afford all the necessary equipment.

So, these were just few of many possible uses of IoT. This interconnection and data sharing of both the technologies allow the user to enjoy the benefit of both the technologies and make a much smarter ecosystem.

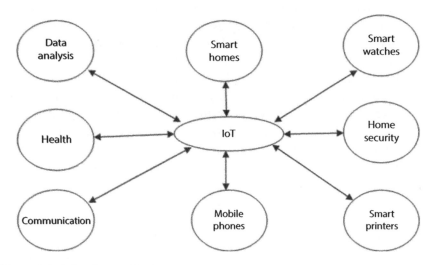

Figure 3.1 IoT and its applications.

3.3   Most Popular IoT and Their Uses

There are various popular IoT in this day and age, we will be discussing few of the most popular IoT [15] which are widely accepted and used. These include various technologies such as Bluetooth and 4G. Most of the other IoT follows or integrates the concepts and working of the following IoT.

LPWANSs: LPWANs or low power wide area networks are networks which help in providing a long range communication on a very low power. These generally consist of small batteries which consist of inexpensive batteries which are small in size and are inexpensive. These are used in large industries to support long range IoT. They are used to connect all sorts of IoT. They can generally support almost all types of sensors; they provide the user with the ability to monitor, metering, and safety of its users. They send small data at low rate which helps them in their longevity. Their low bandwidth ensures its usability and is non-time sensitive.

Cellular: Cellular IoT consists of technologies such as 3G, 4G, and 5G. The cellular technology is extremely popular nowadays and is one of the most used forms of IoT. There, major user database comes from the mobile market where they are comfortably established. They provide the users with sufficient amount of broadband and have various additional features which also includes voice calling, video calling, and video streaming to name a few this broadband does come with a higher cost and power usage. One of the most popular applications also includes smart cars or connected cars which can show you the data and information of your car on your cellular device.

Mesh protocols: One of the most popular mesh protocol is Zigbee mesh protocol; Zigbee is a protocol that requires low power and is used in short range and are wireless. It is quite similar to the LPWANs; the difference being that Zigbee requires more power as compared to the LPWANs on the flip side and it can send larger blocks of data. Their best usage is in the medium range–based IoT where the distribution of node is even. It is often observed that they are used in accordance with Wi-Fi to have a smart and an automated home. Things like smart speaker and smart bulbs use the same technology.

Bluetooth: We all have heard about Bluetooth; it is one of the most popular and widely used applications of IoT. Bluetooth is a subset of WPAN or wide personal area network. What it does is that it creates your own private small network for one to one or one to many data transfers. They are used in carious cellular devices, smart watch, and speakers. The Bluetooth technology is constantly evolving and updating itself in line with the new developments in technology. These are optimized for low power and high data transfer. The use of Bluetooth technology is becoming more and more popular and is an integral part of the IoT.

Wi-Fi: Nowadays, most modern houses have Wi-Fi as their daily driver for their online data transfer and data sharing. It can be used anywhere be it cooperates or your own personal home or offices. The Wi-Fi has helped in integration and connection of various technologies with one another; the only drawback observed of Wi-Fi is that of coverage and scalability. The various applications of Wi-Fi include smart camera, cellular device, watches, and laptops. The latest update in Wi-Fi introduced is Wi-Fi 6 which allows its user less than 96 Gbps. There are various application and usability of Wi-Fi as they are inherently easy to set up and use. This has led to become one of the most popular IoT and is used in a lot of games and transportation vehicles such as cars.

RFID: RFID or radio frequency identification is a popular application which works on the concept of magnetic field and radio frequency; the radio waves are use in the transmission of small data which can later be read with the help of an RFID reader. It has completely revolutionized the way we shop as we can have a more secure shopping as the chances of theft are much lower as they are used as alerts for shoplifters. They are integrated with various other IoT to create smart IoT with many more applications. They are integrated with various other technologies nowadays. It regulates all your data and makes it more efficient all the above mentioned components are displayed in Figure 3.2.

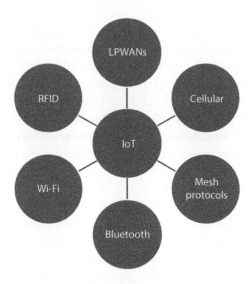

Figure 3.2 IoT and its components.

3.4   Use of IoT in Security

One of the major and most important applications of IoT is in the field of security. We can take many combinations of various technologies to make a safe environment [5]. We can take a combination of electrocuted wires, rotating cameras, and siren alerts. So, Internet of these things will create a system when the person touches a wire or a person is identified in the rotating cameras; the lightning and the sires will automatically initialized, creating a loud noise and giving a shock to a person who is trespassing. Use of IoT is becoming more and more common in the field of technologies these days. Similarly, we can have various technologies like this which use IoT for problem solving. We can also use the combination of RFID cards and the entrance of your house. This model can especially work better in apartments and societies. These gates can only be unlocked when the correct RFID tag reads the data ensuring a safer environment as no unwanted person would be able to enter the society without that key. We can also use the combination of alerts beacon and locking of door. This system can be extremely helpful in the banking sector as soon as we hit the alarm a direct call for police is send which also automatically triggers the command to lock the main gate from the outside preventing any robbers at the bank to leave. The possibilities are endless we can keep on updating it by adding and integrating more and more new developing technologies. We can include cameras in the same setup which can give live feed to the police officers from inside of the bank. So, as we showed you above, we are only limited by our technologies and thinking power in the concepts of IoT.

Over, we see data of industrial IoT security statistics, and we can see over here how people are not ready or prepared to fight the cyber attack and have already recognized a need of protection against IoT attacks; many

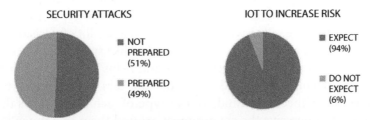

Industrial IoT Security Statistics 2017

SECURITY ATTACKS

- NOT PREPARED (51%)
- PREPARED (49%)

IOT TO INCREASE RISK

- EXPECT (94%)
- DO NOT EXPECT (6%)

Figure 3.3 Industrial IoT security statistics 2017.

of them also believe that the risk of attacked from IoT can be increased a lot in the future and how they are not prepared for it. A statistical depiction is seen in Figure 3.3. Larger companies are at a greater risk of cyber attacks and data leak; due to the IoT, a safer way needs to be updated to already existing system to have a much safer use of IoT. In this discussion, we will be using AI and blockchain method to have a safer IoT interface and make the work not only more efficient but secure as well.

3.5   What is AI?

AI at its very basic level means the ability of machinery to make its own decision without any human help. This is also known as machine intelligence and its main aim is maximize the success rate of any given problem. The most common AIs analyze their environment and take actions accordingly. For an efficient AI, the AI first needs to be trained so it can be done with the help of BLH [6]. BLH or basic learning heuristic is when we strain the AI to do or solve the similar types of puzzles or problems. AI has completely revolutionized the way a device perform tasks. By empowering them to make their own decision, we have removed the need of human interference to an extent and made a machine which is much more efficient in doing the work that would require much more human effort. There majorly four types of AI, each different from other and efficient in its own way. The first type of AI is known as reactive machines; these are the most basic types of AI and only reactive. What I mean by that is that it does not makes its own decision based on its past experiences; one of the examples of the technology is IBM's chess playing supercomputer active in the 1990s; it was able to defeat the current world chess champion at that time which shows the extent to which it can be taught and made intelligent. It purely just knew all the possible moves and predicts what the next move of the opponent could be and then it chose the most appropriate move which ensured higher success rate. Now, coming to the second type that is limited memory, this is a type two class of AI and can look in their past moves or decisions for references. One of the examples of this type of AI can be self-driving cars. The self-driving cars need to make a lot of decisions with a lot of elements that it needs to keep in its mind like speed, turns, and traffic lights. So, this system does exactly this and helps in a much safer right and is also currently being used in self-driving cars. Now, coming to the third type that is theory of mind AI, this type of technology helps the AI understand and perceive the environment around them in a much better way. This is extremely important as these are the qualities which lead to the development of societies in humans. These machines try to understand and feel what their surroundings and then make a decision it helps them to understand each other's motive for future technological advancement; it is extremely important for these AI to understand us and be compatible with human interactions. Now, lastly, coming to the fourth type of AI hat is self-aware AI, these are the machinery which are at the last stage of AI, these are the machinery which can take a conscious decision on their own completely and are aware of themselves, and they are able to predict the feelings of other and work accordingly. These are the type of AI which are not yet created but is the ultimate goal. This type of AI would require no human interference and can completely make its own decisions consciously knowing all the consequences. These were the various types of artificial intelligent which makes the machine smart in a much truer sense. This is the ultimate goal of AI; we are trying to creating a human aiding ecosystem in which all the hard labor is completely performed by AIs making the ease of work much more to humans.

3.6 Applications of AI

There are various applications of AI in almost all sectors of industries as it can make a lot of work easier an automated. We have already discussed few of the applications but some of the major applications [7] in the different fields are as follows.

Communication: AI can be used in the field of communication as it can have a much larger database of language and understand or convey the sentence. The best example for this can be the language translators; some of the language translators can automatically detect the language from the audio input and give the output required. So, for example, a person is speaking in Spanish, it will automatically detect the language and then translate into some other language like English. These are the ways in which AI can be used in communication and help in creating a more global reach.

Smart learning: AI can help in the field of learning as AI can learn from its past experiences and evolve with each new experience which makes it extremely helpful in learning and adapting in different types of conditions from its wide database. It can be used by the military to compute different and the most optimal strategies in war and this is one of many applications that can be created due to the ability of AI to constantly evolve and become better.

Gaming: As we have discussed before, gaming can be a great application of AI. We already discussed how the AI defeated the current chess champion. AI can be used in gaming and improving one's kill and have different opportunities and train ourselves. AI can be used to monitor the game and give us a review how to make it better and train us for a better gaming experience.

Problem solving: One of the major applications of AI is problem solving as it keeps evolving with new equations; we can create a machine to solve tough mathematical equations and help students in solving various equations. It can also help in solving tedious equation and find the most optimal solution. It can perform same task as a human at a much lower time and at a much higher efficiency.

Medicine: We can use the AI technology to have a much better report and monitoring of your health. We can use this and have much better healthcare. We can use this in surgery and avoid any human error as the AI machine can perform the same task with much more accuracy as the past experience keeps on evolving the current system and make it better.

3.7   AI and Security

There are various examples in our technological platforms which very well showcase the integration of AI in the field of security WAN; one of the most commonly used AI in the field of security is CAPTCHA [9]. CAPTCHA is currently used to differentiate between humans and machines as the AI has not yet been able to solve this security which means that if an AI is able to solve this particular point, then we can use this technology then we can try the same technology for different problems as well. To make new technological advancements, we can us the combination various different existing technologies [10] such as radio frequency identifiers and cloud computing if we combine some already existing hardware and integrate with the AI. We can create a smart security solution. We can use the AI in the security of banking as well. We can create a smart system which automatically encrypts your private information and make it available only to the parties concerned.

AI can be extremely helpful in authentication of the user. An AI can be integrated with a smart scanner that can scan the particular document, identify the signature, and compare it to the previous signatures; this model will help in preventing document forgery and tampering in online transfers. It is relatively easier systems as there is already existing technology which can scan and identify and we just have to integrate AI with it and make it a truly smart scanner. If we observe closely IoT is all around us, like the Bluetooth printers, smart speakers, and computers. As the number of IoT increase so does the risk of security. How can we ensure that our data that we are providing to the third party applications just to set up the initialization process will not us affect us in a harmful way in the future. Nowadays, there are various applications which request the use of your camera and microphone while downloading. This raises the question of our safety. The user should beware when which of the following part of our phone is used. These apps can easily access our location as well so a system which can monitor all these apps and when which part of our system is active like Bluetooth and GPS can be detected by an AI and give us a small notification whenever the following component of IoT is used. AI can also be integrated with the object detection algorithm with the help of an AI, then this system can be taught to identify various harmful objects like guns and knives, and this system when applied to a smart camera, we are creating an IoT which can automatically detect danger and send an alert. This system will help us protect a lot of lives and prevent crime from happening to an extent. AI can be extremely helpful in the field of AI as we can create a whole system which will have the database of the number of crimes, types of crimes, and places where they most often happen; then, when we feed this information to the AI, we can optimize and create a system which can tell you the spastics of places and how to control crimes in that particular area. So, let us say that there is area A with a lot of robberies and an area B with a lot of cyber attacks. We have 20 police officers and 10 ethical hackers spread evenly in area A and B; however, if we have this system and we know that area A is inclined more toward robbery and area B is inclined more toward cyber attacks, we can optimize the staff and have 16 police officers in area A with 2 ethical hackers and have 4 police officers in area B along with * ethical hackers. So, what we are doing over here is optimizing our security and arranging our resources in such a way that it suits us the best. This is just one of many ways by which we can use AI in IoT and optimize our strategies toward a more secure environment.

The threat is very real as the same AI that can be used in security can also be used against us in a lot of ways; now, if we look at the study of China in the field of security [11], the Chinese leader Xi Jingping believes that AI is extremely important for the future of the global military and economic power completion. They have a very different and an interesting take on AI in the sense and they are more inclusive with the idea of AI integration and believes that it is inevitable. They believe that AI can provide a tactical advantage to them. We can clearly see how AI can easily be used in warfare to protect us or destroy us. It is better to be first to develop warfare advantages in AI and security and has an edge over others.

3.8   Advantages of AI

In this part, we will be discussing the various advantages of AI and why it is a great technology to be integrated with IoT and security. We will be discussing each of these advantages in details so some of these advantages are as follows:

- Minimal human error
- Less human risk
- Always at our disposal
- Used in tedious work
- Used in chat bots
- Decision making power
- Daily use
- Advancement in other technologies

So, one of the major advantages of AI is that it reduces human effort; it helps in reducing the same amount of work and is self-sufficient in doing the same work. They make life much easier as the humans no longer need to that task anymore and can use that time in a different work or way, for example, there are now various AI-based software which can make the graphical representations and tedious mathematical work for you. Now, the great about AI is that it can act as a dummy or a human replacement in time of danger so I mean by that is that we can use various AI-based robots to be in dangerous situations like defusing a bomb, collecting soil samples from outer space, and aid people which are effected from natural disaster such as tsunami and earthquake. They can be used to provide food and medical supplies in such places. The advantage of AI over other technologies is also that it is at our disposal all the time like humans it does not get tired or need breaks it can work 24/7 without getting tired an continuously perform tedious calculations and other heavy duty work. They can be used in chat bots and helpline as it needs to be available at any given point of time, AI can ensure that we have a system that can work on its own all the time. We as humans often come across some tedious work which has to be done constantly for a long period of time repeatedly; this is where AI can come in handy and help us in creating a system. This system when instructed and can do the same work again and again; these tasks can also include repetitive tasks such as documentation verification and surveillance all these time consuming and difficult tasks can easily be performed by an AI and in a much more efficient way. As we discussed earlier, they can act as a personal assistant and we are already seeing this trend in chat bots such as Siri and Bixby. These chat bots when integrated with our IoT ecosystem we can create a system which can simply function on our voice. They can be of great use for disabled people and help them normalize their living situation. AI is capable of making faster analytic calculation and calculation of the data and its working. As it's a machine, it will perform the calculations faster, thereby reducing time taken to perform various tasks, and they can be used at billing centers where people can just run the barcodes and it will automatically calculate the bill and deduct money from their accounts, thereby reducing the need of a worker. The boom in AI technology has led to advancements in various other technologies as well one such example can be that of prediction of breast cancer. Doctors have successfully used AI-based machinery in predicting breast cancer in the early stages.

3.9   Timeline of Blockchain

To understand better about the blockchain, we will be looking at the complete timeline from its inception to its latest updates as illustrated in Figure 3.4. This technology has constantly being involved and has played a major role in development of crypto currency. First invented in 1991 by Stuart Harber and W Scott Stornetta, blockchain was basically a cryptographically protected chain of data also known as chain of box. It was originally made to act as a watermark on digital data and so that some of the data in banking cannot be back dated. It was made for this purpose which later was evolved into the technology behind the bitcoins. This was how the technology of blockchain was born. Later in the year 1998, Nick Szabo who is a computer scientist and a cryptographer started working on bit gold which was nothing but a digital currency

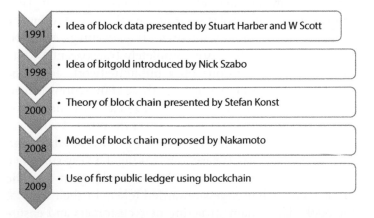

Figure 3.4 Development of blockchain over the years.

which was decentralized this system was never applied however this same system became the building blocks of crypto currency known as bitcoins. In the year 2000, Stefan Konst suggested his theory of blocks connected via a secured chain. Finally, in the year 2008, the model of blockchain was made and then the following year the first public leaguer was made by Nakamoto.

Nakamoto is the person who is credited for the development of bitcoins using the following principles of blockchains. This is just one of examples which have helped in development of a secure cyber ecosystem. This can be applied to many other technologies to add different types of smart systems that can be made to protect your data as well. When combined with AI we can theoretically have a self-sufficient smart system which can be used in banking sectors and IT sectors as well. It can make money transfer and payments much safer a discreet and can avoid any fraud as it cannot be altered as he hash will change with the change of data in the block.

3.10   Types of Blockchain

In this section, we will be studying different types of blockchain in detail, and we will be studying how each of them is different from the other; there are majorly three types of blockchain [14] and we will be studying in this part of the discussion the following three categories as in Figure 3.5:

1. Public blockchain: Public blockchain is one of the most popular and commonly used type of blockchain; the examples of public blockchain include bitcoin and ethereum. These are the two of the most popular applications of block chained security. The public blockchains are open sourced and basically allows any and all types of users to access it. They can choose various roles such as casual users, developers, miners, and community member. The advantage of public blockchain is that they are completely transparent and all the transactions are done on a public network. Everyone can access these transactions. As these transactions can be access by anyone; they are decentralized and no one person has any special privilege or power over the other. As they are decentralized, the chance of it shutting down or edited and censored in any way is very low making it a very suitable a popular platforms to be used. When working on a public blockchain, each user gets rewarded token for their work at the public blockchain attracting new customers and ensuring they stay and work at their blockchain.

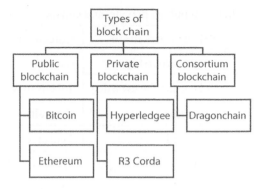

Figure 3.5 Types of blockchain.

2. Private blockchain: Private blockchain is a lot different than that of a public blockchain in the sense that it needs to be requested before use and then only you can access and work on the data, whereas the public blockchain can be joined by anyone. It is a very close knit ecosystem and requires permission to join. The differences to public blockchain does not end there; they are decentralized and not every user or participant is equal in private blockchain. They are often used by huge cooperates who want to share their data within themselves and among others ensuring secrecy and safety of their data. So, few of the examples can be hyperledge and R3 corda. These are the two most popular private blockchains. The token of reward can or cannot be rewarded for your work. There is no guarantee of tokens.

3. Consortium blockchain: Consortium blockchain is more similar to that of private blockchain; the only major difference is that they are owned and governed by a group of entity. The example of consortium blockchain can be dragonchain. They can also be thought of as a subset of private blockchain and the users enjoy the same benefits of that of a private blockchain. They are often observed to be more efficient and have a faster workflow as the work of governance is divided among the group. They can be used by small and big business for their personal use and can be an efficient way of sharing and working on their data.

There are various differences in the nature and how all three of them functions in different ways. The ways in which they differ are shown in Table 3.1.

Table 3.1 Difference between public, private, and consortium blockchain.

Public blockchain	Private blockchain	Consortium blockchain
No ownership	Single ownership	Owned by a group of people
Tokens awarded	Tokens maybe awarded	Tokens maybe awarded
Decentralized	Centralized	Centralized
No censorship	Censored	Censored
Example: bitcoin	Example: hyperledger	Example: dragonchain

Now, if we look at dragonchain, we can also observe that dragonchain can be considered as a hybrid blockchain. Hybrid blockchain takes the best of all the blockchains and makes a very user friendly to use. What it does is it basically can be owned privately or a group of people but the data in the blockchain can be accessed by all and ensures transparency and ensures faster workflow. They are considered to be cooperatively more secure.

They are differentiated on the basis of ownership, tokens, centralization, censorship, and different examples.

3.11 Working of Blockchain

Blockchain which is basically a public ledger has a very simple working to understand the mechanism behind the blockchain we first need to see more about bitcoins and how it was used. So, bitcoin as one of the most popular crypto currencies is used a lot nowadays and its value is constantly increasing day by day so when the finance is transferred and stored that's when block technology is used. This chain is constantly increasing with boxes of data each box containing unique hash or signature which stores your data [1]. In the case of bitcoins, each block of data I of 1 mb and can hold up to roughly 1,000 transactions. Now, coming back to block data, each box of data is divided into three components. These components are as following:

1. Data: The data in the blockchain depends upon the time of blockchain, in bitcoins that data is generally your name, age and some transaction details. However, this data can be transformed into different types of data, so, for example, if we have to make blockchain of customers at a fast food restaurant we can alter the data to input the name, age, transaction details, and favorite food item. This data

can help us in better understand the customer and help in customer acquisition.

2. Hash: Hash is basically a differentiating feature and is unique to all the boxes. It can be compared to a fingerprint as no two fingerprints are the same; similarly, no two hash can be the same, it is used in identifying the block and its contents. The hash is dependent on the data inside the block so change in the data leads to change in the hash of the particular box. So, no two things can be done simultaneously either we can change the data or have the same hash or a digital signature. Hash is generally series of numbers and alphabets which is generated by calculating the data inside the block. The transactions are entered the way there are happening; the order is extremely important for the generation of the correct hash.

3. Hash of previous block: So this part of the block contains the hash of the previous block to maintain a chain-like structure which makes the ability to change the hash extremely difficult, for example, we have a block A with hash A123; then, the next block say block B will contain the hash A123 as well as its own hash B123; then, when we take the third block with hash say C123, it will also have the hash of previous block that is in this case being N123.

Due to this method, we can easily identify where someone is tampering with the records and how it can be prevented as if you tamper with one box, then all the following boxes need to be altered as well and in the case of bitcoins it requires 10 minutes each box. So, this is the reason why this is

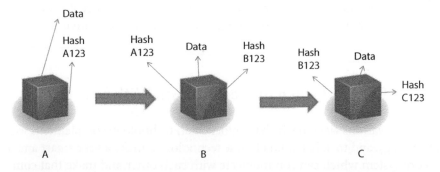

Figure 3.6 Structure of blockchain.

such a secure technology. The results of alteration of one box effects all the other upcoming boxes of data as illustrated in Figure 3.6.

3.12 Advantages of Blockchain Technology

Blockchain technology has various advantages [2]; some of them are given below:

- Avoid information leakage: As tampering of one box leads to the change of hash in all the following box in a domino like effect, it becomes difficult to change and alter which ensures that no personal information is leaked or altered in any kind of way, which in a way prevents any kind of data getting leaked.
- Less transaction time: This is a much faster technology that is present as compared to all the other existing technology as it has a very simple data interface which is secure so each transaction time is low as these are not very heavy files and can easily be processed.
- No transaction intermediates: As we directly add our information and transactions, the need of the third party becomes obsolete. So, this system can help save that third party interest and you no longer have to share your personal data with the other party
- Low risk of fraud: The chances of scam and frauds are much lower due to its secure network. As the data is being added on your own by the end user, the chances of scam and fraud are low. This was the reason it was used in bitcoins as well.
- Real-time transactions: The main reason it is preferred a lot these days because the transactions take place in real time and make the use of them much more viable alternative.

3.13 Using Blockchain Technology With IoT

There are various ways in which the blockchain technology complements IoT technology, and together, both of these technologies make a very smart and a secure system which can communicate with each other and make that communication completely secure [3] some applications are depicted in Figure 3.7.

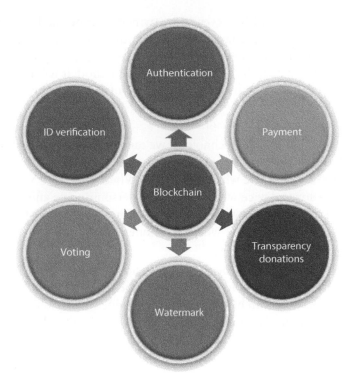

Figure 3.7 Applications of blockchain.

i. Authenticated login system

With the help of IoT, we can create a network which needs to be more user-friendly and secure; at the same time, we can have a onetime login passwords and unique signature which can store all our passwords and sensitive data. This technology can take use of blockchain technology and have a much after database of people without giving it to a third party and making them system much more secure. This when connected with IoT can automatically fill in all your passwords and username and keep all them in a kind of a bank where they are safe due to blockchain technology. This can be one such application where IoT is being secured with the help of blockchain and add an additional line of defense from various hackers. This will provide the user for a one place stop to all their passwords and usernames. All these passwords can be authenticated with the help of blockchain.

ii. Payment at food joint

We can have an automated machine using various technologies together which can take your order and let you pay securely directly to the machine removing the need of a person to take an order and making it much secure as the human error will be lower. The payment can be made secure and fast with the help of blockchain technology and make a much more secure machine that reduces the need of a person to be physically present. As the payment would be with the help of blockchain method, it will more secure and fast; we can use them not only at food joints but at many places like food marts and cafes.

iii. Transparency donations

With the help of blockchain technology, we can create a smart donation system which can track each donation to its source ensuring that your money is being delivered to those who are in need. When integrated with IoT, we are creating a smart device which can help a person donate and ensure fair transaction is taking place, we will be able to create a much more transparent transaction and actually know where are money is being used.

iv. Watermark legal documents

Blockchain technology can be integrated with a scanner and help us in making a smart scanner which can read the documents and look for a special watermark which can help them access the documents and know more about its authenticity. All this data would be very difficult to hack as even if they do imitate the hash the data will remain same and cannot be changed so it can very well be used to check the authentication of a document.

v. Voting machine

We can integrate this same blockchain technology with the voting machine and help in making a fair voting and election if we integrate blockchain to voting machine we can easily track from where the votes are coming and whether they are genuine or not. No person would be able to vote twice as the hash signature is formed with the help of data, and if all the data is the same, then the hash generated will be the same as well and it would not register it and help in ensuring fare election.

vi. Verification id

The blockchain technology can be added to check the authenticity of ids it can be of great help at airports to check whether the presented ids such as passports are genuine or not. When integrated with IoT, we are looking at a system which alerts the person when the presented documents are not genuine.

3.14   IoT Security Using AI and Blockchain

IoT can become one the most unsecure and easy to hack ecosystem due to many active working system. As a lot of systems communicate with each other, the system failure of one system can affect the whole IoT. So, as we discussed before, AI is just the ability of a machine to make its own decision. So, we need to create a system which can automatically detect and predict when and where a malware or an error might occur in the IoT and prevent it from happening. The prediction model and maximum success rate model of AI can help this in the field of IoT. Now, coming to the blockchain, as discussed earlier blockchain is a method which allow the user to store their data which can be accessed by anyone but cannot be altered. This is due to its hash or a signature [12].

Now, if we use this same technology for financial data in the IoT, we can make it accessible to all and ensure security as well. This whole system can be protected with the help of an AI. The blockchain can be the first line of defense from cyber attacks; it will ensure that no data is leaked or altered. It can also prevent identity theft as there is certain amount of anonymity while doing transaction with the help of blockchain. Then, we can use a smart AI which can constantly evolve and predict a cyber threat; it can then take the suitable decision which will ensure the maximum chances of success. There needs to be various models placed in all the sectors as together all these technologies can make a system which is secure smart and reduces human effort. An ecosystem can be created for the banking sectors which can help them securely transfer finances anonymously without any third party interference and prevent data leakage as well. When implemented on a large scale, we are looking at a system which is very difficult to hack into and can have many protections.

As AI is constantly evolving and becoming better the chances of success will also increase accordingly. There are various factors that need to be kept in mind while working on IoT [8]; some of them include problems like data privacy, confidentiality, and accounting. For a system to work us need, it to be in such a way that although we can trace it back to its origin but there is still certain amount of anonyms there to protect the data. The system should also be able to authenticate and access the data to the rightful owner or user of that information only. This is where AI can help and create a system which can authenticate the user it can be a two-step authentication to access the information like an OTP and a fingerprint to prevent data leakage [13]. The system created needs to be efficient as well we need to make sure that the system we are creating should be responsive and efficient; if they alert late or are very slow and have a lot of bugs or is constantly crashing, then this system is of no use. The interface should be clean, easy to operate, and efficient. In the worst case scenario, our personal details or banking details do get lead we can still have them encrypted which will act as a final line of defense.

If the blockchain and AI do not manage to prevent data leakage or corruption, we can have all the data encrypted to an end-to-end user so that only the two responsible parties can access the data. However, we cannot only depend on technologies like AI and blockchain to protect IoT. The amount of security of IoT is also limited to the amount of secure components involved in IoT. The IoT can be easily hacked because of this exact same reason; it is because IoT has so many moving parts of a particular time that to make a system that protects all the parts all the time can be a tedious task. With such advancement in technologies the use of this technology in warfare is inevitable so we need to create a system to counter all this. AI is a great tool but a dangerous one as well we need to be extremely cautious and think about all the ways it might affect us. There is a need of a system which can detect any threat and take actions automatically at a very basic level.

3.15   AI Integrated IoT Home Monitoring System

In this part, we will be discussing a model which can help us in creating an IoT which will give us in depth knowledge about our system [19]. Things required for this are different types of nodes, smart miner, cloud computing, local storage, and AI. So, according to this model, we will have a smart miner that will be in the center of our IoT connected with different nodes such as speakers, fridge, and television so what we are trying to achieve by this mode is to analyze all our homing device understand the power consumptions. We will take all these IoT and connect them with the smart miner; now, the AI in the smart miner will monitor power consumption from the entire device and analyze each of the data separately. We would be able to see and study which appliances are taking up the most power; this system will also help us in identifying faulty component and alert the user. All this analytic data can then be stored in the cloud or a local storage device; preferably, it should be stored in both of the storage device. All this data would give us in depth knowledge and help us in monitoring all our energy consumption. We are looking at various nodes such as fridge, microwave, and washing machine, all with the high power requirement.

As we can see in the above architecture, this how all our systems will be connected ensuring high work efficiency. All the data from the IoT devices will be input in a smart miner; now, this smart miner will study and analyze all the data with the help of an AI and then AI will check for any irregularities. Then, if there are any regularities found in this system then it will notify the smart miner and the user, the history of all the transactions will

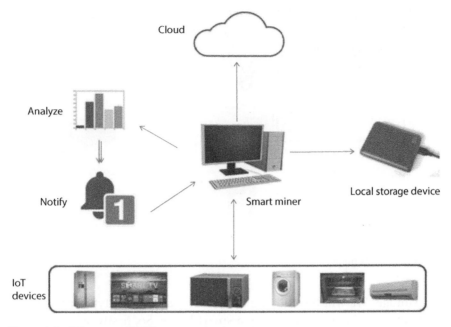

Figure 3.8 AI integrated IoT home monitoring system.

be stored in the cloud and all the analysis can be stored in a local storage device. So, in theory, we are creating a power optimizing system which will give you in depth insight of all the appliances that you are using and alert you for irregularities and saving you from future power failure or worse as even sudden power change will be notified as there will be constant monitoring of all the data that is continuously analyzed by the AI. This system can be extremely helpful for old people and ensure their safety; it can be used by people who are constantly working and their home is unmonitored while they are gone, we can also integrate a SOS notification for a high voltage change beyond a point which can lead to house fire as shown in Figure 3.8. This model will protect its users in more than just one way and give them insights too.

3.16   Smart Homes With the Concept of Blockchain and AI

In this part, we will be discussing about the smart homes concept [16] using blockchain and AI. The IoT will be using blockchain and AI to regulate usability and safety as seen in Figure 3.9. The model of smart homes consists of many parts such as transaction, ledger, smart miner,

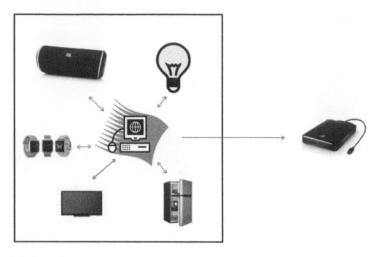

Figure 3.9 Smart home.

and storage. We will be studying each of these different types of components that can be used in making a smart home. So, firstly, when we talk
about transaction, what we mean by transaction is any and all communication taking place between different types of devices is known as transactions. They can be secure ad unsecure transactions. Now, coming to
ledger, ledger, or, in this case, a local BC is a device that keeps track of the
transactions taking place in the whole IoT. All the transactions are connected to each other in a chain-like structure which cannot inherently be
changed. This local BC ledger is keeping its transactions with the help of
blockchain method as each box of record or transaction consist of a hash
of other block of transaction. Now, coming to the smart homeminer, it is
basically a device which is the whole brain of the IoT it ensures smooth
workflow and security. It can be integrated with various anti-malware and
anti-viruses which can be detected with the help of an AI. It helps in creating a secure and a safe network for computing devices to share their
data without the fear of data leakage and malicious attacks from other
devices which are not part of your network. Now, all this data and history of transactions needs to be stored so it can be stored in local storage
devices which can safely keep all your data from attack.

In the above figure, we are looking at a system that showcases us an IoT.
The devices like smart speakers, smart bulb, smart watch, TV, and fridge
are connected to each other. All of the above systems are connected to
each other with the help of blockchain and this system consists of a central
smart miner which regulates and monitors all the information. All this

data then can be stored in a local storage device. This system can be used in home offices, small businesses, or your home. These were all the various components that were required in making of this system and can help in creating a more secure ecosystem for our devices.

3.17   Smart Sensors

In this part, we will be discussing about a device which uses the combination of all homing device [20]. We are looking at a home sensor which is connected to all the other sensors; one such example can be Haier SmartCare device. What this device does is use IoT and AI to create a system which is connected to all the other various sensors such as smoke detector, door indicator, doorbell, fridge, and more. So, this system notifies the user whenever there is an irregularity or danger it acts as a one stop notifying device for all the sensors and nodes. This particular system uses the Zigbee protocol and helps its user in a more in depth monitoring of all their other devices. It can easily be accessed with the help of a mobile application and is easy to set up. Each system can store up to 20 homing devices. This system can be available in various formats 5 to be exact.

This is one of the greatest examples of how IoT and AI are working together to make a system which can help you give more insight about your day-to-day devices. Now, these devices can be modified by including different systems such as ventilators and other medical equipment and can be used in the hospitals for monitoring of their patient. This will help the nurse and the doctor in better understand and studying of their patient. All this data then can be stored in a private blockchain and all the data can be encrypted this system will allow its users to keep a better eye on their patients. This interconnection of system is the core of AI and its principle. This is just one of many IoT applications. This system can be used in both hospitals, home offices, and for your home. There are various such smart devices available in the market which can do all this monitoring work for us. With continuous rise in crime rates, this can act as a defense for all the people who might live at home alone. The mobile application integration provides its user with mobility and can help in ensuring safety even when they are not at home. With mobile application integration, we can also see the live stream of data directly to our mobile phones and we can monitor or check what is going on in our houses when we are not there. The same system can be used in offices and can work in the same manner in the sense same system will help us monitor the office when you are not present ensuring additional layer of security.

3.18   Authentication Using Blockchain

In this part, we will be discussing how we can use blockchain method to make an authentication system which can be seen in Figure 3.10 [17]. We will see how smart contracts can be made using fog nodes in IoT and develop a method for token security in crypto currency. We have briefly already discussed about crypto currency, which is popular and widely used on the internet for example, bitcoin and litecoin. As presented in the research paper by *Almadhoun, Randa, et al. "A user authentication scheme of IoT devices using blockchain-enabled fog nodes."* We can use majorly five technologies/parts which include admin, end user, smart contract, fog nodes, IoT device, and cloud. We will be talking about each of this part and understand how they are used and how they contribute in this system.

In this system, the main role of admin is to give ownership or access to the contract to the people. The admin or a group of admin can decide which user will get what ownership of the contract. He will manage the registration and de-registration of the contracts. The admin will also be responsible for giving the access to the IoT devices. This access is used by fog nodes to identify authenticate IoT access. Now, coming to the end user, end users are basically the people who request access to these IoT network. The access to these networks can only be given to them by the admin. This is where the smart contract comes into play and is a proof of authentication for the user granting them access to that particular IoT. They cannot be given the complete access they are given access only to the node required.

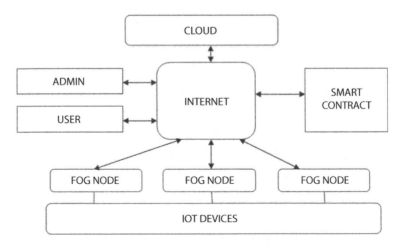

Figure 3.10 Blockchain authentication.

Now, coming to the main part that is the smart contract, smart contracts are basically like a ticket giving you the access to use the nodes. This can be a one ticket system; this contract can give you information about all the nodes that are accessible to you from this contract. All these contracts are integrated with fog node technology which ensures safety and security of the system. So, the fog node which we are discussing over here is basically a node just like a cloud node the only difference being that the storage in the fog node is localized. As it is worked in short range, it is cooperatively faster hence more efficient. Each of the various fog nodes can basically group number of nodes and access. So, there can be various different fog nodes each containing combination of different nodes. In this system there are various devices which can be used each of the device in this IoT can be grouped with other IoT over seen by a fog node which access is to the admin. Over here, the basic wok of cloud is to compute and store fog nodes which and ensures smooth workflow and is one place stop for all your storage needs.

So, this is the basic architecture on how these smart contract works with the integration of fog node technology. With the help of this system, we are creating a safer way for authentication and access to our IoT and it can acts as an addition layer of safety and give some power to those who are admin or in charge of this technology. This will help us in fair use and secure contracts.

3.19   Banking Transactions Using Blockchain

As we have earlier discussed, blockchain in combination with AI and IoT has huge applications. In this part, we will be discussing how we can use blockchain for banking transactions. If we see the case study of china, it is observed that they are facing various issues such as decline in profits and incline in risk, as the technology that is constantly changing the sudden rise is net banking and internet finances have adversely affected the traditional form of banking. To combat that, they need to introduce new and even better way of banking. Blockchain technology is comparatively an unexplored territory when compared to various other technologies such as big data [18]. Now, if we discuss about the inter-banking transactions, they are often done with the help of intermediary firms; now, with the help of blockchain, we can remove this need and have a point to point transfer. This will help us in securing our data and reduce chances of human error. This will help us in prevent sharing data such as personal information, bookkeeping, balance, and other transaction details. Now, coming to the banking transaction between various tasks, it is a very long and a tedious task. Each country has a different set of rules and intermediary stops which makes this whole system lengthy. All this can be avoided just by using blockchain technology for sharing your data cross border. This will help us in having a smoother, faster and a more efficient banking system which will help us in safer transactions as well. There are various banking companies which have already started beta testing on a small level, and one such example can be national Australian bank; they used ledger technology by ripple in making a successful cross border transaction in a much shorter time. Blockchain technology can additionally encrypt your data by doing this method. This will keep our data more secure than existing transaction process. This a more suitable model for developing countries for faster and efficient data share, this dimidiation will help in making a more close knit system where data is such secure and safe.

3.20   Security Camera

When it comes to security, cameras are one of the most popular devices that are used; nowadays, there are various such cameras which come with build in Wi-Fi. We are over here studying about the cameras which help us in monitoring the speed of cars. There are cameras nowadays which can detect the speed of the vehicles and note their number plate. This is also an application of IoT and AI. If we integrate blockchain security to the storage of data, we can create a system that can detect the speed of the vehicle then store the number plate in its database automatically with the help of AI as it is a reparative and a tedious task it can easily be done with the help of an AI.

As we can see in the above system, there is an over speeding car which is detected with the help of a smart traffic camera which then identifies the car, the number plate, and speed at which it is going, then all this data is input in an AI system which can then calculate and compute various such data and then check if it was over speeding, if do this data is then input in a blockchain by the AI itself, the blockchain that we will be using over here would be a public blockchain which can be decentralized and viewed by anyone. It will help us in creating a secure system which can be seen by anyone. A token can be provided to each time you make an enter and then when the numbers of tokens are more than a particular number, say, 5, then the license can be taken or worse. This is a system which is better than the existing model as there is more transparency and less chance of corruption. This method will ensure the authorities to be notified every

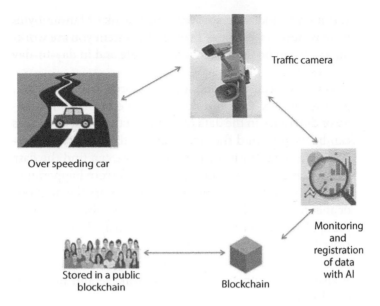

Figure 3.11 Smart traffic security.

time a car breaks the traffic rule and thereby creating a more efficient and a better working system than before as shown in Figure 3.11.

3.21   Other Ways to Fight Cyber Attacks

There are many different types of ways in which we can fight cyber attacks. Each of the cyber attack technique works on different areas and in a different way.

    i.   Access control: Access control is a technique which is used in computing devices and it selects or decides who all can access or use the given data. It is a great method as it restricts other users from accessing your data. It reduces the risk to an extent and can be used in cooperate environments where all people are not required to access all the information.

    ii.   Anti-malware software: Anti-malware software is software which prevents from malware destroying your computing device. Malware is basically software which is made or created just to destroy your computing devices. There are various anti-malware software such as like Malwarebytes from windows which can protect the system you are working on. It can be used both in cooperate and in day-to-day lives as well.

iii. Anomaly detection: Anomaly detector as the name suggests is a part of data mining which detects any abnormality or difference in the data from that of the usual data. This can be used to find the irregularities that might be present in the data. With the help of this, we can find the data irregularities and prevent a cyber attack from happening.

iv. Application security: Application security are the methods or measures which are taken to avoid a cyber attacks by the application; there are various tools in application security which detects various irregularities or error and fix the problem with the tools present in the application security. It also helps in prevention of data leakage and unauthorized access.

v. Data loss prevent (DLP): Data loss prevention software or DLP is a software that can detect future cyber attacks such as data breach. It does by the constant monitoring of the system and blocks sensitive data from users to accessing it. It is mostly used to prevent data leakage and data loss. One such example of a DLP is SolarWinds Data Loss Prevention; it is a DLP and is used to prevent data leakage.

vi. Email security: Email security is a system which prevents unauthorized access to your emails. Email security helps in a secure conversation. This can be used in offices and commercial buildings. If blockchain technology is included with email security, we can have an encrypted and anonymous conversation for everyone except the part concerned in that particular conversation.

vii. Endpoint security: Endpoint security is a system in which we can protect a system from an endpoint in the sense it can be protected from a different devices such as laptop and other mobile devices such as cell phones. However, every endpoint can have an access or an entry point from which there can be a security threat. It is one of the more conventional types of cyber security solution.

viii. Firewall: Firewall is basically a shield which protects the user from incoming and outgoing networks. It basically monitors the network and saves us from outer unsecure network. There are generally of two types of firewall network–based and host-based firewall. Network-based filters the network where as the host-based network is dependent more on the hardware.

ix. Intrusion prevention systems: The intrusion prevention system or IPS is basically a system which can detect or identify a threat and prevent it from happening it does this by constant monitoring. The IPS is constantly searching for unusual activities or abnormality. If and when it detects a possible anomaly, it takes the necessary decision to terminate the irregularity.

x. Network segmentation: Network segmentation as the name suggests is a system in which the network is divided into smaller network, this results in faster and more efficient workflow. By the process of network segmentation, it also ensures network safety to an extent. It monitors the traffic flow. It gives us the option to limit a certain part of the traffic flow or it can shut the entire flow as well.

xi. Security information and event management (SIEM): Security information and event management or better known as SIEM is a service which allows the user to monitor and analyze your data. They can give you real-time alerts and dangers that might be taking place at your system. It can provide the professionals with knowledge and insight about their data usage.

xii. Virtual private network (VPN): Virtual private network or VPN as the name suggest is a private network created by a user; it is very popular nowadays and has proven to be extremely helpful. It allows the user to send and receive the data via a private network. There are various VPN services providing companies such as Cisco.

xiii. Web security: Web security or web application security basically means protection of your web; it detects problem and abnormality on your web and fixes it. This is achieved with the help of various web security tools and monitoring. It follows the same principles of application security and then just applies it to the web thus creating web security.

xiv. Wireless security: As the name suggests, wireless security is the protection of your computing devices via the help of a wireless device; wireless security prevents unauthorized access and ensures restricted entry. There various popular wireless securities such as equivalent privacy and Wi-Fi protected, and both of them are great tools for wireless security.

3.22   Statistics on Cyber Attacks

We have discussed IoT, AI, and blockchain in detail. These all are the building blocks of all future technological advancements in banking sector and security. All the various types of IoT need to be protected from cyber attacks, and the AI and blockchain can help us in that.

Here is the data for all the number of cyber attacks from 2009 till 2017. Over here, we can see that there were more than 800 million cyber attacks in 2019 alone. When we analyze the data we can clearly see the rate at which these cyber attacks are increasing is alarming. Till year 2013, it was still growing at a comparatively slower rate but after that, we have seen a study increase in at least 50 million plus new cyber attacks every year. Over 94% of the malwares delivered to us by an Email.

Over 250,000 people were affected due to the malware in the bank application. This rate is increasing at an alarming rate, and there is no current efficient method to fight these types of cyber attacks. In the second figure, we have a different data; over here, we have the data which shows us the countries that are most affected by these cyber attacks, and as we can see, United States is the most effected place with cyber attacks at 38% percent followed by India at 17% and then Japan at 11% as inferred from Figures 3.12, 3.13 and 3.14.

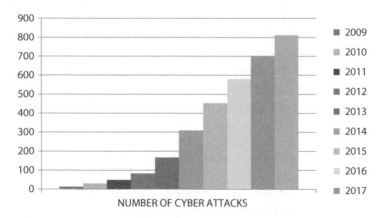

Figure 3.12 Number of cyber attacks.

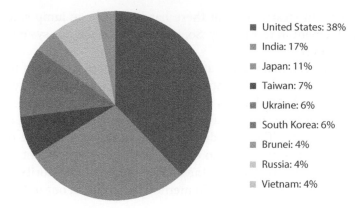

United States: 38%

India: 17%

Japan: 11%

Taiwan: 7%

Ukraine: 6%

South Korea: 6%

Brunei: 4%

Russia: 4%

Vietnam: 4%

Figure 3.13 Cyber attacks across various countries.

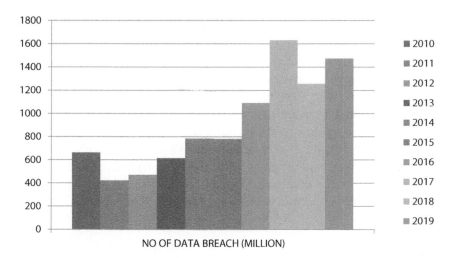

NO OF DATA BREACH (MILLION)

2010
2011
2012
2013
2014
2015
2016
2017
2018
2019

Figure 3.14 Number of data breaches.

We can clearly see over here that is a global issue that needs to be resolved. We need a better system to fight such kinds of threats. We have to develop a system which is smart enough to filter out all these malwares and protect the IoT. We have over seen the extent at which these malwares are working on. India and US are the one of the most effected countries by it. So, to protect IoT we will require various different technologies like AI and blockchain. Now, coming to data breach, data breach is an incident which makes personal information or confidential information public.

So, here, we can clearly see that there has been a huge jump since 2015 with advancement in technology. So, the need to make our system secure is more than ever.

There have been many cyber attacks over the years but one of the most notorious cases was the Mafiaboy cyber attack in 2000. Mafiaboy or better known as Michal Calce was a 15-year old that had initialized a DDoS attack on few of the most popular companies in the world such as eBay, CNN, and Amazon. The total damages due to this attack were over 1.2 billion USD. This is important to our research to see the extent at which the hackers are operating, only if they had a better cyber security. Just like bitcoins, we can use this blockchain method to handle all our online financial exchanges.

3.23   Conclusion

From the discussion presented, we can see how IoT can play such a major role in the development of new technologies. We also discussed how we can use blockchain method and AI to create a much safer internet of thing. We have also introduced many future models which can be used with advancements of technology toward making a smarter ecosystem of technologies. The blockchain technology provides us with a certain amount of anonymity and helps in encrypting our data; blockchain also ensures that our data is very difficult to alter or remove. We also studied about various types of blockchains and different types of AI. We have created many such models which use the combination of blockchain and AI along with IoT and how they are better than existing model or alternative.

References

1. Swan, M., *Blockchain: Blueprint for a new economy*, O'Reilly Media, Inc, 2015.
2. Underwood, S., Blockchain beyond bitcoin. *Commun. ACM*, 59, 11, November 2016, 15–17, 2016. https://doi.org/10.1145/2994581.
3. Pilkington, M., Blockchain technology: principles and applications, in: *Research handbook on digital transformations*, Edward Elgar Publishing, 2016.
4. Wortmann, F. and Flüchter, K., Internet of things. *Bus. Inf. Syst. Eng.*, 57, 3, 221–224, 2015.

5. Kumar, J.S. and Patel, D.R., A survey on internet of things: Security and privacy issues. *Int. J. Comput. Appl.*, 90, 4, 11, 2014.

6. Minsky, M., Steps toward artificial intelligence. *Proc. IRE*, 49, 1, 8–30, 1961.

7. Beck, J., Stern, M., Haugsjaa, E., Applications of AI in Education, in: *XRDS: Crossroads, The ACM Magazine for Students*, vol. 3, no. 1, pp. 11–15, 1996.

8. Gubbi, J. *et al.*, Internet of Things (IoT): A vision, architectural elements, and future directions. *Future Gener. Comput. Syst.*, 29, 7, 1645–1660, 2013.

9. Von Ahn, L. *et al.*, CAPTCHA: Using hard AI problems for security. *International conference on the theory and applications of cryptographic techniques*, Springer, Berlin, Heidelberg, 2003.

10. Xiao, L. *et al.*, IoT security techniques based on machine learning: How do IoT devices use AI to enhance security? *IEEE Signal Process. Mag.*, 35, 5, 41–49, 2018.

11. Allen, G.C., *Understanding China's AI Strategy: Clues to Chinese Strategic Thinking on Artificial Intelligence and National Security*, Center for a New American Security, Washington, DC, 2019.

12. Crosby, M. *et al.*, Blockchain technology: Beyond bitcoin. *Appl. Innovation*, 2, 6-10, 71, 2016.

13. Xu, L. *et al.*, Enabling the sharing economy: Privacy respecting contract based on public blockchain. *Proceedings of the ACM Workshop on Blockchain, Cryptocurrencies and Contracts*, 2017.

14. Niranjanamurthy, M., Nithya, B.N., Jagannatha, S., Analysis of Blockchain technology: pros, cons and SWOT. *Cluster Comput.*, 22, 6, 14743–14757, 2019.

15. Yang, K. *et al.*, Active learning for wireless IoT intrusion detection. *IEEE Wireless Commun.*, 25, 6, 19–25, 2018.

16. Dorri, A. *et al.*, Blockchain for IoT security and privacy: The case study of a smart home. *2017 IEEE international conference on pervasive computing and communications workshops (PerCom workshops)*, IEEE, 2017.

17. Almadhoun, R. *et al.*, A user authentication scheme of IoT devices using blockchain-enabled fog nodes. *2018 IEEE/ACS 15th international conference on computer systems and applications (AICCSA)*, IEEE, 2018.

18. Guo, Y. and Chen, L., Blockchain application and outlook in the banking industry, in: *Financial Innovation*, vol. 2, no. 1, pp. 24, 2016.

19. Tzafestas, S.G., Synergy of IoT and AI in modern society: The robotics and automation case. *Robot. Autom. Eng. J*, 31, 1–15, 2018.

20. Wurm, J. *et al.*, Security analysis on consumer and industrial IoT devices. *2016 21st Asia and South Pacific Design Automation Conference (ASP-DAC)*, IEEE, 2016.

4

Amalgamation of IoT, ML, and Blockchain in the Healthcare Regime

Pratik Kumar[1], Piyush Yadav[1]*, Rajeev Agrawal[1] and Krishna Kant Singh[2]

[1]Department of Electronics and Communication Engineering, G. L Bajaj Institute of Technology and Management, Greater Noida, India
[2]Faculty of Engineering & Technology, Jain (Deemed-to-be University), Bengaluru, India

Abstract

Healthcare plays a critical role in the nation development and its economy. Recent Covid-19 pandemic has witnessed the importance of shifting the conventional healthcare infrastructure toward an automated environment that leverages the emerging paradigms such as Blockchain, Internet of Things (IoT), Machine Learning (ML), and Artificial Intelligence (AI). Further, through this chapter, we demonstrated several technologies which are effective and are essential step into future healthcare system. The amalgamation of these technologies will influence future course of healthcare environment which is pervasive and ubiquitous. This chapter explores such transition and opportunities that would bring the disruptive changes through emerging technologies providing connectivity and interaction among machines and humans for better clinical care irrespective of any ethnic or geographical boundaries.

Keywords: Healthcare, Internet of Things, machine learning, artificial intelligence, blockchain, pervasive, ubiquitous

4.1 Introduction

The kind of revolution that Internet has created in the world by connecting every people, sector, and for all that matter industries with each other

*Corresponding author: piyushyadav1985@gmail.com

Krishna Kant Singh, Akansha Singh and Sanjay Sharma (eds.) *Machine Learning Approaches for Convergence of IoT and Blockchain*, (93–108) © 2021 Scrivener Publishing LLC is something which acts as catalyst that initiates the development of the technology. With the advent of the modern technologies in the recent past years, the world has witnessed technologies like Internet of Things (IoT), Machine Learning (ML), deep learning, and Blockchain that have potential to bring and create a revolution in the healthcare arrangement, business sector, communication field, and the list goes on and on. The major prospect of this chapter is to see what this mentioned technologies can contribute to the healthcare system because medical sector is one such area which can have major impact from these advances [1]. It is a proven fact that the healthcare is one of those sectors which is not yet explored by the technological world in the way it was needed to be; some works are going on but they are still in their dormant state irrespective of the fact that the healthcare field has a lot of potential to concatenate the technological driven world in its setup as it involves a huge amount of sensitive data of the patients, and there is requirement of the continuous monitoring of the patients like those who belong to higher age group that is the elderly people because chances of getting them affected is much more higher, those who are suffering from the chronic diseases where 24/7 monitoring of the patients is needed and many more [2]. So, in this chapter, we will see that how IoT, ML, and Blockchain can create a world of difference in this setup.

IoT is the term particularly used for the amalgamation of the physical devices which involves sensors and other technological stuff which are connected by a means of a router which conveys the information in the connected network of the physical devices. IoT is an immensely a celebrated area because of its all-round versatile nature due to which it finds its area of contribution in the telemedicine, smart retail, connected cars, smart cities, and mobile operations [3]. The IoT in the past few years has come out as a technology that can potentially reduce the pressure in the healthcare regime like in the chronic diseases, persons suffering from the diseases like dementia or Alzheimer, diabetes, and many more. It is also supposed to do commendable job in the sector of the wearable device. Internet of Medical Things (IoMT) is one of the sub-sectors of the IoT which is mainly concerned with the service of IoT in the healthcare regime. In this chapter, we will see that how the whole ecosystem of the IoT works in the healthcare that is how the sensors play their role, we will discuss about the fact that how wearable sensors are transforming the telehealth world and how this sensory data find their place in the cloud ecosystem [6] from wherein our other emerging areas of technology, i.e., the whole concept of neural network and the ML comes in the picture.

In the layman's language, artificial neural networks are similar to that of the biological neural network that are used to perform the given task without being programmed explicitly in the same way that how the human mind works. Some of the famous neural networks which are used in the training are Kohonen neural network, i.e., KNN, backpropagation neural network and many more. With the help of this networks, we can use ML techniques which are used to extract the vital information after processing the obtained data from the sensors in the cloud by performing various steps like data filtering, data mining, and data processing which yield the necessary data we need that includes the data which follows some repetitive trend in their behavior, following fixed kind of patterns, will give some kind of alarming sign if it is needed and will exhibit the condition of the patient over the course of some period and so on [4]. By this technique, we shape the vague and the large data of the patient in an appropriate and user ready form and the work of the health professional that will monitor the patient's data become relatively very easy and the precise information about the patients can be developed [5]. After that, the most important job comes in that is the job of handling the sensitive data of the patient that is subjected to the risk of the many malicious activities on the internet which can drastically hamper the patient's data whose consequences would be fatal [10] So, for this in this chapter, we have also discussed about the security of the patient's data which will be accomplished by the other path breaking technology that is the Blockchain technology. It is an online distributed system that is open to everyone and it consists of the set of the interconnected blocks. Blockchain has the massive opportunity to bring a paradigm shift in a manner of working of the digital ecosystem. It ranges from the medical records, to pharmaceutical supply chains, and it is also validated in the payment distribution models in a massive way and there are other lots of methods to make use of this technology in the healthcare system. Digital medical records are one of the prime examples which have been setup by the Blockchain technology that give the access of the medical record to the patient and to the doctors as well. It can also be used in the supply chain management in the pharmaceutical industry for the supply of medicines and stuff in a more friendly and safe way. With all this, the Blockchain has the immense power to grow in the healthcare industry which will be explained in the detail later in this chapter.

4.2   What is Internet of Things?

The IoT is a whole new framework associated with any other object wherein the exchange of the data is possible between the objects through the computer networks. The things and the data associated with them

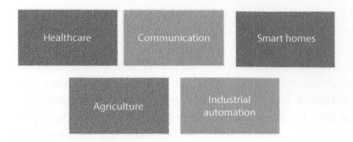

Figure 4.1 Application of the IoT.

could be anything ranging from the sensors, embedded arrangements that can be concatenated with the other system to acquire data such as rainfall activities, moisture content in the soil for agricultural practices, or even in the healthcare, it can be used like observing patient's body movements, heart rate of patient, and body temperature of the patient. It provides all these things about the sense of the environment and makes them intelligent enough to take their own decisions. IoT possesses great sense of deal in healthcare [7, 12]. The power of the IoT is to make them free of human interaction and make them intelligent [13].

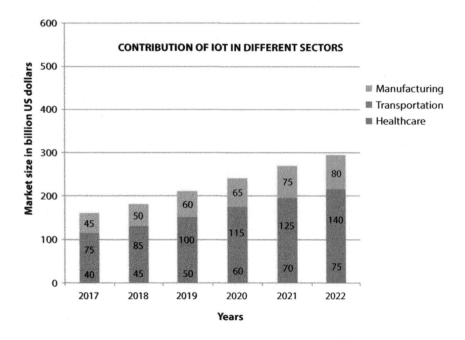

Figure 4.2 Contribution of IoT in different sectors.

Industrial automation, smart homes, agriculture, and communications are some of the sectors which uses the application of IoT as shown in Figure 4.1.

As it is very much clear from the above bar diagram which is represented in Figure 4.2 that the contribution of various industries like healthcare industry, manufacturing industry, and transportation industry is unprecedented in the market of IoT over the years.

Here, in this chapter, our main focus is on the how healthcare industry is integrating and incorporating itself in the IoT regime and how all the system works. So, we will primary discuss about the IoMT, biomedical sensors, and other stuffs like wearable devices which are used nowadays on a huge basis. We will also discuss about the elderly people who are suffering from dementia are making use of wearable sensors and making their life easy with the IoT.

4.2.1   Internet of Medical Things

Nowadays, in the healthcare field, the use of the IoT is something which is arguably the best practice or we can say the application of the IoMT.

The IoMT associates the interconnection of communication oriented medical grade appliances and their amalgamation to larger scale health related networks in order of the betterment of the patient's health. However, as a result of the critical nature of the health associated arrangements, the IoMT still have many challenges majorly in the area of the safety, security, and reliability [14].

4.2.2   Challenges of the IoMT

- Reliability: A reliable system is known by its capacity to obtain its functional aim every time, in the layman's language, it is needed to be failure independent all the times.

In order to achieve the best results, the reliability of the IoMT needed to very high and accurate [14].

- Safety: The working environment must not be hampered by the external source. In the field of the IoMT, especially in the relation of the medical actuators, one must be able to prove that the arrangement will not cause any defect [14].
- Security: The medical arrangement must be strong enough to outer potential threats and attacks because of the sensitive and the personal data they obtain [14].

All of the above parameters are must be considered while designing the IoMT. Despite of these challenges, there is a considerable growth in the IoMT in the recent past years which has been shown by the following graph.

Above graph which is represented in Figure 4.3 shows the trend of the market forecast of the IoMT and its growth analysis per year. Now, we will look about the biomedical sensors and the wearable devices used in the healthcare regime. Wearable devices are the devices that are implant on the patient's body to carry the vital parameters of the body, also known as wireless body area networks [16].

There are many biomedical sensors and wearable sensors [17] which are used in the healthcare regime as they serve a lot of purposes and are very much compatible with the IoT which are given below,

Pulse Sensor: A heartbeat wave is a natural sign that speaks to blood stream volume change in a fringe corridor, for example, a fingertip or an

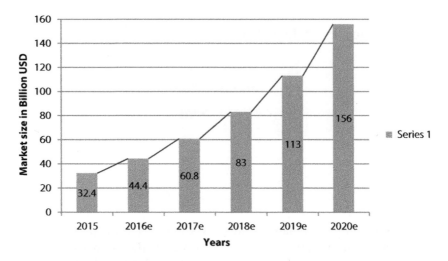

Figure 4.3 Market forecast of IoMT.

ear cartilage. Since the beat wave is influenced by the autonomic apprehensive capacity, it has been utilized for different mental state estimation, for example, stress, exhaustion, and languor [30]. The function of pulse/ heart beat sensor is described as two sided structured working, where on one terminal LED is surrounded with light sensor while the other side is connected with hardware. The connected hardware is responsible for all the intensification of the allotted work or project. The next part, i.e., LED is connected with the human being vein on ear or finger tips for collecting the vitals of the concerned. The LED will fall on the vein legitimate and emanates light.

ECG Sensor: ECG sensor functionality is based on the development in heart muscle by eliminating the polarization that causes pulsating movement of electrical waves in the skin. ECG cathodes are conventional sensors that are wet in nature and required a medium to extend conductivity among skin and terminals. An ECG sensor is utilized to quantify heart movement, which is managed by either Arduino, Rasberry Pi, or any other suitable microcontroller [15]. The obtained data is sent to the cloud server through proper communication medium which will then accessed by the user smartphone and it will give the appropriate directions to the user and make him aware about the potential problems if there is any [15]. Now, we will see about how the role IoT has been utilized in the Alzheimer disease in this section.

4.2.3   Use of IoT in Alzheimer Disease

We will understand this concept using smart healthcare monitoring system which has been in use nowadays for its immense contribution for the dementia patients.

Smart healthcare monitoring system for alzehmier patients is one of its own kind device which is available in the market place, and up to a large extent, it can make a world of difference for its potential users. The present world is suffering a lot because of this fatal Dementia or so called Alzehmier disease and this IoT-based device can bring the positive or by and large optimistic changes in the society through which loT of people can gain advantages and can make use of it. It is not only about the device that is created it is more about the range of advantages; it have from the perspective of elderly people who are suffering from this fatal disease.

The overall conclusion of this device is to make optimistic approach for the Alzheimer patients to monitor their daily life activities [11]. We know that this disease is incurable but with this device we can somewhere manage to make their life normal. Although it cannot guarantee the complete normal routine because it does contain technical equipment's which have their own limits but it can be great initiative.

Wireless care not only records the latest test records but also transmits critical signals to the care personal and their capacities. It also cuts out the duration of the assessment which allows to access the medical cases during the best moment and may improve the better healthcare results. Continuous monitoring of the patient health during their care is critical for those suffering from Alzheimer disease. So, with all this things we need to ensure the fact that currently the world is undergoing through the demographic changes and the population of the elderly people is increasing rapidly day by day and the diseases associated with them also go hand in hand and the Alzheimer is one of the largest contributor to that bucket of disease and in that scenario this device will come into the role play and can help the majority of the sufferers.

As we people are also aware of the fact that technological boost or revolution is its in a way to helping a large amount of crowd there and IoT is one of its main aspects that has already created an ocean of difference in the way many things operate smartly and more intelligently and conveniently and everyone is witnessing it too. Hence, in a nutshell, we can say that smart healthcare monitoring system for the Alzheimer patients for the elderly people and can help majority of the people or the sufferers out there in a very economical way and can be used as a virtual clinic as it is going to provide 24/7 assistance to the people who are needy and can create a beautiful difference in their life.

4.3   Machine Learning

The way ML is flourishing in the healthcare sector is indeed a matter of great appreciation, and it has become possible only because of the fact that the healthcare sector is associated with a lot of data [20] and this data is not in the filtered form and this data redundancy is overcome by the various ML algorithms which performs various processes like data filtering, data sorting, and data mining [8]. ML predicts the patient's condition while IoT is the mode of communication to patient about their actual condition of stress [21].

Artificial neural network forms the backbone of different ML techniques as it is associated with different kinds of learning such as supervised learning, unsupervised learning, and reinforced learning, activities such as pattern classification, pattern recognition is also performed through neural networks [9]. On the basis of these learning, there are various learning techniques such as Kohonen neural network and back-propagation neural network. The data that comes from different sensors which are used in the IoT ecosystem are filtered and processed through this learning technique. Now, we will see about the use of deep learning in the health hector. Particularly, deep learning, a sub-field of Artificial Intelligence (AI) and ML, has seen an massive resurgence in the previous 6 years, generally determined by increments in computational force and the accessibility of enormous new datasets. The field has seen striking advances in the capacity of machines to comprehend and control information, including pictures, language, and discourse. Human services and medication remain to profit colossally from profound learning in light of the sheer volume of information being produced (150 exabytes or 1018 bytes in United States alone, becoming 48% every year) just as the expanding multiplication of clinical gadgets and complete framework [18].

Now, we will see at two instances where neural networks and ML can play a huge role in classifying and using the healthcare data.

4.3.1   Case 1: Multilayer Perceptron Network

In many of the studies, the perceptron neural network is used with other algorithms such as backpropagation neural networks and other neural networks for the analysis of the medical data, as a result of which it had been shown in many researches that multilayer perceptron (MLP) has a great potential in this medical analysis field [22].

MLP is a feed forward neural network and guides the contributions to a fitting set of yields. MLP is comprised of a few layers of hubs inside a chart, so each layer is totally connected to the following one with a nonlinear initiation work, barring the info hubs as shown in Figure 4.4. MLP utilizes a directed learning strategy got back to engendering for preparing purposes and a nonlinear initiation work [22].

The Figure 4.5 shown below represents the architecture of the MLP with input layer, hidden layer, and output layer and notations w01, w00, w02, etc., are the weights associated with the network. The learning calculations expect a MLP design with just one concealed layer. During learning, the loads between the information layer and the shrouded layer, indicated as w01 and the loads between the concealed layer and the yield layer, indicated as w12 are refreshed with isolated calculations. Utilizing the way that the MLP is utilized as a classifier, we characterized a straight and inhumane mistake work that can be planned as a

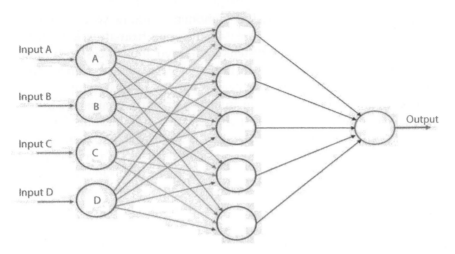

Figure 4.4 A deep neural networks with three hidden layers [19].

piece-wise straight capacity of w01, w02, etc., and to update the values of w12, w13, etc. [24].

4.3.2   Case 2: Vector Support Machine

This type of support machine is basically an application theory based on statistical approach of learning and uses dataset estimators to analyze the model characteristics and performance build on the training set, as a result

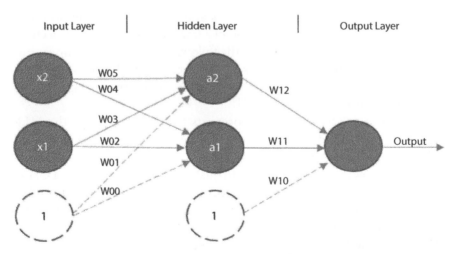

Figure 4.5 Architecture of multilayer perceptron neural network [23].

of which it can handle infinite data sets [22]. Support vector machine (SVM) can deeply a compelled quadratic improvement issue and manufacture ideal isolating outskirts between information sets. SVMs have impressive exploration enthusiasm for the clinical writing exhibitions over the previous years, past that of other AI calculations [22].

Primarily, there are two method of development of classifiers:

1. Parametric approach: based on the prior information derived from data distributions [22].
2. Non-parametric approach: here, the data is not required to fit the normal distribution [22].

4.3.3   Applications of the Deep Learning in the Healthcare Sector

In this present time, the role of deep learning in many forthcoming hot field is immensely celebrated. It is through this learning techniques many industry verticals are shaping their progress in a very sumptuous way and harnessing great success.

It involves all the major field such as communication, automation, and robotics, but its prime role is witnessed in the healthcare setup which involves many sub-sectors such as tracking, patient monitoring, pharmaceutical supply chains, gnemonics, and medical imaging, which is shown in Figure 4.6.

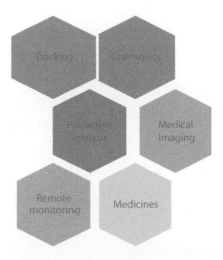

Figure 4.6 Applications of deep learning in the healthcare sector.

4.4   Role of the Blockchain in the Healthcare Field

4.4.1   What is Blockchain Technology?

Blockchain has a huge potential to create revolution and it can perform optimization too across the global infrastructure of technologies connected through internet [27]. This technology uses a distributed ledger on a peer-to-peer network and the processing and storing of data is done in an exceedingly different way [26]. In a layman's language, Blockchain technology is nothing but a short of a distributed online system that can store information and it is based on the set of interconnected blocks which are open to everyone. There are four pillars associated with it, which are given below and shown in Figure 4.7.

- Proof of work: Used to validate the action in the network.
- Ledger: Maintains all the transaction in the network.
- Cryptography: Performs the encryption of the data and it can be decrypted by only legitimate user.
- Smart contracts: Used to verify and validate the user in the network.

Now, we will see that how Blockchain can provide security in the IoT platforms particularly in the field of healthcare.

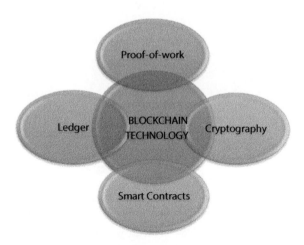

Figure 4.7 Pillars of Blockchain technology [25].

4.4.2 Paradigm Shift in the Security of Healthcare Data Through Blockchain

With the advent of IoT in different industry verticals, it has proven to cut the operation cost and as well as maintenance cost by significant margins and with the rapid growth of IoT; there is an urgent need of finding an optimized way of deploying IoT especially giving attention to the security concern associated with it [25].

As there are lot of patient data coming from biomedical sensors to the cloud servers, they are exposed to lot of vulnerabilities and these data is need to be secured through a proper blockchain implementation. It can be done in the following way:

- Secure communication: The IoT devices which are connected with each other for the purpose of exchanging data between them are required to complete the transaction and to store it in a ledger [25]. Encrypted keys can also be stored in the ledger [25]. Then, the sensors or the devices send the encrypted key using public key of the destination device, and then, it is stored in the blockchain network [25]. After that, the sender will enquire its node to get the public key of the destination device, and then, it will encrypt the message and it can be decrypted only by the destination device through using its private key [25].
- Authentication of the user: Authentication is a dynamic process through which the network decide whether the user accessing the network is valid or not. Authentication serves as the base security of the network. It can be categorized in three categories, i.e., what-you-know, what-you-have, and who-you-are [28]. In order to stop the IoT devices accessing the network, we use public key cryptography to authenticate IoT devices [29].
- Finding legal IoT devices at large IoT ecosystem: There must be a provision or an appropriate framework through which illegitimate devices can be blocked while entering the network. It can be accomplished through creating an enrollment process for the incoming nodes to get credentials of the root server of the network [25]. Root server must authenticate the IoT devices before providing it the node list which are present in the network [25].

With the help of the above mentioned steps, we can secure the healthcare data which are created through IoT ecosystem.

4.5   Conclusion

Healthcare is one of those sectors of our society which possess direct relationship with the people; hence, this sector must be taken care of through our dedicated practice and management and it can be best conquered with the sword of technology. As it had been seen in this chapter that modern technologies like IoT, ML, and Blockchain can create a huge constructive difference in the way healthcare sector operates and it can optimize the results as well as by increasing efficiency of the sector at the same time. As it is very transparent from this review that how IoT can create an integrated ecosystem for the patients by giving them 24/7 assistance, keeping the track of their medical records which will be further optimized through the various deep learning algorithms and neural networks making the task way more easier and error free because there will be no human intervention. At last, the medical data which is exposed to the threat of external world or malicious software will be secured through rock solid Blockchain implementation, hence creating a global decentralized healthcare paradigm which is far more viable than the current conventional healthcare setup.

References

1. Yadav, P., Agrawal, R., Kashish, K., Performance evaluation of ad hoc wireless local area network in telemedicine applications, in: *Procedia Computer Science*, vol. 125, pp. 267–274, Elsevier, Netherlands, 2018.
2. Yadav, P., Agrawal, R., Kashish, K., Heterogeneous network access for seamless data transmission in remote healthcare. *Int. J. Grid Distrib. Comput.*, 11, 8, 69–86, 2018.
3. Nazir, S., Ali, Y., Ullah, N., Internet of things for healthcare using effects of mobile computing: A systematic literature review. *Wireless Commun. Mob. Comput.*, 2019, 20, Article I5931315, 2019. https://doi.org/10.1155/2019/5931315.
4. da Costa, C.A., Pasluosta, C.F., Eskofier, B., da Silva, D.B., da Rosa Righi, R., internet of health things: toward intelligent vital signs monitoring in hospital wards. *Artif. Intell. Med.*, 89, 61–69, 2018.
5. Shahzad, A., Lee, Y.S., Lee, M., Kim, Y.-G., Xiong, N., Real-time cloud-based health tracking and monitoring system in designed boundary for cardiology patients. *J. Sens.*, 2018, 15, Article ID 3202787, 2018.

6. Elmisery, A.M., Rho, S., Aborizka, M., A new computing environment for collective privacy protection from constrained healthcare devices to IoT cloud services. *Cluster Comput.*, 22, 1, 1611–1638, 2019.

7. Qi, J., Yang, P., Min, G., Amft, O., Dong, F., Xu, L., Advanced Internet of Things for personalised healthcare systems: A survey. *Pervasive Mob. Comput.*, 41, 132–149, 2017.

8. Beam, A. and Kohane, I., Big Data and Machine Learning in Healthcare. *J. Am. Med. Assoc.*, 319, 13, 1317–8, 2018.

9. Bishop, C.M., *Neural Networks for Pattern Recognition*, Oxford Univ. Press, New York, NY, USA, 1995.

10. Chacko, A. and Hayajneh, T., Security and privacy issues with IoT in healthcare, in: *EAI Endorsed Transactions on Pervasive Health and Technology*, vol. 4, no. 1, Article ID 155079, 2018.

11. Subasi, A., Radhwan, M., Kurdi, R., Khateeb, K., IoT based mobile healthcare system for human activity recognition. *Proceedings of the 2018 15th Learning and Technology Conference (L&T)*, Jeddah, Saudi Arabia, pp. 29–34, Febuary 2018.

12. Tuan, M.N.D., Thanh, N.N., Tuan, L.L., Applying a mindfulness-based reliability strategy to the Internet of Things in healthcare–A business model in the Vietnamese market. *Technol. Forecasting Social Change*, 140, 54–68, 2019.

13. Aljehani, S.S., Alhazmi, R.A., Aloufi, S.S., Aljehani, B.D., Abdulrahman, R., iCare: Applying IoT technology for monitoring Alzheimer's patients. *2018 1st International Conference on Computer Applications & Information Security (ICCAIS)*, Riyadh, pp. 1–6, 2018.

14. Gatouillat, A., Badr, Y., Massot, B., Sejdić, E., Internet of medical things: A review of recent contributions dealing with cyber-physical systems in medicine. *IEEE Internet Things J.*, 5, 5, 3810–3822, Oct. 2018.

15. Baker, S.B., Xiang, W., Atkinson, I., Internet of Things for smart healthcare: Technologies, Challenges, and Opportunities. *IEEE Access*, 5, 26521–26544, 2017.

16. Kale, S., Mane, S., Patil, P., IOT based wearable biomedical monitoring system. *2017 International Conference on Trends in Electronics and Informatics (ICEI)*, Tirunelveli, pp. 971–976, 2017.

17. Wanjari, N.D. and Patil, S.C., Wearable devices. *2016 IEEE International Conference on Advances in Electronics, Communication and Computer Technology (ICAECCT)*, Pune, pp. 287–290, 2016.

18. Esteva, A., Robicquet, A., Ramsundar, B., Kuleshov, V., DePristo, M., Chou, K., Cui, C., Corrado, G., Thrun, S., Dean, J., A guide to deep learning in healthcare. *Nat. Med.*, 25, 24–29, 2019. 10.1038/s41591-018-0316-z.

19. https://developer.oracle.com/databases/neural-network-machine-learning. htm

20. https://www.google.com/url?sa=i&url=https%3A%2F%2Fdata

21. Pandey, P.S., Machine Learning and IoT for prediction and detection of stress. *2017 17th International Conference on Computational Science and Its Applications (ICCSA)*, Trieste, pp. 1–5, 2017.
22. Naraei, P., Abhari, A., Sadeghian, A., Application of multilayer perceptron neural networks and support vector machines in classification of healthcare data. *2016 Future Technologies Conference (FTC)*, pp. 848–852, 2016.
23. https://www.mlopt.com/?tag=multilayer-perceptron
24. Zhang, Z., Shao, W., Zhang, H., A learning algorithm for multilayer perceptron as classifier. *IJCNN'99H363. International Joint Conference on Neural Networks. Proceedings (Cat. No.99C 39)*, Washington, DC, USA, vol. 3, pp. 1681–1684, 1999.
25. Singh, M., Singh, A., Kim, S., Blockchain: A game changer for securing IoT data. *IEEE World Forum on Internet of Things, WF-IoT 2018 - Proceedings*, pp. 51–55, 2018.
26. Alkurdi, F., Elgendi, I., Munasinghe, K.S., Sharma, D., Jamalipour, A., Blockchain in IoT Security: A survey. *In 2018 28th International Telecommunication Networks and Applications Conference, ITNAC, 2018*, pp. 1–4, 2018, [8615409].
27. Ali, M.S., Vecchio, M., Antonelli, F., Enabling a blockchain-based IoT edge in *IEEE Internet of Things Magazine*, New York, vol. 1, no. 2, pp. 24–29, December 2018.
28. Weaver, A.C., Biometric authentication. *Computer*, 39, 2, 96–97, Feb 2006.
29. Li, D., Peng, W., Deng, W., Gai, F., A blockchain-based authentication and security mechanism for IoT. *2018 27th International Conference on Computer Communication and Networks (ICCCN)*, Hangzhou, pp. 1–6, 2018.
30. Abe, E., Chigira, H., Fujiwarai, K., Yamakawa, T., Kano, M., Heart rate monitoring by a pulse sensor embeeded game controller. *Proceedings of APSIPA Annual Summit and Conference 2015*, pp. 16–19, December 2015.

5

Application of Machine Learning and IoT for Smart Cities

Nilanjana Pradhan[1]*, Ajay Shankar Singh[2], Shrddha Sagar[1],
Akansha Singh[3] and Ahmed A. Elngar[4]

[1]*Analytics, Pune Institute of Business Management (Pune, Maharashthra), PHD
Scholar, Galgotias University, Greater Noida, Uttar Pradesh, India
[2]School of Computer Science and Engineering, Galgotias University,
Greater Noida, Uttar Pradesh, India
[3]Department of Computer Science and Engineering, ASET,
Amity University Uttar Pradesh, Noida, India
[4]Faculty of Computers & Artificial Intelligence, Beni-Suef University, Beni-Suef, Egypt*

Abstract

Internet of Things (IoT) is an evolving technology in which numbers of devices
are connected to the Internet and to number of associated device. The IoT is
large domain in which number of smart devices is connected and individually
is connected together and provides information in a specific way, which they
can be utilized. IoT consist of phenomenal number of objects of every kind that
is from smart microwaves—which naturally cooks food in the specified time,
to self-driving vehicles—whose complex sensors identifies the objects in the
path. Machine learning (ML) is an innovation today and is the procedure of
elimination of human intervention at every possible opportunity. It is enabling
the information to learn design independent from anyone else and take autonomous choices without a coder composing another arrangement of codes.
Each time the IoT sensors assemble information, there must be somebody at
the backend to arrange the information, process them and guarantee data is
conveyed back to the gadget for decision making. ML comes to play with its
algorithm which helps to incorporate discover information from huge data sets
and focus on structure discovery, anticipating classes and qualities, highlight
extraction, and the sky is the limit from there. Distinctive ML methods, for
example, decision trees, clustering, and neural and Bayesian systems, help the

---

Corresponding author: nilanjana.pradhan@gmail.com

Krishna Kant Singh, Akansha Singh and Sanjay Sharma (eds.) Machine Learning Approaches for
Convergence of IoT and Blockchain, (109–128) © 2021 Scrivener Publishing LLC

gadgets to recognize designs in various sorts of informational collections originating from different sources and take proper decision based on their investigation. Such difficulties are confronted particularly on account of embedded system.

Keywords: IoT, machine learning, clustering, decision trees, Bayesian systems

5.1   Functionality of Image Analytics

Post calamity, city organizers need to adequately design response exercises and allot rescue groups to explicit catastrophe zones rapidly. We address the issue of absence of precise data of the debacle zones and presence of human survivors in debris utilizing image analytics from smart city information [1]. Innovative utilization of smart city foundation is proposed as a potential answer for this issue. We gathered pictures from seismic tremor hit smart urban conditions and executed a CNN model for order of these pictures to recognize human body parts out of the trash. TensorFlow backend (utilizing Keras) was used for this arrangement. We had the option to accomplish 83.2% exactness from our model. The epic utilization of picture information from smart city foundation and the resultant discoveries from our model has critical ramifications for successful calamity reaction tasks, particularly in keen urban areas.

Smart urban areas are an endeavor to improve the viability of urban administrations and upgrade the personal satisfaction. They incorporate brilliant structures, keen human services, training, transportation, and different administrations that influence data and correspondence advances. These urbanized regions are based upon huge systems of sensors, cameras, and other associated brilliant gadgets, fit for catching rich, constant data from each alcove and corner of the city ceaselessly [1]. Together with the increasing requirement to successfully oversee and dissect such heterogeneous and unstructured information streams for help in dynamic, these have provoked controllers and different partners to fabricate vital organizations with different private sellers just as academicians to increase rich experiences from the gathered information. Of the different investigation strategies accessible, specialists have exhibited viable use of AI (ML) procedures for fathoming different formative issues, in such brilliant city conditions, similar to traffic executions, medicinal services, crime percentages, and vitality utilization. To guarantee compelling administration during disaster reaction stage, practicality and cooperation of human hands from numerous, geologically dispersed associations and their correspondence are basic. Consequently, information management does a significant job in a disaster response tasks including key intending to guarantee auspicious and viable prioritization and portion of assets among discrete reaction exercises. As per the report of US-based National Research Council (U.S.), "IT can possibly improve how networks, people handle disaster".

Notwithstanding, the presence of contradictory frameworks and advancements because of absence of all inclusive conventions for information sharing and the board in these urban areas makes issues for powerful arranging. The absence of a coordinated and universal framework urges chiefs during calamities to regularly pick an imperfect choice dependent on heuristics. Researchers featured these worries of leaders, particularly for catastrophe executives. They have especially attested the requirement for coordinating distinct information sources and assets for cooperative and convenient way, and there is a requirement for gathering updated data from these appropriated sources through one incorporated data arrangement of the city. This joined with the reception of cutting edge information investigation will help powerful dynamic in a debacle circumstances. In any case, the constrained measure of studies by some researchers features the absence of spotlight on using the abilities of information investigation, comprehensively, for catastrophe executives as a "smart assistance" in a keen city. Because of this gap in the current scenario our present examination endeavors to analyze the adequacy of a particular ML system for disaster executives in brilliant urban areas. The adequacy of calamity reaction tasks is principally controlled by the practicality in distinguishing and organizing catastrophe zones. With existing foundation of cameras all through smart urban communities, visual information is a rich wellspring of data to help such choices. Absence of such foundation in traditional urban situations prevents any chance of catching such information during debacles. Albeit a significant number of these gadgets may be rendered inadequate during fiascos even in keen urban areas, the restricted ones that endure give a speedy look at the catastrophe circumstance and henceforth help such dynamic. Picture investigation methods dependent on ML can be used for such prioritization of salvage endeavors. Roused by this novel utilization of picture investigation, our exploration uses convolution neural systems for arrangement of gigantic measures of picture information with the assistance of Keras with TensorFlow as backend. The proposed model will have high level of precision of the occurrence of human survivors in cargo and fetch from photos of catastrophe areas. Distinguishing proof of survivors noticeable in pictures has been tried to decode from a gigantic dataset of pictures given by brilliant city framework. Subsequently, grouping of these pictures through cloud-based ML systems improves the proficiency of quest tasks for convenient catastrophe reaction. This examination makes a few key commitments. By consolidating a generally less utilized yet amazing strategy on the less used visual substance of large information of savvy urban areas in a novel application and introducing a profound learning-based examination, we represent the capability of ML methods for such settings.

Aside from the curiosity of use, this strategy additionally features a novel and effective system for ML characterization by using backend from Google which is a worldwide market pioneer in ML. Further, our extensive audit of picture information investigation in the space of catastrophe executives with specific spotlight on smart urban areas fills in as an abridgment of information on the theme for future examinations. With an attention on generalizability, the experiences from this investigation will help experts (catastrophe administrators and salvage groups) and all the while grow the information base on picture examination of enormous information.

5.2   Issues Related to Security and Privacy in IoT

Security and protection have become critical worries because of the inclusion of the IoT gadgets for various functionalities. Digital dangers are developing at a hazardous pace making the current security and protection quantifies in satisfactory. Consequently, everybody on the Internet is an item for programmers. Thus, Machine Learning (ML) calculations are utilized to deliver exact yields from huge complex databases. The produced yield examine be utilized to anticipate and distinguish vulnerabilities in IoT-based frameworks [2]. Moreover, Blockchain (BC) procedure is getting well known in present day IoT applications to manage security and protection issues. A few investigations have been led on either ML algorithms or BC methodology. Be that as it may, these examinations focus on the issues related to security and privacy by implementing ML algorithm or a BC methodology that represents a requirement for a joined review on actions made as of late tending to both security and privacy issues utilizing ML algorithms and BC methodology [2]. In this paper, we have given a detailed review of the techniques or methodologies done by the researchers in past related to security and privacy issues. Firstly, we have classified different security and privacy issues in the IoT domain in the previous years. After this, we have discussed on algorithms or methodologies for ML and BC in relation to IoT.

We have seen the enterprises to develop from assembling only the items to building the system of items known as IoT and, in the end, making a savvy system of items. This availability and the exponential development of IoT gadgets have brought about an expanded measure of system traffic. Because of this availability, challenges like security and protection of client information and confirmation and verification of gadgets have emerged. For instance, programmers bargain done billion hurray accounts in 2013. In 2014, 5,000,000 eBay clients were under attack. Figure 5.1 represents the process of literature review of analyzing the challenges in finding the solutions for the threats in IoT in context to ML and blockchain [2].

Figure 5.2 represents various interconnected research domains like machine learning, IoT, blockchain and security and privacy. Following the expanding pattern of assaults, in 2017, upto 3,000,000 clients from Equifax had their own data stolen. Similarly, in a five billion dollar toy industry in 2017 had their 800 and 20,000 customer accounts traded off. It additionally included more than 2,000,000 voice chronicles, out of which a couple were held for ransom. The ongoing digital history is loaded with cyber security calamities; from monstrous information breaks to security defects in billions of smaller scale chips and PC framework lock down until an instalment was

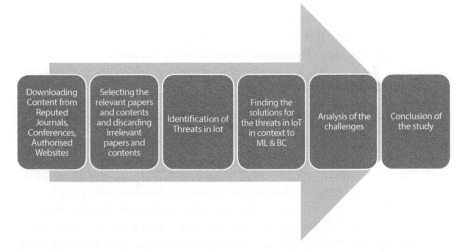

Figure 5.1 Process of literature review.

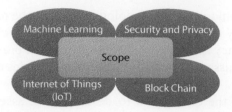

Figure 5.2 Research domains.

made. There is a plenty of security and protection challenges for IoT gadgets, which are expanding every day. Hence, security and protection in complex and asset obliged IoT conditions are huge difficulties and should be handled adequately. The security challenges in IoT are expanding as the assaults are getting refined day by day. Highlighted that ground-breaking registering devices, e.g., desktop PCs, may have the option to distinguish malware utilizing complex resources. However, IoT gadgets have constrained assets. Correspondingly, customary digital security frameworks and programming are not proficient enough in recognizing little assault varieties or zero-day attacks, since both should be refreshed regularly. Moreover, the refreshes are not accessible by the seller progressively, making the system helpless. ML algorithms can be implemented for improving the models for cyber security. In light of the current information on digital dangers, these algorithms can examine network traffic, update threat knowledge at a base, and keep the underlying systems protected from new assaults. Alongside utilizing ML algorithms, the specialists have likewise begun utilizing progressive BC methodologies that can be used for securing the basic frameworks. Despite the fact that ML algorithms and BC methodologies have been created to manage digital issues in the IoT space, a mix of these two is something new that should be thoroughly reviewed through research papers.

5.3   Machine Learning Algorithms and Blockchain Methodologies

With the advancement of the technologies, the business area is a significant part of the complex choice procedure for the business people. On the off chance that a business, for example, mall, café, bistro, medical clinic, and apparel all are opened in renowned areas, for not only satisfying the customers only but also improves with increase in life quality and accommodation, yet in addition, it augments the gains of the business visionaries. Nonetheless, it is unpredictable and with large choice for search of perfect area for a business. Hence, a smart business application that utilizations AI strategies to evaluate the area of a business are being proposed. The proposed framework gathers key component in respect to a specific business and learns a forecast model for potential information. It measures and proposes group of areas that have ideal areas for specific business. The proposed framework is assessed on an operation cases that estimates the most ideal domains for a self-service restaurant which is indicated by fundamental attributes taken as contributions from business people through a networking-based application. These qualities are meal price per client, family type, gender, and age. The main choice for process which is assessed on the basis such as house price per region and nearby populace having a place with various household type, In keen urban areas, and the business area is an important part of the unpredictable choice process for the business people. On the off chance that a business, for example, mall, restaurant strike through bluster, café, clinic, garments, and so forth, is opened in ideal area; for not only fulfilment level of the clients are upgraded through extended quality of life and accommodation, yet in addition it boosts the gains of the business people. In any case, it is mind-boggling and long-haul choice to found perfect area for a business. Along these lines, we recommend an intellectual business model which utilizes AI techniques to enhancing the domain of a business. The proposed framework gathers key component esteems for a business and learns an expectation model for future information. It estimates and proposes bunches of regions which have specific areas for that business. The proposed framework is assessed on a utilization case that appraises the most ideal areas of an eatery as indicated by principle attributes taken as contributions from business people through a web-based application. These attributes are meal price per client, household type, gender, and age. The first period of choice procedure is evaluating referenced highlights, for example, house price per area and nearby populace having a place with various household types.

The business people struggles in deciding list of capabilities as well as sets aside a lot of effort to give any outcome. So as to quicken choice procedure and arrive at future achievement rapidly, the conduct of the highlights ought to be considered by potential years. The prerequisite of the element for prediction of the following a long time with less blunder rate so as to improve profit of business people close to the upgrading life comfort of residents. In the second point for business people, there can be numerous regions bunches that has comparable highlights. Rather than checking the highlights of areas individually, there ought to be a suggestion that quickens choice procedure for the business people. In this way, we accept that the choice procedure is implied for business visionaries by thinking about groups of locale. The gatherings of them can be appeared with comparative component subtleties. To do this, various levelled bunching is required to deal with region bunches that are total to a gathering as per comparative highlights. In light of these two focuses, the savvy city ought to be represented by means of powerful eatery area estimation model that illuminates business people with a fewer error rate. Hence, the researchers have proposed a novel brilliant city application named as Business Location Estimator which can find ideal region for wanting to open eatery through utilizing AI techniques.

5.3.1   Intrusion Detection System

Sooner rather than later, transportation will experience an intermediary phase which can shape the business to the point of being unrecognizable. Savvy vehicles have assumed a noteworthy job in the progression of canny and associated transportation frameworks [4]. Consistent vehicular cloud administration accessibility in smart urban communities is turning into an essential endorser need which requires improvement in the vehicular help the board engineering. In addition, as smart urban communities keep on sending broadened advancements to accomplish different and elite cloud administrations, security issues with respect to imparting substances share individual requester data despite everything wins. To alleviate these worries, we present a robotized secure ceaseless cloud administration accessibility system for brilliant associated vehicles that empowers an interruption location instrument against security assaults and offers types of assistance that meet clients' nature of administration (QoS) and nature of experience (QoE) necessities [4]. Constant assistance accessibility is accomplished by bunching keen vehicles into administration explicit groups. Bunch heads are chosen for correspondence purposes with confided in outsider elements (TTPs) going about as middle people between administration of demand and supply. The most ideal management is then conveyed from the chose specialist organizations to the demand. Besides, interruption recognition is practiced through a three-stage information traffic examination, decrease, and order strategy used to distinguish positive believed administration demands against bogus solicitations that may happen during interruption assaults. The arrangement receives profound conviction and choice tree AI components utilized for information decrease and characterization purposes, separately. The system is approved through reproductions to show the viability of the arrangement as far as interruption assault location. The proposed arrangement accomplished a general precision of 99.43% with 99.92% identification rate and 0.96% fake optimistic and false negative pace of 1.53%. In the due course of time, the transportation will experience a drastic change in the era of the business to the point of being indistinguishable. Savvy motor vehicles have assumed a significant increase in the job of smart and associated transportation frameworks. Consistent mobile cloud administration accessibility in brilliant urban areas is turning out to be a crucial endorser that needs improvement in the mobile that helps in the boarder framework. In addition to a perceptive urban areas keep on sending distinct innovations for accomplishment of different cloud administrations, security issues with respect to imparting elements share individual requester data despite everything wins. To moderate these worries, we present a robotized secure consistent cloud administration accessibility system for brilliant associated vehicles that empowers an interruption location component against security assaults and offers types of assistance that meet clients' nature of administration (QoS) and nature of experience (QoE).

Persistent assistance accessibility is accomplished by grouping smart vehicles into administration specific groups. Group heads are chosen for correspondence purposes with confided in outsider substances (TTPs) going about as middle people between administration requesters and suppliers. The most ideal administrations are then conveyed from the chose specialist co-ops to the requesters. Besides, interruption recognition is cultivated through a three-stage information traffic examination, decrease, and classification method used to recognize positive believed administration demands against bogus solicitations that may happen during interruption assaults. The arrangement embraces profound conviction and choice tree AI instruments utilized for information decrease and classification purposes, separately.

TTPs repeat a similar procedure from all cluster heads' request, where TTPs are allowed for a hub trust score. Information is then examined to distinguish the component it has a place with. Information is additionally decreased by eliminating excess information. The approaching suspicious traffic is classified as per the sort of intrusion, for example, for swearing of-administration (DoS), probing, user to root (U2R), and remote to user attack (R2L). The final phase of this phase is to either acknowledge the service request for additional handling at the SP or reject it and afterward add it to the arrangement of intrusive traffic for future traffic investigation. The final phase rehashes a similar procedure engaged with stage II yet applied to approaching traffic from TTPs. By receiving such a multi-stage intrusion detection mechanism, traffic is guaranteed against nosy security assaults. Client information shared among the cloud entities may be open with the communicating hubs.

5.3.2   Deep Learning and Machine Learning Models

Profound learning [deep learning (DL)] and AI (ML) algorithms have as of late added to the headway of models in the different parts of expectation, arranging, and vulnerability investigation of keen urban areas and urban improvement. This paper presents the cutting edge of DL and ML strategies utilized right now. Through an original scientific classification, the enhancement in model improvement and innovative application areas in built-up supportability and savvy urban areas are introduced. Discoveries uncover that five DL and ML algorithms have been generally implemented for addressing the various parts of keen urban communities. These are counterfeit neural systems; bolster vector machines; choice trees; groups, Bayesians, cross breeds, and neuro-fluffy; and profound knowledge. It is additionally revealed that vitality, well-being, and urban vehicle are the primary areas of keen urban communities that DL and ML algorithms contributed in to deal with their issues.

To recognize the most applicable writing in the domain of utilizing DL and ML algorithms for smart urban communities and maintainable urban advancement, we studied Web of Sciences (WoS) and Scopus with the accompanying hunt watchwords: "keen urban communities" or "supportable urban improvement" and all the current DL and ML algorithms.

5.3.3   Artificial Neural Networks

After doing thorough review of research papers, we have concluded that very few researchers have implemented artificial neural systems (ANNs) with regard to smart urban areas. ANNs have numerous applications in keen urban communities, including risk location, water supply, vitality, and urban vehicle. One researcher has developed a framework for smart lightning location framework helped by ANNs. The proposed model provides the way to deal with strengthening of the wind turbines in smart cities. A well-organized strategy identifies water spills in smart city communities by using ANNs.

A support vector machine (SVM) is another AI technique which is utilized to manage smart city issues. SVMs are implemented in various parts of a smart city like water supply, energy, assessment, and the executives of savvy and well-being areas. Many researchers have explored the different areas for the implementation of SVMs in the smart cities, for improving water use in keen urban communities by using SVM. Chui proposed a creative way to deal with assess vitality supportability in smart urban areas. Eventually, SVMs to give answers for the well-being business of keen urban areas are used.

Decision tree (DT) is one of the methodology in which various issues related to smart cities by using ML algorithm. Many researchers have used DTs to deliver the problems identified with organizations, atmosphere contamination, urban vehicle, and nourishment to build up a smart city. Some researchers' versatile edge examination makes a significant client experience and see brand commitment for smart urban areas. A plan for smart action to gauge air quality for intellectual urban communities for utilizing IoT and SaaS is proposed by some researchers. A structure for motivator system for a clever traffic framework was developed by researchers that are dependent on activity game hypothesis. A smart dairy model by using IoT sensor is used for estimating steers' medical problems, milk creation expectation, and profitability improvement.

5.3.4   Hybrid Approaches

Number approaches of AI techniques (ANNs, SVMs, and DTs) have being used in smart cities very efficiently. Hence, we can also implement hybrid approaches (Bayesian, hybrids, and neuro-fuzzy) that have been implemented to resolves the problem in the domains like energy, urban governance, evaluation, and management. A sustainable model for urban countryside advancement city has been developed by the researchers. Researchers have proposed a structure to fabricate a zero-emanation neighborhood utilizing responsive structure envelope. A system for applying resident has focused on enormous information for administration insight in keen urban communities. Building up a versatile neuro-fuzzy framework for estimating the maintainability of urban areas can be considered. At long last, researchers have given a quality computer aided blood investigation framework to find and include the white platelets in blood tests. Their methodology adds to making the social insurance industry keen in the brilliant city.

5.3.5 Review and Taxonomy of Machine Learning

The utilization of ML in smart building applications as represented in Figure 5.3 is reviewed in this paper. We have split existing activities into two principle classes that is occupant centric vs. energy/gadgets centric. The higher segment group of researchers is fully utilizing ML for different segments that are identified by the inhabitants that consist of the following: firstly, occupancy estimation and identification; secondly, action acknowledgment; and last, valuating inclinations and conduct. Some researchers are doing utilization of ML for assessing perspectives that are related either to vitality or gadgets. They are segmented into three classifications that are (a) vitality report and request prediction, (b) machines outline and issue location, and (c) induction on sensors. Solutions in every classification are introduced, talked about, and looked at, just as open points of view and research trends. Compared to related cutting edge overview papers, the commitment here in is to give an exhaustive and all-encompassing audit from the ML viewpoints instead of compositional and specialized angles

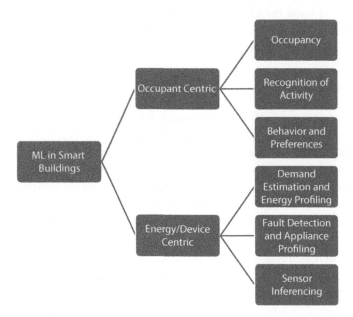

Figure 5.3 Implementation of ML in smart buildings.

existing structure the board systems. This is by considering a wide range of ML tools, structures, and a few classes of uses, and by organizing the scientific categorization accordingly. The paper closes with a rundown conversation of the introduced works, which center around exercises learned, challenges, and open and future headings of research right now.

5.4   Machine Learning Open Source Tools for Big Data

Storing huge volume of information for future handling has been accomplished for quite a long time, while "enormous information" idea picked up energy in the mid-2000s because of the mechanical progressions that improved Internet get to speed, diminished expense of capacity, and expanded computational force. The enormous information idea contrasts from putting away a lot of information as in the pace of information provided has expanded to such a degree that it meets the criteria for another information source. Likewise, the information obtaining recurrence has expanded to a level that new calculations and systems for top-to-bottom degree of investigation are required. Developing traffic, expanding populace, and open well-being are serious issues of creating urban communities. Numerous urban areas face social and natural maintainability difficulties, for example, contamination and ecological weakening. Some have issues of offering types of assistance, for example, water, sanitation, sewage removal, and trash assortment. One testing application region of enormous information examination and AI that can possibly upgrade our lives is savvy urban communities. A keen city foundation offers interoperable types of assistance between residents, organizations, and legislative associations to accomplish effective and supportable urban areas. Structuring a design for the keen city is thus an exceptionally perplexing errand, predominantly due to the enormous assorted variety of gadgets, correspondence advancements, and quantity of administrations. Continually varying nature of keen urban communities and need of constant dynamic require versatile calculations and AI methods. With a gigantic development rate in day-by-day delivered information, it was tested in such a way that the production processes gains from it. From one perspective, large information gives incredible chances to specialists to create calculations that can separate hidden examples and to fabricate prescient models then again it makes difficulties, for example, versatility. This section gives definitions and clarifies accessible apparatuses, libraries, and motors that can be utilized for large information handling dependent on criteria, for example, extensibility, adaptability, convenience, and accessibility. Additionally, it gives a thorough audit of open source devices alongside an examination of the points of interest and disadvantages of every innovation such as MapReduce, Spark, Flink, Storm, and H2O and the library which are used are as follows Mahout, MLlib, and SAMOA.

In open research issues recently, well-known innovation answers for different smart urban communities and purpose has risen as a noteworthy progression for Internet and distributed computing standards. Enormous information is one of the original cloud ideal models which have associated elements that become some part of the keen city foundations, and the progressions in distributed computing makes it in mainstream where the customary media transmission frameworks encourage fundamental interchanges between the cloud elements. Huge information has united advances as far as administrations, registering, data preparing, organizing, and controlling clever advances. Among the key innovations merged is the enormous information handling because of its processing capacity and cost viability. Abundance of different methodologies has been projected and intended for thinking about the implementation on the cloud in the current scenario. Nonetheless, there are key open research issues still to be settled in the enormous information time. Since, as a rule, empowering advances have limited confirmation benefits for versatile clients, various systems are presented for the expansion of client validation over the cloud-based conditions. Commercialization of isolated application and security issues in huge information has increased a lot of consideration of the analysts to fulfill the security properties of verification and key in understanding conventions. As long as the advancement of the security conventions is all the more testing and ought to likewise considering moderation of the calculation and correspondence cost. In addition, allowing for the huge information preparation and the vitality of the cloud utilization for assorted systems in smart cities is an additional key for testing. In energy utilization models, it considers the considering previously mentioned smart city planning that are obligatory for progressively estimating while taking into consideration distinctive access types. The wide coverage of the mass region along with the streamlined organization of the cloud architecture and covering number of administration requirements with cautious thought so as to understand an effective large information worldview in the keen city time.

5.5   Approaches and Challenges of Machine Learning Algorithms in Big Data

Smart urban communities offer types of assistance that profit by the city-scale organization of the sensors, the actuators, and keen articles. Such administrations are for the most part strong-minded by information and can be widely named for creators of information, purchasers of information, or a blend of together. For instance, a leaving administration that sends Message Queue Telemetry Transport (MQTT) agent is distributing the parking areas' accessibility information that is viewed as a maker while vehicles that buy in to that dealer are considered as buyers. Autos can be delivering other information for making use of other intense parts of the city such as autos use Device-to-Device (D2D) interchanges to alarm close by vehicles and walkers of their essence and possible traffic risks [7]. In a city-scale organization of smart administrations, information is created at high a rate which presents new difficulties for smart city creators and developers. Smart city sensors data are big data due to their huge volume and are scalable and helps in providing smart services. Smart city data can be sampled and used in smart analytical services. The major problem of smart cities from ML viewpoint is that information determined by three V's that is volume, variety, and velocity, which are having different types of problems from analytics and ML algorithms. Regrettably, just a small part of the extremely large city information is regularly used by brilliant administrations to improving the lives of the city's occupants. The primary offender is lacking a huge amount of tagged data. This requires the need to use ML algorithms which exploits the accessibility of untagged and tagged data in relation to smart cities. Closely resembling the procedure for reuse of waste and models in smart societies, where there is a need for measures and mechanism for data reusing in smart societies where hundreds or thousands of Gigabytes of data is created every moment. Data analytics methodologies and ML algorithms must have the option for removing information and helpful data from information to eliminate the measure of computerized squander. Regardless of the ongoing progressions in figuring and capacity innovations, the vast majority of the information explanatory methodologies misuse testing strategies that are proficient as far as time multifaceted nature however disregard an enormous piece of information that may contain significant examples that are not spoken to by the examples. Then again, using Deep Neural Networks (DNNs), datasets with a huge number of parameters can be measured to remove clever investigation. Narrative information demonstrates that when keen city information is not utilized for learning and investigation in a present moment, it is improbable that it would be utilized later. It is evaluated that by 2012, just about 0.5% of every single 2.8 Zettabyte (ZB) of put away information have been examined and 3% of them are marked dependent on an investigation.

This features the test of possibly squandering shrouded data in 99.5% of the produced information. Recently, there have been dynamic conversations on the administration, the executives, and capacity of smart cities large information, yet there is no unmistakable answer on the best way to utilize the colossal measures of gathered information. Would it be advisable for it to be straightforwardly joined into examination and AI exercises? Or, on the other hand, would it be a good idea for it to be tested? Despite the fact that by and large inspecting approximates the arrangement, for smart city administrations where the inclination of residents comes to play, or individual exercises influence the entire network, examining may not be perfect. For instance, to foresee oddities in a city's foundation considering every single gathered datum from the different sensor sources would assist with acknowledging such administrations. Another model incorporates administrations that anticipate criminal or unfair exercises through Internet-based life remarks (e.g., Twitter and Facebook). For such administrations, considering a more extensive scope of information is essential, since the crook or prejudicial remarks may establish a little part of the entire information. Savvy city biological systems have the accompanying attributes from an AI point of view: Humans' requirements for communicating with the frameworks for providing criticism. Numerous sensors and smart gadgets create information at a high rate. Not all the information can be checked on by people for avocation, yet the framework ought to take in and develop itself from past encounters. They need a general, dynamic, and consistent learning instrument as the setting of a keen city application is not constantly fixed and the working condition of brilliant city applications advances over the time. The data which is produced by smart city applications is energetic or has some point of weakness. In view of these qualities, we accept a mix of DNNs, Reinforcement Learning (RL), and semi-directed learning can deal with the matter and convey total versatile arrangements. The requirement for profound taking in approaches comes from the desire to extricate significant level reflections from the crude information. Each level of a DNN produces a conceptual portrayal of its info information. To get more degrees of reflection, increasingly shrouded layers of neurons are required. Fortification learning has been read well for control frameworks and frameworks that need to achieve automatic activities. In support knowledge, there is no yield (that is, order) for the preparation information—which is the situation for some savvy city applications, rather picking the correct activities is compensated. The objective of a RL framework is to discover an activity for every condition of the framework with the end goal that the all-out remuneration of the learning specialist is amplified in the long haul. Then again, it is infeasible or amazingly repetitive for the clients to give a prize input to all the preparation information. This issue can be tended to using semi-directed learning approaches where information is in part marked.

Semi-managed AI approaches are a promising technique to address the shortage of explained information in enormous information streams. Besides, Deep Reinforcement Learning (DRL) approaches additionally have demonstrated promising outcomes in frameworks where a prize criticism from the earth is expected to get better the exhibition of the framework rather than a class mark as on account of managed knowledgeable strategies. The mix of these strategies can assist with extricating the most incentive from the large information produced by savvy urban communities. The authors have projected a technique; we join the quality of these methodologies for conveying semi-directed DRL operators that gain from the keen smart cities data to play out the best activities on the earth. The proposed methodologies is an empowering influence for intellectual keen city administrations since the knowledge specialist advances as the states of the earth change and carry out autonomic activities without human intercessions.

Consumer Internet of Things (CIoT) is another examination which conveys a subjective structure for IoT applications [4]. Figure 5.4 presents communications among subjective assignments including observation activity cycle, gigantic information investigation, semantic induction and information revelation, keen dynamic, and on-request administration provisioning. They recognized two territories that are needed for objects in an intellectual area for comprehending and learning, to be specific, getting the semantic from dissected data, and finding important examples and rules as information. The creators characterized a subjective structure for smart homes dependent on psychological powerful frameworks and IoT [5]. Inside of their subjective reminiscence, they utilized a Bayesian model, a Bayesian channel, and support learning. The Bayesian channel measures the condition of the architecture, and strengthening learning provides the instrument to choosing the most perfect actions dependent on the all-out rewards.

As opposed to brought together insight and investigation on the cloud, the creators proposed to incorporate man-made brainpower in mist processing to encourage savvy city massive data examination. They explained

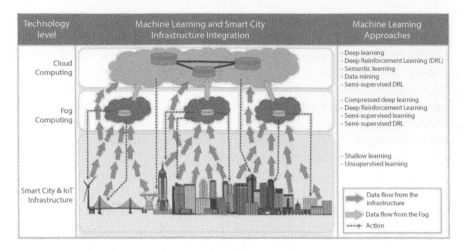

Figure 5.4 Intelligence levels for smart cities [8].

various leveled haze figuring model to dissect vast data for smart city applications [6]. Making use of this model, the all-purpose implementation is upgraded throughout diminishing the broadcast capacity that interchanges by not conveying every single crude datum to the cloud and performing continuing examination for the reason of the nearness of the haze to the wellspring of data. They utilized Hidden Markov Model (HMM) approach in their model to help enormous information examination in a brilliant pipeline observing framework. Bridges the works right now shows which levels of large information age are secured by their knowledge and investigation. It likewise demonstrates the situation of this examination comparative with these works. Contrasted with the previously talked about works that bring examination to the mist or cloud levels, our methodology intends to convey scientific arrangements on the haze and the cloud, which thus covers an enormous amount of smart city application including time-delicate and non-time-touchy ones. Besides, so as to get better the exactness of the investigation, the proposed approach dives into the bigger assortment of information where information is undiscovered and no names or meta-information are given [6]. Insight for smart cities. In this area, we present the general system for knowledge in savvy urban areas. The system proposes three degrees of knowledge, in particular: the degree of smart city and IoT foundation, haze figuring, and distributed computing. The general situation of AI techniques inside the chain of command of brilliant city framework where every part of the smart city framework is constrained by a smart programming specialist is conveyed in the haze or the cloud contingent upon the attributes of the required investigation (e.g., time affectability). Subsequently, crude information can be moved to the mist or to the cloud. The running investigation specialist at that point restores a proper activity to the foundation gadgets dependent on forecasts (e.g., modify traffic light planning dependent on traffic clog information from the relating streets).

5.6 Conclusion

As the urban communities turned out to be progressively packed and the appearance of thoughts, for example, IoT, sending sensors all around the urban areas for clever dynamic turned into a characteristic advance. As the measure of information expanded essentially, scientists grew new procedures for dealing with both spilling and put away information starting from various sources. Right now, a portion of the infrastructure for large information examination is seen and systems that can be utilized are talked about. There is no single instrument or structure that covers all or even most of enormous information preparing assignments; one must consider the exchange offs that exist between convenience, execution, and calculation determination while looking at changed arrangements. Up until now, the conventional calculations and devices have for the most part assisted with understanding the information preparing prerequisites; however, as the size of information develops, the versatility issue emerges.

References

1. Chaudhuri, N. and Bose, I., Application of image analytics for disaster response in smart cities. *Proceedings of the 52nd Hawaii International Conference on System Sciences*, 2019.
2. Waheed, N., He, X., Usman, M., Security & Privacy in IoT Using Machine Learning & Blockchain: Threats & Countermeasures. *arXiv preprint arXiv*, 2002, 03488, 2020.
3. Bilen, T. *et al.*, A smart city application: Business location estimator using machine learning techniques. *2018 IEEE 20th International Conference on High Performance Computing and Communications; IEEE 16th International Conference on Smart City; IEEE 4th International Conference on Data Science and Systems (HPCC/SmartCity/DSS)*, IEEE, 2018.
4. Aloqaily, M. *et al.*, An intrusion detection system for connected vehicles in smart cities. *Ad Hoc Networks*, 90, 101842, 2019.

5. Nosratabadi, S. *et al.*, State of the art survey of deep learning and machine learning models for smart cities and urban sustainability. *International Conference on Global Research and Education*, Springer, Cham, 2019.
6. Djenouri, D. *et al.*, Machine learning for smart building applications: Review and taxonomy. *ACM Comput. Surv. (CSUR)*, 52, 2, 1–36, 2019.
7. Ulusar, U.D., Ozcan, D.G., Al-Turjman, F., Open Source Tools for Machine Learning with Big Data in Smart Cities, in: *Smart Cities Performability, Cognition, & Security*, pp. 153–168, Springer, Cham, 2020.
8. Mohammadi, M. and Al-Fuqaha, A., Enabling cognitive smart cities using big data and machine learning: Approaches and challenges. *IEEE Commun. Mag.*, 56, 2, 94–101, 2018.

6

Machine Learning Applications for IoT Healthcare

Neha Agarwal[1], Pushpa Singh[2]*, Narendra Singh[3],
Krishna Kant Singh[4] and Rohit Jain[5]

[1]Dept. of Computer Science & Engineering, Amity University, Noida,
Uttar Pradesh, India
[2]Dept. of Computer Science and Engineering, Delhi Technical Campus,
Greater Noida, Uttar Pradesh, India
[3]Dept. of Management Studies, GL Bajaj Institute of Management & Research,
Greater Noida, India
[4]Faculty of Engineering & Technology, Jain (Deemed-to-be University),
Bengaluru, India
[5]Dept. of Computer Science & Engineering, Penn State University, United States

Abstract

Healthcare sectors are gradually accepting technology that provides various remote healthcare facility, disease prediction, and in-home diagnostics capabilities, which combine Machine Learning (ML) and the Internet of Things (IoT). ML offers tools for management of electronic records, integration of data, and techniques for computer-aided diagnosis which helps in disease diagnosis, prediction, and treatment suggestion. The IoT connect all type medical devices, patients monitoring tools, and wearable devices that can send immediate data to concern authority like doctor. In this chapter, authors focus on ML applications for IoT-based healthcare. In this chapter, first, we introduce the basic concepts of ML and IoT and summarize the advantages of the techniques over traditional approaches of healthcare. We described the challenges of using ML and IoT in research and finally presented applications of ML like identifying diseases and diagnosis, drug discovery, personalized medicine, and smart health records that are augmented with IoT that significantly have an impact on delivery of healthcare.

Keywords: IoT, machine learning, healthcare, application, convergence

---

Corresponding author: pushpa.gla@gmail.com

Krishna Kant Singh, Akansha Singh and Sanjay Sharma (eds.) Machine Learning Approaches for Convergence of IoT and Blockchain, (129–144) © 2021 Scrivener Publishing LLC

6.1   Introduction

Recently, healthcare is gradually leveraging with emerging technologies such as Internet of Things (IoT), Machine Learning (ML), and cloud computing for providing smart healthcare systems to enhance effective health diagnostics and treatment. ML approaches in healthcare system offers smart services for healthcare monitoring and medical automation in various perspectives and environments (hospitals, offices, home, etc.). IoT and cloud architectures are exploited to make smart healthcare systems capable of connecting real-time applications. IoT devices can communicate with each other and collect enormous amount of health data every day by wearable sensor networks [1]. To analyze and extract meaningful information from IoT device'collected data, human intervention is required. AI- and ML-based techniques perform intelligent automation, analyzing and predicting meaningful information and able to learn from their collected data, without the need of human being [2].

The conventional diagnosis and prognosis system was designed poorly which could hinder the proper diagnosis and treatment of patients. The conventional system had very poor integration among the equipment used to gather information and communication between the equipment and several healthcare sectors. Integration of IoT and ML had provided a smart and intelligent decision support clinical system which helps in detecting diseases at an early stage improving the survival rate of the patient. The ML techniques, supervised and unsupervised learning, have made a key contribution in the diagnosis of disease in healthcare, therefore permitting a significant reduction of doctor visit costs and a general improvement of patient care quality. Integrating the power of IoT and ML for healthcare builds a lot of prospects to increase outcomes and drive wellness by reducing the strain points of current healthcare system. IoT with ML offers a better diagnostic care and heath monitoring application to the patient.

This chapter elaborates the role of IoT and ML technique in the healthcare industry. Section 6.2 represents basics of ML and its types with regard to the healthcare. IoT Architecture is represented in Section 6.3 for the healthcare in order to make smart and intelligent healthcare. Section 6.4 discusses application of IoT and ML in healthcare. Finally, Section 6.5 concludes the chapter.

6.2   Machine Learning

ML has bring in revolution and is getting widely adopted in healthcare because of its extra ordinary performance in various versatile tasks such as

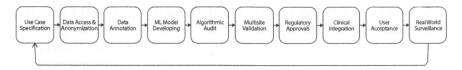

Figure 6.1 ML development phases for healthcare.

recognizing the organs of a body using images [3], classifying and detecting the disease [4–6], and segmenting and reconstructing the medical images [7–9]. The technique is used in variety of healthcare applications ranging from one dimensional heart signals to multi-dimensional medical images for computer-aided diagnosis. It is believed that in near future, the expert applications will assist doctors for examining patients. The ML model has achieved intelligence competing with human intelligence in several clinical areas like radiology [10] and dermatology [11]. The latest advanced technologies like big data, cloud computing, and data science [12] has added an edge to it for producing more accurate results. These technologies have together played a crucial role in enabling health services in the remote rural areas. Figure 6.1 depicted the foremost phases for development of ML-based healthcare systems.

6.2.1 Types of Machine Learning Techniques

6.2.1.1 Unsupervised Learning

Unsupervised learning is an ML technique which trains the machine with unlabeled data and so is also referred as self-organizing maps. The algorithms under this method cluster the data on the basis of their similar attributes, trend, patterns, etc. Several clustering techniques used are partitioning, overlapping, agglomerative, and probabilistic. The method extracts the regularities from the dataset for reducing the high dimensional data to low dimensional. The method can be implemented on all kind of data but the main disadvantage of this method is that the outcome is unpredictable. Clustering and principal component analysis (PCA) is two important unsupervised learning techniques that is used in healthcare. One of the example of using unsupervised learning is prediction of heart diseases based on clustering techniques [13] and PCA is using for predicting hepatitis [14].

6.2.1.2 Supervised Learning

Supervised learning is a ML technique which trains the machine with labeled data. While training the machine is provided with an input data along with the expected output once the training is complete, the machine is expected to predict the correct label for new data inserted as in input. The two most widely used supervised learning techniques are classified on the basis of the output generated. If the output is discrete, then it is classified as classification; however, if output is continuous, then its classified as regression. One of the examples in healthcare using supervised learning is analyzing the medical images and recognizing the different organs of the body [3] and classification of lung diseases [15].

6.2.1.3   Semi-Supervised Learning

Semi-supervised learning is a ML technique which trains the machine with labeled as well as unlabeled data; typically, the labeled data is very small, whereas the unlabeled data is in large amount. With this algorithm, first, using unsupervised learning method, the unlabeled data is clustered, and then, they are labeled using the existing labeled data. Few of the healthcare application using semi-supervised learning are speech analysis and protein sequence classification.

6.2.1.4   Reinforcement Learning

Reinforcement learning is a ML technique in which machine learns from the consequences of actions within an environment rather than being explicitly taught with given sets of input and corresponding correct and expected output. The machine learns from past experiences (exploitation) and at the same time takes instant new decision on the basis of trial and error learning (exploration). This technique is widely used in healthcare applications to make an expert system.

6.2.2   Applications of Machine Learning

ML is enabling the analysis of huge heterogeneous data being generated in healthcare on daily basis from several sources as displayed in Figure 6.2. ML benefits four major application of healthcare, namely, prognosis, diagnosis, treatment, and clinical workflow.

6.2.2.1   Prognosis

It is the medical terminology used for predicting the development of disease, complications generated by disease on health, its impact on life,

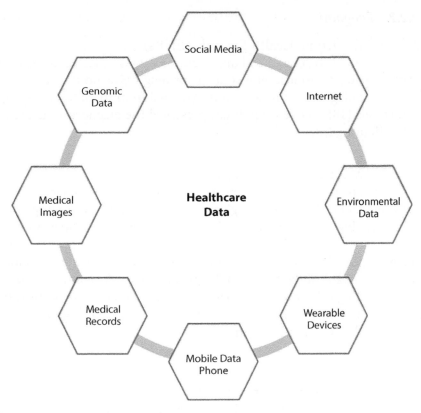

Figure 6.2 Sources of data for healthcare.

prediction on the duration of how long the disease will take to be cured, and whether the symptoms will remain stable or gets worsen or improve with the phase of time, its impact on the lifestyle whether a patient would be able to do his daily activities, and its impact on life expectancy. It is made on the basis of disease diagnosis, the physical and mental condition of patient, and the possible available treatment; it also defines the description and duration of the disease. In the clinical settings, patients' data is collected through different sources, namely, medical images, pathological labs, and genomics; this data enable the ML model to define prognosis, diagnoses, and according define treatment. Several models are developed on ML for classification of several kind of cancers, namely, lung cancer [16] and brain tumor [17]. The healthcare applications are still working on designing models for suggesting medicines; however, this requires enormous exploration on several areas like validations bioinformatics.

6.2.2.2   Diagnosis

6.2.2.2.1   Electronic Health Records (EHRs)

A vast amount of structured and unstructured data is collected as medical reports of patients from several sources forming EHRs on the daily routine. For the diagnosis, clinical data is extracted from these records using ML methods [18]. Reference [19] has presented the diagnosis of diabetes from EHR using ML.

6.2.2.2.2   Medical Image Analysis

For therapeutic purpose and diagnosis, medical images are collected from several modalities like X-ray, angiography, and Computed Tomography (CT). A typology of commonly used medical imaging modalities is ultrasound, X-rays, MRI, CT, PET, etc. [20], as shown in Figure 6.3. These modalities provide critical information while detecting the abnormalities in different organs of the body. ML helps doctors in efficiently and effectively extracting information for diagnosis of diseases from these images. The analysis of images includes detection, classification, segmentation, retrieval, and reconstruction of images.

6.2.2.2.3   Treatment

Once the image is examined, the report for the treatment is to be generated by physician or radiologist which is a challenging and time-consuming task so the researchers are attempting to design framework collaborating

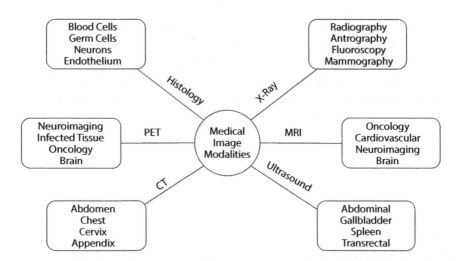

Figure 6.3 Commonly used medical imaging modalities.

NLP (Natural language Processing) and ML; few of the frameworks are discussed in [21–23].

6.2.2.2.4   Clinical Flow

ML is widely adopted in healthcare for its potential toward predictive analysis of disease so that timely treatment is possible. For example, ML has proved to provide an efficiency in risk prediction in cardiovascular [24], cancer and several other diseases, namely, fatty liver, and diabetes [25]. ML is also implemented for interpretation of medical images of severe diseases like fatty liver in clinical services using computer-aided detection (CADe) and computer aided-diagnosis (CADx). ML has also facilitated the clinical environment by automating transcription of patient's conversation and generating reports and discharge summaries. The clinical speech and audio processing have been used to identify various diseases whose symptoms are related to speech disorder, namely, Alzheimer's [26], dementia [27], and vocal hyper function [28].

6.3   IoT in Healthcare

Currently, IoT gained an excessive attention of researchers and developers. It permits communications between objects, machines, and everything together with peoples. The most common applications of IoT are smart homes [29], connected vehicles [30], smart cities [31], smart retail [32], and smart agriculture [33] and, of course, healthcare is not also exception in this line. IoT is generating a global network of smart connected devices that can enrich Healthcare system. IoT in the healthcare sector offers the security and the integrity of the medical data. IoT-based healthcare system can monitor their patient'data remotely and continuously. These data are processed and stored in data center such as cloud storage [34]. ML techniques can enhance the functionality of system which significantly increases the effectiveness, flexibility, and quality that too in reduced cost. ML algorithm such as decision tree, Bayesian, KNN, and SVM are used to diagnosis several diseases like cancer, diabetes, epilepsy, heart attack, and other prominent diseases [6].

6.3.1   IoT Architecture for Healthcare System

The main strength of IoT and ML-based applications is the high impact on changing aspects of the potential users' everyday life. Consider the IoT architecture for healthcare system as depicted in Figure 6.4.

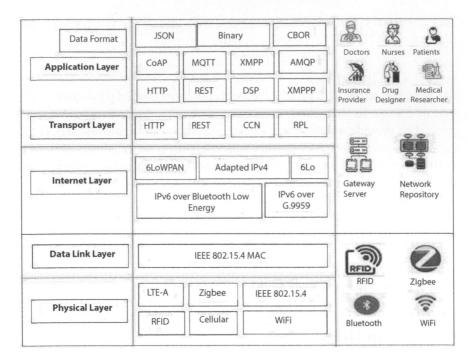

Figure 6.4 IoT architecture for healthcare.

6.3.1.1   Physical and Data Link Layer

The physical and data link layer contains of the IoT objects and physical networks joining them with other objects or network. This layer dedicated on the identification of things and accumulating the information from users. This layer encoded information data bit into electrical and mechanical specification that can travel over wireless or wired link and vice-versa. There are various protocols and technologies for physical and network access protocols. Some of the popular physical and data link layer protocols are shown in Figure 6.4. Data link layer specific-IEEE 802.15.4 MAC and physical layer specific protocol are LTE-A, Zigbee, IEEE 802.15.4, Wi-Fi, RFID, BLE, etc. Physical layer is also called as perception layer.

In healthcare system, physical objects and detection devices are in form of RFID, bar code, or distance sensors, available as body temperature sensor, ECG sensor, and blood pressure sensor. Activity tracker, smart cloth, continuous glucose monitor (CGM), etc., are some device that is based to continuously monitor of specific attribute like blood glucose level and heartbeat for several days at a time, by taking readings at regular intervals. The collected data is transmitted to the upper layer for transmission.

6.3.1.2   Network Layer

The network layer is called as infrastructure layer in the IoT architecture. Network layer is responsible to map the information gathered by the IoT devices in the physical layer to the telecommunication protocols [35]. The network layer processes the received data from the physical layer and communicate the data to the application layer through several network technologies such as wired or wireless networks. If healthcare application is distributed geographically, then local area network such as Wi-Fi, Bluetooth Zigbee, and Infrared technology is used and 4G, 5G, and LTE-A is used to connect long area distance [36]. The standard network layer level protocols are IPv4, IPv6, 6LoWPAN, 6TiSCH, 6Lo, IPv6 over Bluetooth Low Energy, etc., as shown in Figure 6.4. IPv4 has limited number of address space which is insufficient for increasing number of IoT connected devices. The IPv6 standard has been established to accommodate more address space that is necessary to address the billions of IOT devices.

6.3.1.3   Transport Layer

The transport layer transfers the sensor data from the physical layer to the application layer and application layer to physical layer via networks layer [36]. Transport layer alters and transfers sensor data between layers and through networks such as 5G, 4G, Wi-Fi, Bluetooth, and LoRaWAN [37] like a typical IoT gateway.

6.3.1.4   Application Layer

End user IoT device communicate with the software application through application layer. Application layer outline entire application on which IoT have installed [38]. This layer offer the facilities to the applications. The services may be varying according range of application like smart city, smart home, smart agriculture and smart health since services rely on the information that is collected by sensors. The health related data is extracted, stored, and processed by cloud-based product embedded with ML and deep learning techniques for further analysis and prediction. Application layer supports different data formats, and applications protocols. Data format like JSON, CBR, and binary format. The developers prefer JSON (JavaScript Object Notation) as the standard data format to exchange clinical data between the platform components and services [39]. Application protocols such as CoAP, MQTT, REST, and XAMPP are shown in Figure 6.4. Doctors, nurses, patients, insurance providers, medical researcher, and drug designer are the users that interact with IoT-based application.

6.4   Machine Learning and IoT

Today, smart watches, Fitbit, IoT sensors, and smart wearable devices are attracting health conscious people which monitor their health and generate data; this data is then transferred to cloud for being analyzed by ML algorithms and results are returned back with suggestions. However, security is one of the major concern due to several challenges being faced during the transit of data to cloud that is on the network as well as cloud being a third party is also partially reliable. Researchers are also working in the area of security of the data during transit as well as when stored in cloud.

6.4.1   Application of ML and IoT in Healthcare

Healthcare industry today is leveraging with IoT and ML that offer diverse remote health monitoring, in-home diagnostics capabilities. IoT and ML are restructuring the conventional healthcare system into a more consistent and accurate diagnosis and treatment with safe and secure data sharing [6]. AI and ML in the healthcare system are used to accurate disease classification, diagnosis, prediction, and monitoring and medicine suggestion. IoT connect doctors, patients, and diagnosis center to assist in constant monitoring of patient data in real time. ML permits healthcare experts to move to a personalized care system, which is recognized as precision medicine. ML and deep learning became one of the most incredible revolutions in the healthcare sector. The following are the application of integrating ML and IoT in healthcare.

6.4.1.1   Smart Diagnostic Care

The bio-module devices, wearable devices, and smart pills perform some diagnostic for patient. ML can examine the wide amount of collected data from IoT devices and simplify the diagnostic process. Smart diagnostic system can fulfill the lack of qualified doctors, pathological staff, and medical instrument operator in isolated areas [40]. Critical patients can be 24-hour under observation of doctors and medical staff due to IoT and ML-based smart diagnostic care. The patient's state and disease status are more precisely defined which supports to develop a personalized treatment plan [41]. Hence, diagnostic service with IoT and ML can greatly advance the personal diagnostic care.

6.4.1.2   Medical Staff and Inventory Tracking

IoT and ML-based technology also assist to monitoring the medical staff, availability of expert, tracking of instruments, and biological samples. Smart healthcare system helps in the pharmaceutical industry for drug prediction, drug production, circulation, and inventory management. RFID technology plays vital role in the tracing and monitoring of drugs and equipment and the regulation of the market for medical products [42]. AI and ML techniques predict daily demand and classification of product. Support vector regression, deep learning algorithm, and time series algorithm ensure significant accuracy for demand forecasting process [43].

6.4.1.3   Personal Care

IoT and ML-based application offer personal care to hospital discharged patients, remote patient, and elderly people living alone. IoT devices monitor the health status; the patients' particular health information can be stored into the cloud server for investigation and suggestion. ML-based techniques analyze the patients/device holder and intimate the timings of medicine, level of glucose, consult with doctor, etc.

6.4.1.4   Healthcare Monitoring Device

Various devices are available in market for healthcare monitoring based on IoT and ML. IoT sensor–based devices such as glucose monitors and biosensors can embed the power of ML approaches for monitoring and decision-making. Integrating IoT devices and the necessary high-speed data transfers are making a strong healthcare monitoring device. HelpAgeSensor [44] device for elderly person can be enhanced by using ML.

6.4.1.5   Chronic Disease Management

IoT with ML is used to manage chronic diseases such as diabetes, cardiovascular ailments, and cancer. Chronic diseases management comprises combining sensors, data, and algorithms along with medical specialists in four steps:

   a. Sensor device that capture biological signals in the hospital and at home.
   b. Collect data from several sources to offer a holistic picture of the patient's health and create a profile of patient.

  c. Analyze the profile with ML techniques to perceive the presence and evolution of the chronic diseases.

  d. Monitor the patient profile to manage their health.

IoT and ML-based must support the heterogeneous environment. Heterogeneous environment is referred where different protocol, architecture, devices, service providers, hardware, and software platforms can work in seamless manner [45]. IoT and ML support disease diagnosis system in an effective manner [6]. Success of ML and IoT-based healthcare application relies on best connected channel model [46]. Further, this chapter can be extended with blockchain for transparent and secure transaction that work efficiently in a distributed environment [47, 48].

6.5 Conclusion

This chapter outlines the potential of ML and IoT to transform the delivery services of traditional healthcare. Several kinds of ML techniques, namely, unsupervised learning, unsupervised learning, semi-supervised learning, and reinforcement learning are also discussed along with the layered architecture of IoT designed for healthcare services. We have also discussed several applications using integration of IoT and ML such as smart diagnostic care, personal care, and chronic disease management. IoT and ML-based solution makes a promising solution to the implementation of trustworthy, secure, and distributed healthcare applications.

 Further, healthcare industry can also be integrated with Blockchain along with IoT and ML. Blockchain technology offers protected transactions, safe data storage, immutable data record, and transparent data flow service, transaction validation process, and secure data exchanges between organizations. A smart contract is one of the Blockchain features that can be used as a real agreement in the healthcare industry. IoT, ML, and Blockchain adoption in healthcare industry will focus on smart health supply chain, drug supply chain management, and claim management.

References

1. Greco, L., Percannella, G., Ritrovato, P., Tortorella, F., Vento, M., Trends in IoT based solutions for healthcare: Moving AI to the edge. *Pattern Recognit. Lett.*, 135, pp. 346–353, 2020.

2. Agrawal, V., Singh, P., Sneha, S., Hyperglycemia prediction using machine learning: A probabilistic approach. *International Conference on Advances in Computing and Data Sciences*, Springer, Singapore, pp. 304–312, 2019.
3. Yan, Z., Zhan, Y., Peng, Z., Liao, S., Shinagawa, Y., Zhang, S., Zhou, X.S., Multi-instance deep learning: Discover discriminative local anatomies for bodypart recognition. *IEEE Trans. Med. Imaging*, 35, 5, 1332–1343, 2016.
4. Anthimopoulos, M., Christodoulidis, S., Ebner, L., Christe, A., Mougiakakou, S., Lung pattern classification for interstitial lung diseases using a deep convolutional neural network. *IEEE Trans. Med. Imaging*, 35, 5, 1207–1216, 2016.
5. Shen, W., Zhou, M., Yang, F., Yang, C., Tian, J., Multi-scale convolutional neural networks for lung nodule classification. *International Conference on Information Processing in Medical Imaging*, Springer, Cham, pp. 588–599, 2015.
6. Singh, N., Singh, P., Singh, K.K., Singh, A., *Diagnosing of Disease using Machine Learning, accepted for ML & Internet of medical things in healthcare*, Elsevier Publications (In Press), United States, 2021.
7. Schlemper, J., Caballero, J., Hajnal, J.V., Price, A.N., Rueckert, D., A deep cascade of convolutional neural networks for dynamic MR image reconstruction. *IEEE Trans. Med. Imaging*, 37, 2, 491–503, 2017.
8. Mehta, J. and Majumdar, A., RODEO: robust DE-aliasing autoencoder for real-time medical image reconstruction. *Pattern Recognit.*, 63, 499–510, 2017.
9. Havaei, M., Davy, A., Warde-Farley, D., Biard, A., Courville, A., Bengio, Y., Larochelle, H., Brain tumor segmentation with deep neural networks. *Med. Image Anal.*, 35, 18–31, 2017.
10. Rajpurkar, P., Irvin, J., Zhu, K., Yang, B., Mehta, H., Duan, T., Lungren, M.P., Chexnet: Radiologist-level pneumonia detection on chest x-rays with deep learning. *arXiv preprint arXiv*, 1711, 05225, 2017.
11. Gulshan, V., Peng, L., Coram, M., Stumpe, M.C., Wu, D., Narayanaswamy, A., Kim, R., Development and validation of a deep learning algorithm for detection of diabetic retinopathy in retinal fundus photographs. *Jama*, 316, 22, 2402–2410, 2016.
12. Latif, S., Asim, M., Usman, M., Qadir, J., Rana, R., Automating motion correction in multishot MRI using generative adversarial networks. *arXiv preprint arXiv*, 1811, 09750, 2018.
13. Singh, R., Rajesh, E., Prediction of heart disease by clustering and classification techniques Prediction of Heart Disease by Clustering and Classification Techniques. *International Journal of Computer Sciences and Engineering*, 7, 5, pp. 861–866, 2019.
14. Polat, K. and Güneş, S., Prediction of hepatitis disease based on principal component analysis and artificial immune recognition system. *Appl. Math. Comput.*, 189, 2, 1282–1291, 2007.
15. Afshar, P., Mohammadi, A., Plataniotis, K.N., Brain tumor type classification via capsule networks. *2018 25th IEEE International Conference on Image Processing (ICIP)*, IEEE, pp. 3129–3133, 2018.

16. Zhu, W., Liu, C., Fan, W., Xie, X., Deeplung: Deep 3d dual path nets for automated pulmonary nodule detection and classification. *2018 IEEE Winter Conference on Applications of Computer Vision (WACV)*, IEEE, pp. 673–681, 2018.

18. Wang, Z., Shah, A.D., Tate, A.R., Denaxas, S., Shawe-Taylor, J., Hemingway, H., Extracting diagnoses and investigation results from unstructured text in electronic health records by semi-supervised machine learning. *PLoS One*, 7, 1, e30412, 2012.

19. Nestor, B., McDermott, M., Boag, W., Berner, G., Naumann, T., Hughes, M.C., Ghassemi, M., Feature robustness in non-stationary health records: Caveats to deployable model performance in common clinical MLtasks. *arXiv preprint arXiv*, 1908, 00690, 2019.

20. Anwar, S.M., Majid, M., Qayyum, A., Awais, M., Alnowami, M., Khan, M.K., Medical image analysis using convolutional neural networks: A review. *J. Med. Syst.*, 42, 11, 226, 2018.

21. Jing, B., Xie, P., Xing, E., On the automatic generation of medical imaging reports. *arXiv preprint arXiv*, 1711, 08195, 2017.

22. Wang, X., Peng, Y., Lu, L., Lu, Z., Summers, R.M., Tienet: Text-image embedding network for common thorax disease classification and reporting in chest x-rays. *Proceedings of the IEEE conference on computer vision and pattern recognition*, pp. 9049–9058, 2018.

23. Xue, Y., Xu, T., Long, L.R., Xue, Z., Antani, S., Thoma, G.R., Huang, X., Multimodal recurrent model with attention for automated radiology report generation. *International Conference on Medical Image Computing and Computer-Assisted Intervention*, Springer, Cham, pp. 457–466, 2018.

24. Weng, S.F., Reps, J., Kai, J., Garibaldi, J.M., Qureshi, N., Can machine-learning improve cardiovascular risk prediction using routine clinical data? *PloS One*, 12, 4, e0174944, 2017.

25. Fatima, M. and Pasha, M., Survey of ML algorithms for disease diagnostic. *J. Intell. Learn. Syst. Appl.*, 9, 01, 1, 2017.

26. Fraser, K.C., Meltzer, J.A., Rudzicz, F., Linguistic features identify Alzheimer's disease in narrative speech. *J. Alzheimer's Dis.*, 49, 2, 407–422, 2016.

27. Pou-Prom, C. and Rudzicz, F., Learning multiview embeddings for assessing dementia. *Proceedings of the 2018 Conference on Empirical Methods in Natural Language Processing*, pp. 2812–2817, 2018.

28. Ghassemi, M., Van Stan, J.H., Mehta, D.D., Zañartu, M., Cheyne II, H.A., Hillman, R.E., Guttag, J.V., Learning to detect vocal hyperfunction from ambulatory neck-surface acceleration features: Initial results for vocal fold nodules. *IEEE Trans. Biomed. Eng.*, 61, 6, 1668–1675, 2014.

29. Vijayalakshmi, A.V. and Arockiam, L., A secured architecture for IoT healthcare system. *International conference on Computer Networks, Big data and IoT*, Springer, Cham, pp. 904–911, 2018.

30. Bui, K.H.N. and Jung, J.J., ACO-based dynamic decision making for connected vehicles in IoT system. *IEEE Trans. Ind. Inf.*, 15, 10, 5648–5655, 2019.

31. Dubey, S., Singh, P., Yadav, P., Singh, K.K., Household waste management system using iot and machine learning. *Procedia Comput. Sci.*, 167, 1950–1959, 2020.

32. Jayaram, A., Smart Retail 4.0 IoT Consumer retailer model for retail intelligence and strategic marketing of in-store products. *Proceedings of the 17th International Business Horizon-INBUSH ERA-2017, Noida, India*, vol. 9, 2017.

33. Prathibha, S.R., Hongal, A., Jyothi, M.P., IoT based monitoring system in smart agriculture. *2017 international conference on recent advances in electronics and communication technology (ICRAECT)*, IEEE, 2017.

34. Vijayalakshmi, A.V. and Arockiam, L., A secured architecture for iot healthcare system. *International conference on Computer Networks, Big data and IoT*, Springer, Cham, pp. 904–911, 2018.

35. Song, Y.E., Liu, Y., Fang, S., Zhang, S., Research on applications of the internet of things in the smart grid. *7th International Conference on Intelligent Human-Machine Systems and Cybernetics (IHMSC)*, vol. 2, pp. 178–181, 2015.

36. Sethi, P. and Sarangi, S.R., Internet of things: architectures, protocols, and applications. *J. Electr. Comput. Eng.*, 2017, pp. 25, 2017.

37. Calihman, A., Architectures in the IoT civilization. Online access from: https://www.netburner.com/learn/architectural-frameworks-in-the-iot-civilization/. 2019.

38. Burhan, M., Rehman, R.A., Khan, B., Kim, B.S., IoT elements, layered architectures and security issues: A comprehensive survey. *Sensors*, 18, 9, 2796, 2018.

39. Barroca Filho, I. D. M., Architectural design of IoT-based healthcare applications. Ph.D thesis submitted to Federal University of Rio Grande do Norte, Exact and Earth Sciences Center, 2019.

40. Ahamed, F. and Farid, F., Applying Internet of Things and machine-learning for personalized healthcare: issues and challenges. *2018 International Conference on MLand Data Engineering (iCMLDE)*, IEEE, pp. 19–21, 2018.

41. Tian, S., Yang, W., Le Grange, J.M., Wang, P., Huang, W., Ye, Z., Smart healthcare: Making medical care more intelligent. *Global Health J.*, 3, 3, 62–65, 2019.

42. Zhang, L., Applications of the Internet of Things in the Medical Industry (Part 1): Digital Hospitals, IoT Zone, 2018. https://dzone.com/articles/applications-of-the-internet-of-things-in-the-medi-1.

43. Kilimci, Z.H., Akyuz, A.O., Uysal, M., Akyokus, S., Uysal, M.O., Atak Bulbul, B., Ekmis, M.A., An improved demand forecasting model using deep learning approach and proposed decision integration strategy for supply chain. *Complexity*, 2019, pp. 15, 2019.

44. Pandey, R.S., Upadhyay, R., Kumar, M., Singh, P., Shukla, S., IoT-based help age sensor device for senior citizens. *International Conference on Innovative*

Computing and Communications, Springer, Singapore, pp. 187–193, 2020, 2020.

45. Singh, P. and Agrawal, R., A game-theoretic approach to maximise payoff and customer retention for differentiated services in a heterogeneous network environment. *Int. J. Wireless Mob. Comput.*, 16, 2, 146–159, 2019.

46. Singh, P. and Agrawal, R., A customer centric best connected channel model for heterogeneous and IoT networks. *J. Organiz. End User Comput.*, 30, 4, 32–50, 2018.

47. Singh, P. and Singh, N., Blockchain with IoT and AI: A review of agriculture and healthcare. *Int. J. Appl. Evol. Comput. (IJAEC)*, 11, 4, 13–27, 2020.

48. Singh, P., Singh, N., Deka, G.C., Prospects of machine learning with blockchain in healthcare and agriculture. *Multidisciplinary Functions of Blockchain Technology in AI and IoT Applications*, IGI Global, pp. 178–208, 2020.

7

Blockchain for Vehicular Ad Hoc Network and Intelligent Transportation System: A Comprehensive Study

Raghav Sharma[1]*, Anirudhi Thanvi[1], Shatakshi Singh[2], Manish Kumar[3] and Sunil Kumar Jangir[2]

[1]*Department of Information Technology, Jaipur Engineering College and Research Center, Jaipur, India*
[2]*Department of Computer Science and Engineering, School of Engineering and Technology, Mody University of Science and Technology, Lakshmangarh, India*
[3]*Department of Biomedical Engineering, Mody University of Science and Technology, Lakshmangarh, India*

Abstract

Vehicular Ad Hoc Network (VANET) is advancing in recent ages, with the furtherance in the Internet of Things and the technology of sensors. The scientific provocations of contemporaneous VANET are the decentralized deployment of architecture and protection of privacy. Considering this, blockchain governs the attributes of being dispersed, collective, preserving, non-tampering, and decentralized, designing a novel decentralized structure utilizing the automation of blockchain, also known as VANET based on blockchain. It can successfully inscribe the issues of mutual distrust and centralization in the middle of organizations in recent VANET. Intelligent Vehicle (IV) is coming across thorough going growth in industry and research still it goes through many risks to security. Standard protection methods are incapacitated to provide protected IV sharing of data. A verification agreement based on Public Key Infrastructure gives the basic services of security for the VANET. This chapter will review technologies working for cryptocurrency and Bitcoin, which is currently being used to create trust and dependability in associated networks also it analyzes how movability influences productivity in a system of blockchain run in a VANET.

Corresponding author: rs1151015@gmail.com

Krishna Kant Singh, Akansha Singh and Sanjay Sharma (eds.) Machine Learning Approaches for Convergence of IoT and Blockchain, (145–174) © 2021 Scrivener Publishing LLC

Keywords: Vehicular Ad hoc Network (VANET), blockchain, Intelligent Vehicle (IV), Intelligent Transportation System (ITS), security, smart vehicle, cloud computing, networking

7.1   Introduction

With the fast improvement in urban sprawl, the brilliant metropolis has pulled in broad consideration in both industry and scholarly community. It is assessed that the count of vehicles around the globe will rise to 2 billion in the following two decades [1]. The rise of Vehicular Ad hoc Networks (VANETs) draws incredible benefits and congenial experience of driving for individuals. Two kinds of transmission, to be specific the vehicle-to-infrastructure (V2I) transmission and the vehicle-to-vehicle (V2V) transmission are set up in VANETs to advance participation among the vehicles and offer significant driving of data through the committed short-extended communication (DSRC) radio [2]. Adding to this, it accomplishes environment-friendly mode by diminishing the consumption of numerous open assets and lessening the car crashes and clog on the roads.

A VANET can enhance the progression of rush to encourage quick conveyance also give advantageous data administrations. The objective of VANET is focused upon to give identity-arranging information communication abilities for automobiles making progress toward empowering utilization, for example, held in driving vehicles and security alerts [3]. In recent times, different VANET applications have discovered an incentive in this innovation to advance responsibility and believability of the information [4]. Blockchain is an innovation that uses an appropriate record to permit exchanges between nobles of system, lacking some requirement on behalf of a focal standard [5]. For example, as automobiles turn to be independent, progressively, they are required to trade information through "trust" in an assortment of intelligent transportation situations, for example, smart contacts, further which can profit by the use of the technology of blockchain [6]. In a blockchain framework, nodes do not confide in one another, and in this way, they track a procedure of validation each and every time a fresh different block is introduced [7]. A node confides in a block simply next to an accord by implementing this approval procedure. This procedure is known as a proof-of-work (PoW) process, that gives a way to build up an accord on which a specific exchange is legitimate inside the system. The perfect thing is if a block is approved through all full nodes (FNs) in a system [8], that requires the proliferation of a block to all the FNs over a complete system. This makes various factors huge than others in the exhibition of a net of blockchain, e.g., the amount of nodes, all-out engendering interval, and so forth.

The blockchain is globally praised advancement dependent on the technology of dispersed records, which started from the endeavors of unknown creators to provide security to e-money. Advanced monetary forms that depend on the blockchain are explained as cryptocurrency, as it depends on cryptographic scientific devices. The very first blockchain began through the means of a manuscript secretly distributed in the year 2008 on metzdowd.com in its cryptography mailing list [9]. Since 2008, an incredible turn of events, which has been done on starting ideas, has prompted the production of many circulated and dynamic blockchains. The concept of blockchain includes various types of information and is, in fact, it is tedious to fact that Bill Gates freely stated in a conversation on television regarding this innovation: "I think it's a technical tour de force." Countless petitions have been envisioned for blockchain information frameworks, numerous researchers and monetary specialists anticipate that extraordinary developments should be focused on this imaginative idea, particularly in the coordination's segment [10–13]. A few writers have also described this latest innovation as problematic, regarding the transportation field [14].

In request to expand their own solaces, humans in day-to-day life schedules have been in part or finished and supplanted by mechanized and inserted types of machinery in every part of the business. Embedded frameworks study their ecological environmental factors and in this manner react or control the circumstance with no human mediation [15]. In the recent time, with the improvement in the wireless communication and the progression in the industry of vehicles, VANETs have become an experienced exploration region. VANET comprises a gathering of moving and fixed vehicles associated by means of a wireless system. As of not long ago, the fundamental utilization of VANETs was to give solace and wellbeing to drivers in a vehicular domain [16]. Be that as it may, this view is changing the framework toward intelligent frameworks of transportation where vehicles are associated and impart utilizing keen gadgets.

We normally describe the associated vehicle which is outfitted with remote web availability and in general with VANET. Improvements in programming and equipment innovation head toward automobiles under complete mechanized astute control. The modern intelligent associated vehicle has become a personal computer framework like a cell phone, constrained by a perplexing system with a remote transmission network organized and internal in-vehicle arrangement. The smart vehicles associated with nearly everything are developing quickly as a digitalized substantial framework from the customary enriched mechanical framework. Nonetheless, the presentation of a vehicular cloud arrangement dependent on remote web availability implies an exceptional increment in the dependence on the networked software. This prompts an issue in cybersecurity, just as security-related capacity issues in the automobile world. In view of these previously mentioned realities, the most significant tasks related to smart vehicles is to utilize a confided system to make sure about them in opposition to vindictive hacking.

Figure 7.1 portrays a quintessential network of vehicular blockchain where objects of IoT (I1, I2,..., I6) are associated among a few companions. Additionally, the vehicles are contemplated as different peer nodes in the systems which are additionally isolated into smaller nodes relying on their administration rules. Smaller nodes are answerable for approving the trust of outstanding nodes or IoT gadgets while peer nodes are a piece of the whole blockchain.

The major benefaction of this chapter is to majorly address problem of centralization in traditional VANET and its collaboration with blockchain to form an Intelligent Vehicle (IV). This chapter provides an insight of blockchain technology and projects a novel dispersed design, blockchain-based VANET. This also covers the importance and need of blockchain in this area. In this chapter, we familiarize the key traits of cyber security problems when integrating blockchain to vehicles creating vehicle an IV. Also, implementation of blockchain supported IVs with ITS-oriented blockchain model.

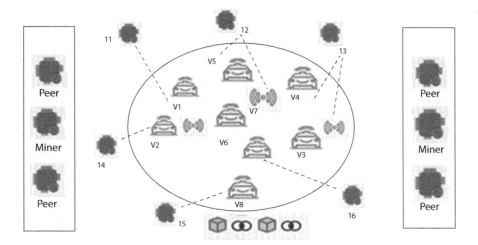

Figure 7.1 System design of blockchain.

7.2   Related Work

In the current years, protection of privacy has become a problem area in the investigation of VANET [17, 18]. As indicated by the articles secured by analysts, we can isolate the protection of privacy into three sorts: protection of location privacy [19–22], protection of trajectory privacy [23–25], and protection of identity privacy [26].

In [25], it is introduced by authors that a stratagem of privacy of trajectory utilizing the different mix zones. By continually evolving nom de plumes made the pen names and ensured the privacy of vehicular trajectory. At the moment, numerous researchers utilize the k-obscurity system in VANET. The guideline of max entropy, they discover a number of k suitable automobiles by means of the nearest chronicled demand likelihood. At that point, the genuine vehicle is covered up in these k vehicles, and vehicle security is ensured.

In the current year, a couple of specialists have brought blockchain in relevance to VANET, thinking about the qualities of dispersion, excess stockpiling, aggregate upkeep, and non-breakable blockchain. For instance, Joy et al. [27] introduced the idea of block-tree. Further onward, the mark was placed by the vehicle in the blockchain. Greg et al. [28] confirmed the achievability of the blockchain and broke down the start to finish delay and an opportunity to gather, compose, and enhance blockchain substance.

To more readily consolidate the blockchain in accordance with VANET, Dorri et al. [29] introduced a finely adaptable blockchain. Furthermore, in light of this, in accordance to [30] introduced a blockchain design with dispersed security assurance for smart vehicle frameworks. While Lei et al. [31] introduced another system topology dependent on blockchain architecture to disentangle disseminated key administration in heterogeneous vehicle transmission frameworks. Moreover, the utilization of the blockchain as a method for protection saving verification of area has been introduced in crafted by [32].

One body centers around the progress of credibility and security in information traded in a VANET. The current work introduces a triple layer design for guaranteeing the safety of information in VANET [33]. Alternative most recent study introduces blockchain-based unknown notoriety framework so as to discontinue the relation between genuine characters plus open keys to protect security [34]. Likewise, their found a study that reads a consortium blockchain for making sure about information sharing and capacity framework in a VANET [35]. Additional investigation utilizes consortium blockchain and shrewd agreement innovations so as to make sure the accomplishment about information stockpiling and partaking in vehicular edge systems [36], that accepts the vehicular edge processing attendants comprised of the side of the road units (RSUs) that cannot be completely reliable and hence might bring about genuine security and protection challenges. Another body shows enthusiasm for settling vitality utilization in a blockchain framework that are utilized to vehicular system. Late effort illustrates a significant knowledge of the blockchain utilization in a vehicular system [37].

The undeveloped-access domain produced by VANETs acquires incredible difficulties at area of security and privacy which are in poor condition to be actualized in reality [37]. Zhang et al. [38] stated an Identity-based Batch Verification (IBV) plot designed for V2V and V2I transmission in VANETs, that are utilized for sealed gadget so as to secure privacy, and each gadget put away the framework's main key to create pseudo characters locally.

Calandriello et al. [39] introduced an amalgamation strategy that reinforces the structure utilizing nom de plumes self-affirmation, which is not important to oversee them without trading off the vigor of the framework. Tan et al. [40] introduced a non-verified confirmation convention among vehicles and side of the road entities to understand vehicle's identification validation; also, Vijayakumar et al. [41] planned unique key administration and safe validation system so as to improve client's major concern in VANETs. The exchange procedure of blockchain brought together a framework and does not give the conveyed security. Wu et al. [42] used one-time validation and gathering marks to distinguish vindictive clients. In any case, it is ineffective to follow dubious messages because of costly bilinear blending activities at the phase of the following.

Numerous scientists in VANETs concentrate on improving proficiency, ensuring protection, and security by means of blockchain innovation. Yuan and Wang [43] introduced a dispersed and secure blockchain-based independent smart transportation framework. Rowan et al. [44] introduced a novel open key foundation based on blockchain and a vehicle meeting key foundation convention to make sure about V2V transmissions. Chuang et al. [45] introduced a privacy preservation authentication scheme (PPAS) for correspondence among vehicles and foundations in this network, which accomplished the vehicle and the RSU to verify one another and fulfilled the majority of the security necessities. Be that as it may, this plan gives no disseminated framework and is utilized to speak with vehicles. Peng [46] introduced an onboard organized unknown validation protocol. Lu et al. [34] structured a blockchain-based unknown notoriety framework for ad hoc network, and Malik et al. [47] introduced blockchain-based mysterious confirmation for vehicular systems. Regardless of [34] and [47] are understood that save clients' protection in the confirmation procedure, none of their plans present a technique for vehicle declaration, and just are appropriate in Bitcoin without similarity.

An earlier framework that is nearest to our own is Blockchain ITS [43] introduced by Yuan and Wang. They were among the founders to investigate the utilization of blockchain to help ITS. B2 ITS depends on a seven-layer calculated design that empowers equal transportation administration for ITS [48].

Furthermore, Leiding *et al.* [49] introduced a framework to provide administration in a self-guided and dispersed framework. A few uses incorporate traffic guideline applications and vehicle duty and protection apps. Dorri *et al.* [50] stated that utilizing a blockchain elective that enhances for IoT so as to ameliorate surviving ITS apps. Singh and Kim [51] introduced a framework known as Trust Bit, based on a prize framework that urges smart vehicles to impart honestly. Michelin *et al.* [52] brought up another Blockchain that permits associated automobiles to allocate information safely in a dispersed manner and alter a safe way. These frameworks addressed a few parts of ITS frameworks, for example, decentralization, compelled asset, and information trade; nonetheless, these investigations just managed a constrained arrangement of specialized difficulties and did not mean to incorporate various ITS frameworks together.

There are a few research associations and enterprises which are dealing with blockchain innovation usage for smart automobiles. Yuan *et al.* [53] introduced blockchain innovation for ITS to set up protected, faithful and dispersed self-sufficient environment and a seven-layered reasonable structure for the blockchain. Mainly, if you consider VANET, Benjamin *et al.* [54] likewise introduced blockchain innovation [49]. They have consolidated blockchain-based on Ethereum's shrewd agreements framework with vehicle impromptu systems. Introducing a blend of two applications, compulsory applications (traffic guideline, vehicle charge, vehicle protection) and discretionary (apps which give data and updates on congested driving conditions and climate estimates) of vehicles. They have tried to associate the administrations of VANET with blockchain. Blockchain can utilize various different functions, for example, correspondence in between the vehicles, give security, give distributed correspondence without revealing individual data, and so forth. Ali Dorri *et al.* [50] have introduced the blockchain innovation instrument without revealing any exclusive data of vehicle clients to give and modernize the outlying programming and different rising vehicle administrations. Sean Rowen *et al.* [44] have portrayed the blockchain innovation aimed at making sure about smart vehicle correspondence through the obvious acoustic and light side channels. They have checked their introduced instrument through another meeting cryptographic key, utilizing dual side-channels and blockchain open key frameworks.

7.3   Connected Vehicles and Intelligent Transportation System

We, by and large, characterize the associated vehicle which is equipped with remote web availability and normally additional with VANET. Improvisation in programming and equipment innovation concludes to vehicles under complete automated smart control. Figure 7.2 depicts the common engineering of a shrewd associated vehicle. Smart vehicles incorporate various arranged check units with detectors guaranteeing different vehicle performance. The essential equipment gadgets acknowledging savvy and associated vehicle capacity can be grouped into worked in or acquired association frameworks.

Associated vehicles nowadays been developed with a smartphone-like PC framework with web association, while it has progressively tedious controller with in-vehicle connection for supervision of movement elements, electronic frill, drive train, and prolusion related to an assortment of capacities giving solace and comfort to tenants.

In due course, VANET is alluded as the remote system known as smart transportation framework (ITS), which is meant to empower protected, productive flow of traffic, earth cognizant smart transportation administrations,

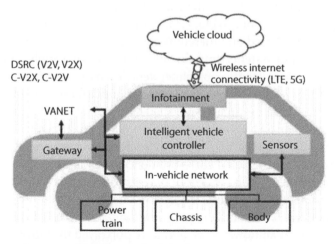

Figure 7.2 Architecture of intelligent vehicle [55].

just as extra explorer data administrations. ITS is intended to help the vehicle to share or to trade data among vehicles and infrastructure through the correspondence conventions, for example, vehicle-to-(side of the road) infrastructure (V2I), vehicle-to-network (V2N), and vehicle-to-vehicle (V2V), or vehicle-to-everything (V2X) transmission.

The self-governing vehicle is the best in the class of frameworks where incitation and dynamic moves work simultaneously with adapting to approaching natural data from detectors and correspondence systems while driving. Shrewd vehicles will be associated with nearly each and everything, and ending up being a piece of "IoT." The presentation of a remote connection of internet-based vehicle cloud will activate the wonderful increment in dependence on organized programming, therefore, prompting issues of cyber threats for information security, spillage of protection, just as safety-related capacities in vehicles.

7.3.1   VANET

These days, the field of intelligent transportation systems (ITS) is a difficult research zone due to the capability of new vehicular applications. Examination endeavors in vehicular specially appointed systems (VANETs) are in actuality part between modern consortia and the scholarly network. VANET is an extraordinary wire ad hoc network, which gives correspondence administration to V2V and V2I situations. As a significant piece of the ITS, the fundamental objective of VANETs is to offer complete types of assistance for the running condition of vehicles as per distinctive useful necessities of vehicles as indicated by various utilitarian prerequisites. VANETs incorporate three elements: CA, RSU, and Vehicle (V). CA is responsible for creating framework boundaries and the enrolment of V. RSU is introduced on the two roadsides, chiefly answerable for vehicle validation and correspondence administrations. The vehicle arranged the on-board unit (OBU) can speak with different elements remotely.

7.3.2   Blockchain Technology and VANET

Technology in the blockchain is a segregated, open record, kept by individual node in the system, that eventually self-sustained by every nodule. It gives a shared system devoid of the obstruction of the another authority. The blockchain trustworthiness depends upon solid cryptography that approves and link squares self-possessed on exchanges, constructing it difficult to mess with any specific exchange devoiding of being identified [9]. Figure 7.3 illustrates the blockchain innovation highlights, for example,

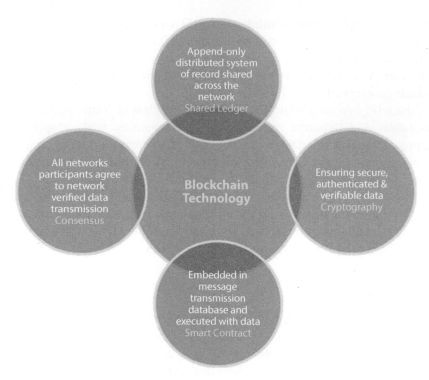

Figure 7.3 Blockchain technology.

shared record, cryptography, signed squares of exchanges, and advanced marks [9].

In the current centuries, a couple of research scholars have brought blockchain into VANET, thinking about the attributes of dispersion, excess vault, aggregate upkeep, and carefully designed block-tree. For instance, Joy *et al.* [27] introduced the idea of block-tree. What is more, the vehicle installed its mark into the blockchain. Greg *et al.* [28] confirmed the attainability of block-tree and examined the start to finish delay and an opportunity to gather, compose, and update blockchain substance. To more readily join the blockchain with the VANET, Dorri *et al.* [29] introduced a feathery adaptable blockchain. Also, in light of this, the reference of [30] introduced blockchain engineering with dispersed security assurance for astute vehicle frameworks. While Lei *et al.* [31] introduced another system geography dependent on blockchain structure to disentangle appropriated key administration in diversified vehicle correspondence frameworks. Moreover, the utilization of the blockchain as a method for security safeguarding verification of area has been introduced in crafted by [32].

7.4   An ITS-Oriented Blockchain Model

This portion displays an ITS-aligned, seven-layer theoretical structure for portraying and normalizing the common engineering and significant segments of blockchain systems and quickly depicts its fundamental key methods. Because of area confinements, the specialized subtleties for usage are past the extent of this paper and along these lines are precluded. As shown in Figure 7.4, likewise as the noteworthy open structure interrelationship testimonial representation [56], the blockchain representation has seven-layers piled-up as underneath:

1. Physical Layer: The physical layer epitomizes various types of physical establishments (e.g., devices, vehicles, resources, and other natural items) associated with ITSs, for, e.g., traffic signals, latest technology cameras, vehicles, etc. The key method is IoT in the given layer [57], which promotes upgraded device protection and data security when incorporated with blockchain.

2. Data Layer: This layer provides the fastened data blocks, along with the connected strategies containing asymmetric encode, hash calculations, time-stamping, and Merkle trees. In a blockchain structure, each figuring hub winning the accord competition will be engaged to make a different square, compiling all related to transportation data created within a particular timespan into Merkle-tree-organized data obstruct with time-stamps showing the making time of this square.

3. Network Layer: The system layer indicates the components of dispersed systems administration, data transmission, and confirmation. Most ITS models, structures, and usage scenarios are composed of large numbers of distributed, autonomous, non-static decision-making devices or vehicles, in this manner a blockchain ITS can be topologically displayed as a P2P organization.

4. Consensus Layer: The consensus layer bundles all conceivable consensus computation. As a rule, productively arriving at an agreement in decentralized structure has for quite some time been a standard query in conveyed figuring and ITS exploration [58]. One of blockchain's key plus points is promoting all dispersed junctions approaching consensus

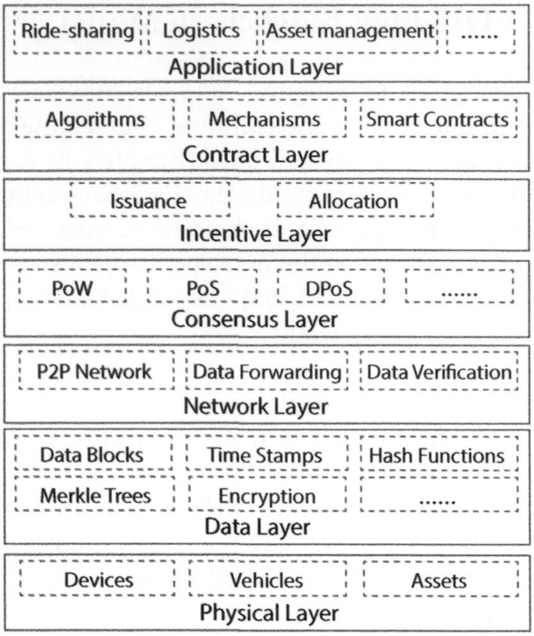

Figure 7.4 An ITS-oriented blockchain model [59].

on information rationality, which is the base of reciprocal trust among the junctions.

5. Incentive Layer: This layer joins economical prizes into blockchains and determines its allotment and issuance systems.

6. Contract Layer: This layer piles up various contents, computation and smart contracts, which fulfills in as significant catalyst to the non dynamic data, cash or resources kept away in the blockchain.

7. Application Layer: This layer compiles potential usage situations and utilizations instances of Blockchain ITS. In practice, blockchain revolution is still in its early stages, majorly in transportation models.

7.5   Need of Blockchain

Wireless internet access too joined with other correspondence components is turning out to be fundamental highlights of smart vehicles. Smart vehicles are advancing quickly by way of a digital-physical framework since customary rich mechanical framework. Associated smart vehicles offer a scope of complex assistance that advantage the automobile makers, clients, proprietors, vehicle drivers, specialists of transport the executives, and other specialist organizations. At whatever point a gadget is associated with the web, it is presented to a hazard from different malevolent cyber-attack. Advanced vehicles outfitted with advanced innovation have the utmost mechanized highlights also organized to interconnect with one another, which opens up new streets for malware. The assault surfaces of intelligent associated vehicle are expansive and may stretch out a long way past the defenselessness of hacking the vehicle itself.

Potential privacy attack and threat surface of savvy related vehicles can be requested into the following four classes as shown in Figure 7.5: Cyberattack through the web endeavored unapproved association with the in-vehicle organize engineering, inactive assault by altering sensors information, and remote assault through VANET.

- Cyberattack through the internet: Internet association transforms smart vehicles into a digital-physical framework and every vehicle carries something sort of hubs in the IoT [60].
- Endeavoring direct assaults on the in-vehicle system: An aggressor can endeavor to make an unapproved association with the in-vehicle organize, whereas we can regulate center ter elements of vehicles over the entryway of the in-vehicle system.
- Passive attack: A noxious attack that makes the vehicle detects inaccurate data by duplicating traffic signs or street signs or by giving phony signs or fake signals.
- The threat of V2X Transmission: V2X trades can compel more or less authentic dangers contrary to the protection and

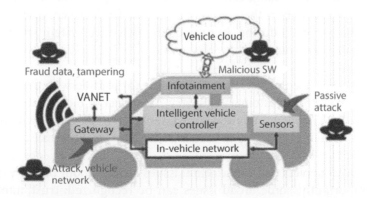

Figure 7.5 Expected potential attack surface [55].

precautions of vehicles and can incite upset traffic stream. Smart vehicles are needed to assemble data, for example, the traffic condition, momentary traffic circumstances at imperceptible separations, and information for agreeable driving.

Transportation is coming across an advanced development in examination and industry and are named as IVs, yet experience the harsh possessions of several security exposures. To sort most of the chances of IVs as another foundation of data innovation, mandatory task required is to conquer various difficulties in actualizing a safe reliance organization for smart vehicles. These days' security correspondence, all information correspondence is programmed and established developing an open/individual key framework with endorsement based common confirmation between associated hubs or cloud servers. Albeit mutual validation guarantees that the two gadgets can confirm the credibility of one another, these customary security strategies are as yet powerless against secure information partaking between keen vehicles [30, 61, 62].

A central necessity of ITSs is the assurance of origin, unchanging nature, and an error strong system between smart vehicles. The features are portrayed as follows:

1. Provenance: Each member identifies from where is the benefit originated and how its possession is transformed from exchanges.
2. Immutability: No member can mess with exchange after it has been documented in the data warehouse (Ledgers).
3. Resilience: Uncertainty an exchange is in blunder, debasement is promptly clear, and everybody is made heedful of it. Another exchange can be utilized to recoup the mistake, and the exchange is then re-established. If a few hubs are disconnected or enduring an onslaught, the entire system works not surprisingly.

Blockchain has been perceived as an uprising innovation with the possibility to derange every customary industry. The effect of blockchain innovation has been knowledgeable about the financial part as of now with digital forms of money called cryptocurrency like Bitcoin, Ethereal, and other crypto coins.

Figure 7.6 depicts the fundamental issues rising up out of our writing. Most importantly, some broad issues can be recognized: trust, administrative consistency, decentralization, data sharing, and flexible request

General Issues

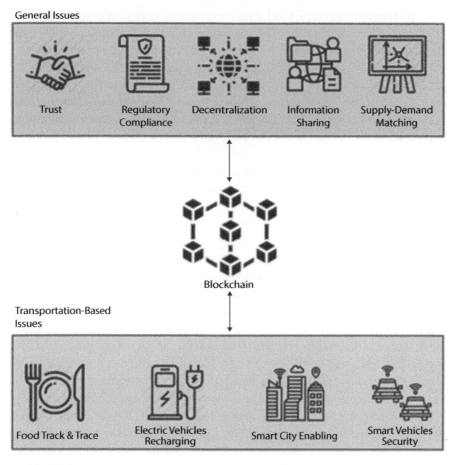

Figure 7.6 Issues emerging in the application of blockchain technology with transportation [63].

coordinating (i.e., utilization of smart contracts). In any case, around additionally four primary transportation-based issues are there: intelligent city enabling, electric vehicle reviving, food track and follow, and keen vehicle security.

These last four are investigated beneath, remembering for the argument the five recognized common issues also, featuring the present status of the art and the possible future examination points of view.

7.5.1   Food Track and Trace

One of the principal investigation difficulties of previous scarcely at any time is food detectability. A few methodologies have been introduced by researchers to expand food eminence and security: NFC, cosmology, QR Code, RFID, and so on. The fundamental intention is to give the last customer all the data about the procedures that an item on the rack has experienced. Specifically, the following methods having the option to gather every data about the different strides of the food flexibly anchor from downstream to upstream, while following is capacity to remake the item history in reverse [64]. The advantages of foodstuff discernibility are two-fold:

- Growing the apparent estimation of products
- Ensuring administrative consistency [65].

However, even now around, a few inadequacies in light of the fact that numerous discernibility frameworks are inadequate: fakes are still very far-reaching [66], while the review costs are regularly exceptionally high on account of food outrages on the grounds that the granular recognisability is burdensome, particularly on account of batch mixing [67]. In this specific circumstance, blockchain innovation comprises a huge chance to improve food recognisability: the decentralization of the general framework maintains a strategic distance from the presence of outsiders, and this makes the data trade between the on-screen characters quicker and progressively effective; the data recorded stays after some time and it is very simple to follow the entertainer who embedded it into the framework.

Moreover, there is no issue of incongruence among the data frameworks of the different substances included, in light of the fact that a solitary stage can be utilized. The fundamental future examination points of view are the accompanying: the need to have genuine contextual analyzes in light of the fact that the reproductions present in the writing are insufficient to show the possibility of the blockchain; a few organizations are for all intents and purposes applying this innovation in the food gracefully chains, yet not many genuine information is available on the scholarly side. Additionally, taking into account that, particularly in horticulture, many flexibly chains are not very innovation-based, we ought to examine progressively about how the presentation of cell phones would be elements in question: the expenses to prepare the entertainers and to rethink the chain procedures ought to be utmost researched area in following barely any years.

7.5.2   Electric Vehicle Recharging

Electric vehicles are getting progressively boundless, just like the stations for reviving them. The use of blockchain innovation here is somewhat innovative and a bit investigated. Some rare type of the fundamentally resolves worries the privilege of coordinating vitality requests and flexibly. From one viewpoint, there are drivers gathering who are based on their geological area, which show the requirement for an energize inside a specific time window, and on the other, a lot of vitality providers are ready to choose costs, in light of interest and competitors. This mechanism could support the two players since drivers could pick, each time, the least expensive proposal in their general vicinity, and providers could powerfully shift their costs, augmenting the normal benefit. Indeed, the utilization of savvy agreements could empower closeout instruments. In any case, significant endeavors are expected to make the blockchain-based designs adequately versatile [68]; truth be told, throughout the ages the amount of drivers and providers one who wish to choose link the electronic vehicle biological system possibly will drastically develop. The utilities of the blockchain may, perhaps, as it may establish the prompt to provide complete drive for electric vehicles spread.

7.5.3 Smart City and Smart Vehicles

Numerous urban communities remain characterized "smart" as and when the accompanying highlights become available: broadband availability, information labor force, and computerized presence. Some of principal objectives of shrewd urban communities is on way to advance the administrations offered to residents, decreasing authoritative expenses using innovation. Taking into account that the utilization of IoT, although valuable, prompts security issues in information the board, the presentation of blockchain innovation could explain this significant issue. In upcoming days, practically automobiles that are manufactured and advertised would be termed smart; truth be told, they will have the option to interface with web and interconnect through one another. Also, for this situation, the primary issues concern protection and security [50]; truth be told, the utilization of incorporated frameworks represents the disturbing subject of information handled by means of a particular unit. Executing blockchain innovation can cause creation drivers progressively safe in allocating data around the continuous position, traffic conditions, and any startling occasions, for example, street mishaps. In any case, even for this situation, there is an incredible requirement for down to earth tests: there is an absence of genuine executions inside keen urban areas and the penchant of drivers to share extremely secret data (e.g., geological area) ought to likewise be firmly assessed and investigated (e.g., drivers receiving a few polls, so as to be with a total picture).

Note that traffic blockage is one of the primary issues of present-day urban communities and one of the fundamental drivers of air contamination; its decrease is a major test these days. Conventional endeavors to take care of clog issues have been focused in endeavors to move the interest on the travel framework [69] and on a superior administration of street traffic-utilizing devices, for example, traffic reproduction [70–75], unique system stacking equilibria, and dynamic models [76, 77] for the re-enactment, and the board of client course decision [78–82]. New advances, for example, ITS and cooperative ITS (C-ITS) have been additionally reflected as expansion in street traffic maintainability [83–85]; however, the genuine development is perhaps originating from the group of people yet to come of vehicles that will be power-driven, "associated", and "self-ruling". New vehicles are been assumed by frequent, the way headed for will totally change traffic systems regarding decreased vitality utilization, improved safety, and diminished contamination. The forthcoming presenting self-ruling automobiles and the change since petroleum-based advancements to electronic and rechargeable automobiles has been developing, truth be told, totally alter the street rush division: merchandise and individuals shall be stimulated via driverless self-sufficient vehicles in shrewd urban areas. Human focused taxi administrations will be subbed via self-sufficient vehicles and new plans of action will develop where portability as help could replace the current vehicle possession worldview.

The trust the board issue in vehicular systems [53] can be fathomed by blockchain advancements, and different, secure frameworks dependent on this innovation might bolster the turn of events and send of power spark and self-governing portability where all exchanges are "communicated" and put away on a protected, open, and unalterable information base. The advancement of savvy urban areas, where the above-recorded administrations and advances are executed, can make an interest in blockchain innovation. For instance, blockchain frameworks could fulfill the future needs of residents and specialists to trade and store individual information securely.

Regarding the recently broke down blockchain and maintainability shows an extraordinary correlation between them in transportation-based issues:

1. The more prominent viability of detectability frameworks might limit amount of parcels been reviewed on or after the marketplace in such case of food outrages, restricting food squander.
2. The utilization of smart contract might invigorate development of the rechargeable vehicle showcase, through resulting

welfares for the globe, bearing in mind decrease of fumes outflows.

3. The data distribution between drivers, invigorated via compensating instruments through proper cryptographic money, might diminish rush in packed urban regions, refining personal satisfaction.

4. The blockchain innovation could prompt a persistent increment in the quantity of keen urban communities, preferring reasonable urban turn of events.

Other likely uses of blockchain are expected to rise up out of the union of developing administrations and advances, for example, Mobility as a Service (MaaS), IoT, man-made consciousness known as artificial intelligence (AI), and Deep Learning (DL), 5G, and disseminated keen products. This intermingling will get rise request of blockchain innovations and may decide the conditions for the improvement of blockchain applications in different parts like transportation, that have not been at this point broadly shrouded in the writing: travel, rail, sea, and air transportation. Blockchain advancements are relied upon to be presented in these segments once the degree of the improvement of the transportation frameworks arrives at that of what is plainly imagined for street transportation and that includes the future reception of self-ruling or self-ruling and associated vehicles. With respect to now, the writing examination, which was completed for this paper, shows that blockchain advancement with regard to rail, oceanic, and air transportation is not viewed as a rising subject.

In the real world, there are a few "impediments" for utilizing blockchain in the transportation segment. A few obstructions for utilizing blockchain in economical flexible chains have been identified in [86]. These obstructions are ordered into intra-hierarchical hindrances (e.g., absence of information and skill; money related limitations), frameworks related boundaries (e.g., the adolescence of innovation; delay to embrace blockchain innovation because of bogus open observation), between authoritative boundaries (e.g., social contrasts of flexibly chain accomplices), and outer boundaries (e.g., absence of government approaches and absence of outside partners' association). Other noteworthy constraints incorporate absence of readiness of the entertainers of the blocks to share data [87], bounds on the amount of exchanges per unit of time, contrasted with different players, for example, Visa or Mastercard (i.e., execution and adaptability issues) [88] and administrative vulnerability [11]. In addition, exchanging on a blockchain framework could be costly, in light of the fact that any error is irreversible and expands the exchange costs [89]. These are a couple of boundaries among those bantered in the writing; extra data can be found in [90–93]. This innovation is as yet juvenile and not prepared for the enormous scope spread in the current world.

7.6   Implementation of Blockchain Supported Intelligent Vehicles

We are now investigating the principal question of "By what can the trust arrange among unknown members be framed by blockchain technology?" Blockchain is a dispersed record which consists of information of every exchange implemented over a distributed system. At that point, by what means can the idea of a mutually circulated record create safe and changeless evidence of all exchanges and deals on the system?

Figure 7.7 depicts an outline of the essential instrument of Blockchain. Blockchain utilizes a notable uneven personal/open cryptographic hash and key system to approve the verification of exchanges. The individual key is utilized to sign the exchanges created by every hub. All exchanges marked with an individual key are communicated with system hubs. Entirely mining hubs of the system gather different exchanges and take a shot at finding a goal for a given accord rule. At the point when a hub locates an accord of the given system, it communicates the square to all hubs. Every other hub gets the square and, just if all exchanges in that are

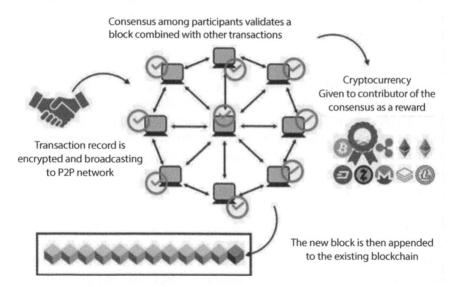

Figure 7.7 Basic mechanism of blockchain [94].

substantial, all hubs prompts their acknowledgment about square by making the following through chain of blocks.

The primary hub which exemplifies every block effectively, i.e., locates an agreement goal, acquires an award of cryptographic money, which might be an advantageous objective, to rouse each mining hub to expound to discover accord of the following square. This accord with remuneration and motivations framework turns into the main impetus for members to keep up the blockchain without being broken. The exchange information consisted in these blocks becoming unchanging, and this can be viewed as believed and made sure about, on the grounds that exchanges are stored by coordinated time stamps and gathered into cryptographically made sure about hinders that are composed in chains [95]. Contingent upon its transparency, we group the blockchain with open engineering like Ethereum and Bitcoin that work by mysterious doubtful members by non-consented access, or with permission to get to, that manages approved individuals. In the open blockchain, every hub can take partake in according to the procedure, where exchanges are naturally endorsed and recorded by mass support [96].

7.7 Conclusion

While blockchain innovation has a lot of advantages, the foundation of one of every VANET causes difficulties because of the hubs' portability. To examine the recital of a blockchain framework functional to VANET, this chapter presents a primer report on the developing blockchain innovation and it is possible uses in transportation research. We plan on an ITS-origin, seven-layer conceptual structure, introduce the exploration structure of the Blockchain Intelligent Transportation framework, and examine its key examination issues. In this framework, a correspondence is accomplished between different advancements, for example, V2I. At that point, an ongoing way of arranging the framework is depicted that depends on the improved transportation framework. Additionally, a portion of the security highlights is given in the said innovation, which causes security to vehicle correspondence. Last, however, not the least, portability strategies are introduced in building up ITS applications for V2V.

The presentation of blockchain advances is regularly identified with the dispersion of the network of associated frameworks and gadgets (i.e., IoT). The blockchain records must remain associated with the physical ecosphere, and with numerous mechanisms, it is predicted as association will remain supported by IoT gadgets. The "associated" automobiles will turn into piece of the IoT and so stays the purpose behind the developing reputation of blockchain advances in smart cities and street rush management. Supportive information distribution, exchanges, and some information (cash) trade that is conceivable among "self-sufficient(autonomous)" and "associated" automobiles might encourage by utilization of blockchain innovations that be able to ensure explicit highlights cannot have been ensured by traditional databanks.

The discussion will continue pending numerous submissions that have been organized and utilized, and until the particular handy arena of blockchain advancements is appropriately "framed". The constructive and target opinion, which rises up out of our survey, it came out as there is a developing enthusiasm for the logical ecosphere, in blockchain presentations in the transport area. Nonetheless, plentiful exertion is as yet required, for the most part with respect to transportation building analysts, so this promising innovation can arrive at its last level of development.

7.8   Future Scope

During the previous years, vehicles have become progressively dependable and agreeable. The requirement for unwavering quality and solace is joined by a few security necessities identified with driving and the information on the inward and outside ecological boundaries. Various administrations are as of now sent in present-day vehicles, including restriction, way choice, and crash evasion. To offer such types of assistance, propelled correspondence frameworks have been presented. They basically guarantee V2V, V2I, and vehicle-to-home (V2H) communication administrations.

ITS grips a legitimate sort of correspondence related applications intended to limit environmental effect, improve traffic the executives, and boost the upsides of transportation to both business clients and the overall population. A portion of the noticeable instances of shrewd transportation is Tollgate Management Systems and frameworks for driver help. These frameworks are being bolstered by the composed endeavors of governments and different associations. The administration association, which outlines the governing principles, principally considers the constant situations for vehicles and the clients inside the vehicles. To achieve compelling ITS, vehicular guidelines go about as a boundary as a result of contrasts in different normalization gatherings. Moreover, alongside that, there is a tremendous provincial variety among various nations.

The information approval is as yet a challenge. A vindictive vehicle can look out for creating ecological information and produce real information simultaneously. When it accomplishes that, it can supplant the real information produced with noxious information. For this situation, genuine information must be approved. While this case is exceptionally impossible because of the way, this requires time for creating the real information, and consequently, it can downsize the measure of assaults being conveyed, it is as yet a chance. So as to defeat this assault, the arrangement is to approve the real information being sent by the vehicle, other than the approval of the ecological information. In spite of the fact that the ecological information must be approved consistently, genuine information can be approved at a lower rate.

One of the tests is to make a notoriety system attached to the character of the vehicle. Because of the way that there is a real physical contact between the vehicles (they are in a similar region), the personality of the vehicle can be found in the picture of the vehicle. Vehicles are not indistinguishable because of the presence of tag numbers; henceforth, the picture of the vehicle can be considered as a unique mark. This can be accomplished through picture preparing strategies, and this is getting all the more a chance dependent on the way that vehicles are being outfitted with high innovation remembering cameras for a request to take into consideration the self-ruling vehicle innovation and keen vehicles.

References

1. Eze, E.C., Zhang, S., Liu, E., Vehicular ad hoc networks (VANETs): Current state, challenges, potentials and way forward. *ICAC 2014 - Proceedings of the 20th International Conference on Automation and Computing: Future Automation, Computing and Manufacturing*, pp. 176–181, 2014.
2. J., V. R.-N. M., News and undefined 2019, in: *EU parliament finally votes for WiFi to connect cars.*
3. Jia, D., Lu, K., Wang, J., Zhang, X., Shen, X., A survey on platoon-based vehicular cyber-physical systems. *IEEE Commun. Surv. Tutorials*, 18, 1, 263–284, Jan. 2016.
4. Li, Y. (Jeff), An overview of the DSRC/WAVE technology. *Lecture Notes of the Institute for Computer Sciences, Social-Informatics and Telecommunications Engineering, LNICST*, vol. 74, LNICST, pp. 544–558, 2012.
5. Zheng, D., Jing, C., Guo, R., Gao, S., Wang, L., A traceable blockchain-based access authentication system with privacy preservation in VANETs. *IEEE Access*, 7, 117716–117726, 2019.
6. B. Parno and A. Perrig, Challenges in securing vehicular networks, Wksp. Hot Topics in Networks (HotNets-IV), pp. 1–6, 2005.
7. Zhang, T. and Zhu, Q., Distributed privacy-preserving collaborative intrusion detection systems for VANETs. *IEEE Trans. Signal Inf. Process. over Networks*, 4, 1, 148–161, Mar. 2018.

8. Thanvi, A., Sharma, R., Menghani, B., Kumar, M., Jangir, S.K., A study on uninterrupted security in IoT based healthcare system, in: *IoT and Cloud Computing based Healthcare Information System*, p. 10, 2020.

9. Nakamoto, S., *Bitcoin: A peer-to-peer electronic cash system*, Charles Sturt Univ., p. 9, 2008. https://bitcoin.org/bitcoin.pdf

10. Friedlmaier, M., Tumasjan, A., Welpe, I.M., Disrupting industries with blockchain: The industry, venture capital funding, and regional distribution of blockchain ventures. *SSRN Electron. J.*, pp. 1–10, Jun. 2017.

11. Hackius, N. and Petersen, M., Blockchain in Logistics and Supply Chain: Trick or treat? *Reinf. Plast.*, 9783745043, April, 23, 2017.

12. B., D.-T., Crunch and undefined 2016, in: *Blockchain has the potential to revolutionize the supply chain*.

13. Casey, M. and P., W.-H., business review, and undefined 2017, in: *Global supply chains are about to get better, thanks to blockchain*.

14. Carter, C. and L. Koh. Blockchain disruption in transport: are you decentralised yet?. The National Academies of Sciences, Engineering, and Medicine, Jun. 2018

15. Tonguz, O., Wisitpongphan, N., Bai, F., Mudalige, P., Sadekar, V., Broadcasting in VANET. *2007 Mobile Networking for Vehicular Environments, MOVE*, pp. 7–12, 2007.

16. Sharma, R., Thanvi, A., Menghani, B., Kumar, M., Jangir, S.K., An approach towards information retrieval through machine learning and its algorithms: A review. *FICR Int. Conf. Rising Threat. Expert Appl. Solut. IIS Univ*, p. 10, 2020.

17. Zheng, Z., Zha, H., Zhang, T., Chapelle, O., Chen, K., & Sun, G. A general boosting method and its application to learning ranking functions for web search. Advances in Neural Information Processing Systems 20: Proceedings of the 2007 Conference, 2007.

18. Sun, Gang, Yuxia Xie, Dan Liao, Hongfang Yu, and Victor Chang. User-defined privacy location-sharing system in mobile online social networks. *Journal of Network and Computer Applications*, Elsevier, 86, 34–45, 2017.

19. Tyagi, A.K. and Sreenath, N., Location privacy preserving techniques for location based services over road networks. *2015 International Conference on Communication and Signal Processing, ICCSP 2015*, pp. 1319–1326, 2015.

20. Ullah, I., Wahid, A., Shah, M.A., Waheed, A., VBPC: Velocity based pseudonym changing strategy to protect location privacy of vehicles in VANET. *International Conference on Communication Technologies, ComTech 2017*, pp. 132–137, 2017.

21. Ying, B., Makrakis, D., Mouftah, H.T., Dynamic mix-zone for location privacy in vehicular networks. *IEEE Commun. Lett.*, 17, 8, 1524–1527, 2013.

22. Kang, J., Yu, R., Huang, X., Zhang, Y., Privacy-Preserved pseudonym scheme for fog computing supported internet of vehicles. *IEEE Trans. Intell. Transp. Syst.*, 19, 8, 2627–2637, Aug. 2018.

23. Zhang, S., Wang, G., Liu, Q., Abawajy, J.H., A trajectory privacy-preserving scheme based on query exchange in mobile social networks. *Soft Comput.*, 22, 18, 6121–6133, Sep. 2018.

24. Zhu, L., Xie, H., Liu, Y., Guan, J., Liu, Y., Xiong, Y., PTPP: Preference-aware trajectory privacy-preserving over location-based social networks. *J. Inf. Sci. Eng.*, 34, 4, 803–820, Jul. 2018.

25. Memon, I., Chen, L., Arain, Q.A., Memon, H., Chen, G., Pseudonym changing strategy with multiple mix zones for trajectory privacy protection in road networks. *Int. J. Commun. Syst.*, 31, 1, e3437, Nov. 2018.

26. Cui, J., Xu, W., Zhong, H., Zhang, J., Xu, Y., Liu, L., Privacy-preserving authentication using a double pseudonym for internet of vehicles. *Sensors*, 18, 5, 1453, May 2018.

27. Joy, J. and Gerla, M., Internet of vehicles and autonomous connected car - Privacy and security issues. *2017 26th International Conference on Computer Communications and Networks, ICCCN 2017*, 2017.

28. Joy, J., Cusack, G., Gerla, M., Poster: Time analysis of the feasibility of vehicular blocktrees. *SMARTOBJECTS 2017 - Proceedings of the 3rd Workshop on Experiences with the Design and Implementation of Smart Objects, co-located with MobiCom 2017*, pp. 25–26, 2017.

29. Dorri, A., Kanhere, S.S., Jurdak, R., Towards an optimized blockchain for IoT - IEEE Conference Publication. *2017 IEEE/ACM Second International Conference on Internet-of-Things Design and Implementation (IoTDI)*, 4AD, pp. 173–178.

30. Sharma, P.K., Moon, S.Y., Park, J.H., Block-VN: A distributed blockchain based vehicular network architecture in smart city. *J. Inf. Process. Syst.*, 13, 1, 184–195, 2017.

31. Lei, A., Cruickshank, H., Cao, Y., Asuquo, P., Ogah, C.P.A., Sun, Z., Blockchain-based dynamic key management for heterogeneous intelligent transportation systems. *IEEE Internet Things J.*, 4, 6, 1832–1843, Dec. 2017.

32. Amoretti, M., Brambilla, G., Medioli, F., Zanichelli, F., Blockchain-based proof of location. *Proceedings - 2018 IEEE 18th International Conference on Software Quality, Reliability, and Security Companion, QRS-C 2018*, pp. 146–153, 2018.

33. Zhang, X., Li, R., Cui, B., A security architecture of VANET based on blockchain and mobile edge computing. *Proceedings of 2018 1st IEEE International Conference on Hot Information-Centric Networking, Hot ICN 2018*, pp. 258–259, 2019.

34. Lu, Z., Liu, W., Wang, Q., Qu, G., Liu, Z., A privacy-preserving trust model based on blockchain for VANETs. *IEEE Access*, 6, 45655–45664, Aug. 2018.

35. Vyas, A. and Jangir, S.K., Advances in approach for object detection and classification. *National Conference on Information technology & security applications*, no. 978, pp. 1–3, 2019.

36. Vatsal Babel, S.K.J. and Kumar Singh, B., Evaluation methods for machine learning. *J. Anal. Comput.*, XI, I, 1–6, 2018.

37. Sharma, V., An energy-efficient transaction model for the blockchain-enabled Internet of Vehicles (IoV) - IEEE Journals & Magazine. *IEEE Commun. Lett.*, 23, 2, 246–249, Feb. 2019.

38. Zhang, C., Lu, R., Lin, X., Ho, P.-H., Shen, X., An efficient identity-based batch verification scheme for vehicular sensor networks. *IEEE INFOCOM 2008 - The 27th Conference on Computer Communications*, pp. 246–250, 2008.

39. Calandriello, G., Papadimitratos, P., Hubaux, J.P., Lioy, A., Efficient and robust pseudonymous authentication in VANET. *VANET'07: Proceedings of the Fourth ACM International Workshop on Vehicular Ad Hoc Networks*, pp. 19–28, 2007.

40. Wang, D., Tan, H., Choi, D., Kim, P., Pan, S., Chung, I., Secure certificateless authentication and road message dissemination protocol in VANETs. *Hindawi Wirel. Commun. Mob. Comput.*, 2018, 13, May 2018.

41. Vijayakumar, P., Azees, M., Kannan, A., Deborah, L.J., Dual authentication and key management techniques for secure data transmission in vehicular ad hoc networks. *IEEE Trans. Intell. Transp. Syst.*, 17, 4, 1015–1028, Apr. 2016.

42. Wu, Q., Domingo-Ferrer, J., González-Nicolás, Ú., Balanced trustworthiness, safety, and privacy in vehicle-to-vehicle communications. *IEEE Trans. Veh. Technol.*, 59, 2, 559–573, Feb. 2010.

43. Yuan, Y. and Wang, F.Y., Towards blockchain-based intelligent transportation systems. *IEEE Conference on Intelligent Transportation Systems, Proceedings, ITSC*, pp. 2663–2668, 2016.

44. Rowan, S., Clear, M., Gerla, M., Huggard, M., Goldrick, C.M., Securing Vehicle to Vehicle Communications using Blockchain through Visible Light and Acoustic Side-Channels. *Cryptography Secur.*, pp. 1–10, 08-Apr-2017.

45. Chuang, M.C. and Lee, J.F., PPAS: A privacy preservation authentication scheme for vehicle-to-infrastructure communication networks. *2011 International Conference on Consumer Electronics, Communications and Networks, CECNet 2011 - Proceedings*, pp. 1509–1512, 2011.

46. Peng, X., A novel authentication protocol for vehicle network. *2016 3rd International Conference on Systems and Informatics, ICSAI 2016*, pp. 664–668, 2017.

47. Malik, N., Nanda, P., Arora, A., He, X., Puthal, D., Blockchain based secured identity authentication and expeditious revocation framework for vehicular networks - IEEE Conference Publication. *2018 17th IEEE Int. Conf. Trust. Secur. Priv. Comput. Commun. 12th IEEE Int. Conf. Big Data Sci. Eng*, pp. 674–679, Aug. 2018.

48. Wang, F.Y., Parallel control and management for intelligent transportation systems: Concepts, architectures, and applications. *IEEE Trans. Intell. Transp. Syst.*, 11, 3, 630–638, Sep. 2010.

49. Leiding, B., Memarmoshrefi, P., Hogrefe, D., Self-managed and blockchain-based vehicular ad-hoc networks. *UbiComp 2016 Adjunct - Proceedings*

of the 2016 ACM International Joint Conference on Pervasive and Ubiquitous Computing, pp. 137–140, 2016.

50. Dorri, A., Steger, M., Kanhere, S.S., Jurdak, R., Blockchain: a distributed solution to automotive security and privacy. *IEEE Commun. Mag.*, 55, 12, 119–125, Dec. 2017.

51. Singh, M. and Kim, S., Trust Bit: Reward-based intelligent vehicle commination using blockchain paper. *IEEE World Forum on Internet of Things, WF-IoT 2018 - Proceedings*, vol. 2018-January, pp. 62–67, 2018.

52. Michelin, R.A. *et al.*, SpeedyChain: A framework for decoupling data from blockchain for smart cities. *ACM International Conference Proceeding Series*, pp. 145–154, 2018.

53. Kerrache, C.A., Calafate, C.T., Cano, J.C., Lagraa, N., Manzoni, P., Trust management for vehicular networks: an adversary-oriented overview. *IEEE Access*, 4, 9293–9307, 2016.

54. Minhas, U.F., Zhang, J., Tran, T., Cohen, R., A multifaceted approach to modeling agent trust for effective communication in the application of mobile Ad Hoc vehicular networks. *IEEE Trans. Syst. Man Cybern. Part C Appl. Rev.*, 41, 3, 407–420, May 2011.

55. Kim, Shiho. Blockchain for a trust network among intelligent vehicles. In *Advances in Computers*, vol. 111, pp. 43-68. Elsevier, 2018.

56. Modiri, N., The ISO Reference Model Entities. *IEEE Netw.*, 5, 4, 24–33, 1991.

57. Li, S., Da Xu, L., Zhao, S., The internet of things: a survey. *Inf. Syst. Front.*, 17, 2, 243–259, Apr. 2015.

58. Lakshman, T.V. and Agrawala, A.K., Efficient decentralized consensus protocols. *IEEE Trans. Softw. Eng.*, SE-12, 5, 600–607, 1986.

59. Yuan, Y. and Wang, F.Y., Towards blockchain-based intelligent transportation systems. *IEEE Conf. Intell. Transp. Syst. Proceedings, ITSC*, pp. 2663–2668, 2016.

60. Connected Vehicle Cloud—Under the Road, Ericsson, www.ericsson.com

61. Singh, Madhusudan, and Shiho Kim. Safety requirement specifications for connected vehicles. arXiv preprint arXiv:1707.08715, 2017.

62. Park, J. and Park, J., Blockchain security in cloud computing: use cases, challenges, and solutions. *Symmetry (Basel)*, 9, 8, 164, Aug. 2017.

63. Astarita, V., Giofrè, V.P., Mirabelli, G., Solina, V., A review of blockchain-based systems in transportation. *Inf.*, 11, 1, 1–24, 2020.

64. Pizzuti, T., Mirabelli, G., Sanz-Bobi, M.A., Goméz-Gonzaléz, F., *Food* track & trace ontology for helping the food traceability control. *J. Food Eng.*, 120, 1, 17–30, Jan. 2014.

65. Charlebois, S., Sterling, B., Haratifar, S., Naing, S.K., Comparison of global food traceability regulations and requirements. *Compr. Rev. Food Sci. Food Saf.*, 13, 5, 1104–1123, Sep. 2014.

66. Charlebois, S., Schwab, A., Henn, R., Huck, C.W., Food fraud: An exploratory study for measuring consumer perception towards mislabeled food products and influence on self-authentication intentions. *Trends Food Sci. Technol.*, Elsevier, 50, 211–218, Apr. 2016.

67. Thakur, M., Wang, L., Hurburgh, C.R., A multi-objective optimization approach to balancing cost and traceability in bulk grain handling. *J. Food Eng.*, 101, 2, 193–200, Nov. 2010.

68. Knirsch, F., Unterweger, A., Engel, D., Privacy-preserving blockchain-based electric vehicle charging with dynamic tariff decisions. *Comput. Sci. – Res. Dev.*, 33, 1–2, 71–79, 2018.

69. Marzano, V., Tocchi, D., Papola, A., Aponte, D., Simonelli, F., Cascetta, E., Incentives to freight railway undertakings compensating for infrastructural gaps: Methodology and practical application to Italy. *Transp. Res. Part A Policy Pract.*, 110, 177–188, Apr. 2018.

70. Astarita, V., Florian, M., Musolino, G., A microscopic traffic simulation model for the evaluation of toll station systems. *IEEE Conference on Intelligent Transportation Systems, Proceedings, ITSC*, pp. 692–697, 2001.

71. Astarita, V., Giofré, V., Guido, G., Vitale, A., Investigating road safety issues through a microsimulation model. *Procedia - Soc. Behav. Sci.*, 20, 226–235, Jan. 2011.

72. Young, W., Sobhani, A., Lenné, M.G., Sarvi, M., Simulation of safety: A review of the state of the art in road safety simulation modelling. *Accid. Anal. Prev.*, 66, 89–103, May 2014.

73. Astarita, V. and Giofré, V.P., From traffic conflict simulation to traffic crash simulation: Introducing traffic safety indicators based on the explicit simulation of potential driver errors. *Simul. Model. Pract. Theory*, 94, 215–236, Jul. 2019.

74. Osorio, C. and Punzo, V., Efficient calibration of microscopic car-following models for large-scale stochastic network simulators. *Transp. Res. Part B Methodol.*, 119, 156–173, Jan. 2019.

75. Martinez, F.J., Toh, C.K., Cano, J.C., Calafate, C.T., Manzoni, P., A survey and comparative study of simulators for vehicular ad hoc networks (VANETs). *Wirel. Commun. Mob. Comput.*, 11, 7, 813–828, Jul. 2011.

76. Gentile, G., New formulations of the stochastic user equilibrium with logit route choice as an extension of the deterministic model. *Transp. Sci.*, 52, 6, 1531–1547, Nov. 2018.

77. Gentile, G., Solving a dynamic user equilibrium model based on splitting rates with gradient projection algorithms. *Transp. Res. Part B Methodol.*, 92, 120–147, Oct. 2016.

78. Trozzi, V., Gentile, G., Kaparias, I., Bell, M.G.H., Effects of countdown displays in public transport route choice under severe overcrowding. *Networks Spat. Econ.*, 15, 3, 823–842, Sep. 2015.

79. Papola, A., Tinessa, F., Marzano, V., Application of the Combination of Random Utility Models (CoRUM) to route choice. *Transp. Res. Part B Methodol.*, 111, 304–326, May 2018.

80. Papola, A., A new random utility model with flexible correlation pattern and closed-form covariance expression: The CoRUM. *Transp. Res. Part B Methodol.*, 94, 80–96, Dec. 2016.

81. Kucharski, R. and Gentile, G., Simulation of rerouting phenomena in dynamic traffic assignment with the information comply model. *Transp. Res. Part B Methodol.*, 126, 414–441, Aug. 2019.

82. Marzano, V., Papola, A., Simonelli, F., Papageorgiou, M., A Kalman filter for quasi-dynamic old flow estimation/updating. *IEEE Trans. Intell. Transp. Syst.*, 19, 11, 3604–3612, Nov. 2018.

83. Astarita, V., Giofrè, V.P., Guido, G., Vitale, A., *A single intersection cooperative-competitive paradigm in real time traffic signal settings based on floating car data.* Energies, 12, 3, 409, Jan. 2019.

84. Astarita, V., Guido, G., Mongelli, D., Giofrè, V.P., A co-operative methodology to estimate car fuel consumption by using smartphone sensors. *Transport*, 30, 3, 307–311, Jul. 2015.

85. Astarita, Vittorio, Vincenzo Pasquale Giofrè, Giuseppe Guido, and Alessandro Vitale, The use of adaptive traffic signal systems based on floating car data. Wireless Communications and Mobile Computing 2017, pp 1-14, 2017.

86. Saberi, S., Kouhizadeh, M., Sarkis, J., Shen, L., Blockchain technology and its relationships to sustainable supply chain management. *Int. J. Prod. Res.*, 57, 7, 2117–2135, Apr. 2019.

87. Kembro, J., Selviaridis, K., Näslund, D., Theoretical perspectives on information sharing in supply chains: A systematic literature review and conceptual framework. *Supply Chain Manag.*, 19, 609–625, Sep. 2014.

88. Astarita, Vittorio; Giofrè, Vincenzo P.; Mirabelli, Giovanni; Solina, Vittorio. 2020. A review of blockchain-based systems in transportation Information 11, no. 1: 21. https://doi.org/10.3390/info11010021

89. Jason Bloomberg, Eight Reasons To Be Skeptical About Blockchain, forbes 2017. https://www.forbes.com/sites/jasonbloomberg/2017/05/31/eight-reasons-to-be-skeptical-about-blockchain

90. Lindman, J., Tuunainen, V.K., Rossi, M., Opportunities and risks of blockchain technologies – A research agenda. *Hawaii Int. Conf. Syst. Sci. 2017*, Jan. 2017.

91. Li, X., Jiang, P., Chen, T., Luo, X., Wen, Q., A survey on the security of blockchain systems. *Futur. Gener. Comput. Syst.*, 107, 841–853, Jun. 2020.

92. Thanvi, A., Sharma, R., Menghani, B., Kumar, M., Jangir, S.K., Bitcoin exchange rate price prediction using machine learning techniques: A review. *Int. Conf. Information Management and Machine Intelligence, Algorithms for Intelligent Systems, Proc. of ICIMMI 2020*, p. 8, 2020.

93. Queiroz, M.M. and Fosso Wamba, S., Blockchain adoption challenges in supply chain: An empirical investigation of the main drivers in India and the USA. *Int. J. Inf. Manage.*, 46, 70–82, Jun. 2019.

94. Singh, M. and Kim, S., Branch based blockchain technology in intelligent vehicle. *Comput. Networks*, 145, 219–231, 2018.

95. Cachin, Christian, and Marko Vukolić. Blockchain consensus protocols in the wild. arXiv preprint arXiv:1707.01873, pp. 1-24, 2017.

96. Xu, C., Wang, K., Guo, M., Intelligent resource management in blockchain-based cloud datacenters. *IEEE Cloud Comput.*, 4, 6, 50–59, Nov. 2017.

8

Applications of Image Processing in Teleradiology for the Medical Data Analysis and Transfer Based on IOT

**S. N. Kumar[1], A. Lenin Fred[2]*, L. R. Jonisha Miriam[2],
Parasuraman Padmanabhan[3], Balázs Gulyás[3] and Ajay Kumar H.[2]**

[1]Amal Jyothi College of Engineering, Kanjirapally, Kerala, India
*[2]Mar Ephraem College of Engineering and Technology, Elavuvilai,
Tamil Nadu, India*
*[3]Cognitive Neuroimaging Centre (CONIC), Lee Kong Chian School of
Medicine, Nanyang Technological, University, Singapore, Singapore*

Abstract

Every day, a huge amount of medical images is generated for disease diagnosis and therapeutic applications. The analysis and storage of medical data is a crucial task and transfer of data is also a needy one from the perspective of telemedicine. The preprocessing, segmentation and compression algorithms gain importance in the analysis, storage and transfer of medical data. This chapter focuses on the importance of image processing techniques for disease diagnosis and detection. The medical images are corrupted by noise and an appropriate filtering algorithm is required prior to subsequent process. The medical images are stored in lossless format; however efficient lossy compression algorithms are also there for medical images. The Picture Archiving and Communication System (PACS) require an efficient compression algorithm, thereby minimizing the degradation of reconstructed image quality. The classification algorithms are used to classify the tumor stages. This chapter also discusses the hardware implementation of image processing algorithms for teleradiology applications. For preprocessing of input CT/MR images, nonlinear tensor diffusion filter was used, segmentation was done by improved FCM based on crow search optimization and compression was done by prediction-based lossless technique. The hardware implementation of algorithms was done on Raspberry Pi B+ embedded processor.

**Corresponding author*: leninfredip@gmail.com

Krishna Kant Singh, Akansha Singh and Sanjay Sharma (eds.) Machine Learning Approaches for Convergence of IoT and Blockchain, (175–204) © 2021 Scrivener Publishing LLC

Keywords: Teleradiology, nonlinear tensor diffusion, crow search optimization, lossless compression, embedded system

8.1   Introduction

Image processing interprets the usage of computerized algorithms for the analysis of images with respect to an application. It plays a vital role in domains like biometrics, medical, and archaeology. The different stages in image processing are as follows: acquisition, storage, processing, communication, and display. The processing of digital image comprises of the following; denoising or enhancement, segmentation, classification, and compression.

The teleradiology is a vital part of telemedicine that refers to the transfer of medical images and reports through the dedicated cloud network. The medical imaging modalities like CT, MRI, and US have created a big revolution in modern medicine for accurate disease diagnosis. There are two modes of data transfer in telemedicine: store and forward concept and real-time telemedicine. In real-time telemedicine, data are transferred between two places simultaneously. The medical council ethics states that unauthorized transfer of medical data such as through Email, USB should be avoided. The teleradiology offers an attractive solution for the analysis and transfer of medical data. The other applications of telemedicine are teleconsultation through video conferencing, telepathology, telecardiology, and tele-education. The video conferencing facility helps for the transmission of both audio and video information.

Medical images acquired from the scanning equipment are corrupted by noise. The role of preprocessing is unavoidable in many applications to yield fruitful results for subsequent operations such as segmentation, compression, and classification. Various denoising techniques are used for noise filtering and the choice of filtering approach relies on the medical imaging modality. The noise is an unavoidable component in most of the measurements. Apart from the physiological and environmental noise, in image acquisition systems, the electronic noise gains importance. In general, the noise is a random variable and CT images are affected by random noise whereas MR images are affected by Rician noise [1]. The selection of a filtering algorithm is vital since it should not induce any artifacts, thereby blurring the resultant image. The spatial domain filter operates directly on the pixels of the image, while the transform domain approach operates on the transformed coefficients of the image by applying the appropriate mathematical transform [2]. The FIR is a classical linear filtering algorithm; the filter coefficients are convolved with the input image. Mean filter is efficient for suppressing random and uniformly distributed noise. The mean filter induces the blurring effect and can cause the loss of fine details and texture. The median filter generates better restoration results, especially for impulse noise, when compared with average filter. The edge preservation is poor in median filter as the non-noisy image elements are exaggerated by the median operation. The Weiner filter relies on the power spectrum density of the noise and blurs the sharp features and edges in the resultant image.

The diffusion filtering is an edge preservation technique and relies on the diffusion model of liquid or gas. The selection of filtering technique relies on the modalities of medical imaging and type of noise. In medical field, the main goal of image segmentation is to find out the desired region of interest (ROI), i.e., anatomical organ or irregularities like tumor and cyst [3]. It is a "broad and active field" that gains importance not only in medical imaging but also in machine vision and satellite imagery [4]. The segmentation role is vital prior to pattern recognition and classification and in some cases; it is used in compression also. It is categorized into contextual and non-contextual techniques. In contextual, the spatial relationship of image pixels is not taken into account. Also, the extraction of ROI depends on global attribute like gray value. Examples include classical, adaptive, and color thresholding. In non-contextual, the spatial relationship of image elements is considered. Examples include region growing and clustering. Moreover, it is validated by appropriate performance metrics based on the availability of ground truth image for better efficiency.

Storage and transmission is an imperative problem due to the huge size of medical data [5]. For example, each slice of CT medical data set is of size 512×512 (16 bits) and each data set comprises of generally 200 to 400 images. The average size of the data set is of 150 MB and hence the compression technique is prevalent for the transfer and storage of data. The compression is characterized as a procedure that reduces the storage volume of data by encoding and decoding through the appropriate algorithm. The compression techniques are divided into lossy and lossless algorithms. More specifically, it is meant for lowering the number of bits in order to represent the image pixel data by the elimination of redundancy. The redundancy is defined as repetitive data that is present implicitly or explicitly in an image. The types of redundancy are interpixel redundancy, psychovisual redundancy, and coding redundancy. Some information is of relatively less important for the perception by human observers and it is termed as psychovisual redundancy [6]. The inter-pixel redundancy deals with the neighboring pixel correlations (spatial/geometric redundancy) in an image [6]. There is a considerable loss in the reconstructed image for a lossy compression scheme. The advances in telemedicine aids the physicians for better diagnosis and treatment planning with the usage of computer aided signal processing and image processing algorithms [7]. A hybrid watermarking scheme was employed for ensuring security in medical images for telemedicine applications [8]. The role of telemedicine in ophthalmology was highlighted in [9]. The tele ophthalmology was employed for the screening of retinal diseases. The medical imaging applications in telemedicine were discussed in detail in [10]. The role of big data analytics in healthcare sector was described in [11]; current challenges and future works are also discussed. Artificial intelligence is gaining importance in healthcare sector providing solutions to therapeutic diagnosis and preplanning of surgery [12, 13]. In this present research work, preprocessing, segmentation, and compression work are carried out for the analysis of medical data. The chapter organization is as follows: preprocessing approach is discussed in Section 8.2. ROI extraction is highlighted in Section 8.3. Section 8.4 comprises of simulation results and discussion. Section 8.5 describes the conclusion.

8.2   Pre-Processing

The role of anisotropic diffusion filter is vital in both image quality improvement and denoising [14]. The edge preservation is poor and fine details are also not preserved in classical diffusion approach. This chapter proposes improved algorithms of Perona Malika (PM) model, the classical diffusion filtering algorithm, Non-Linear Scalar Diffusion (NLSD) filter, and Non-Linear Tensor (NLTD) filter.

8.2.1   Principle of Diffusion Filtering

The principle of diffusion filtering algorithm is described as image intensity is taken as the material intensity; noise is taken as density variation. The process of diffusion is accomplished in an iterative fashion such that density inhomogeneity leads to denoised image. In anisotropic diffusion, the preservation of boundary happens by restricting the diffusion across edges.

For diffusion, flux "i" is produced at an arbitrary location (x, y) in 2D image which is denoted in Equations 8.1 and 8.2.

$$i(x, y) = - D(x, y) \times \nabla v(x, y))$$
(8.1)

$$i(x,y) = -D(x,y) \times \left(\frac{\frac{\partial \nabla v(x, y)}{\partial x}}{\frac{\partial v(x, y)}{\partial y}} \right)$$
(8.2)

Here, D indicates diffusion tensor, ∇v (density gradient) determines the quantity of diffusion appear in any direction.

The homogeneous diffusion does not rely on the strength and direction of the gradient vector. The diffusion coefficient "ε_0" multiplied by identity matrix is the diffusion tensor which is expressed in Equation 8.3.

$$D(x, y) = \varepsilon_0 \begin{bmatrix} 1 & 0 \\ 0 & 1 \end{bmatrix}$$
(8.3)

The inhomogeneous diffusion relies on the gradient strength and the diffusion tensor is expressed in Equation 8.4.

$$D(x, y) = \left(\begin{matrix} \varepsilon \|\nabla v(x, y)\|^2 & 0 \\ 0 & \varepsilon \|\nabla v(x, y)\|^2 + \lambda^2 \end{matrix} \right)$$
(8.4)

The diffusion decreases with an increase in gradient length $\|\nabla V\|$. When $\lambda = \infty$, inhomogeneous diffusion becomes homogeneous diffusion. The maximum diffusion per step is determined by "ε_0". A small value of ε_0 delays the diffusion process, while a high value causes fluctuation of density values. Also, the presence of diffusion "λ" will cause the edge contrast to increase rapidly than contrast to reduce. The anisotropic diffusion produces smooth but false boundaries and it is commonly employed for noise removal applications due to the satisfying result of the output image.

The key functionality of NLSD and NLTD algorithm is Gauss gradient approach. One-dimensional Gauss gradient kernel is computed from the Gaussian distribution and is illustrated in Equation 8.5.

$$g(X,Y) = \frac{1}{2\pi\sigma^2} e^{-\left(\frac{X^2+Y^2}{\sigma^2}\right)} \tag{8.5}$$

where "σ" denotes the scale of diffusion.

In normalized form, the Gaussian distribution is expressed in Equation 8.6.

$$g_X = e^{-(-X*X/2*\sigma^2)} \tag{8.6}$$

The first-order derivative of the Gaussian function is represented in Equation 8.7.

$$I_X = \frac{\partial g_X}{\partial X} = \frac{-X}{\sigma^2} g_X \tag{8.7}$$

Similarly,

$$I_Y = \frac{\partial g_X}{\partial Y} = \frac{-Y}{\sigma^2} g_X \tag{8.8}$$

$$\frac{\partial^2 g_X}{\partial X} = \frac{X^2 - \sigma^2}{\sigma^4} g_X \tag{8.9}$$

"σ" must be greater than or equal to 1, and it can be scaled down to 0.7.

The smoothed image was generated by performing the convolution of the Gaussian kernel. The final image after Gaussian smoothing is represented in Equation 8.10.

$$I_G = \sqrt{I_X^2 + I_Y^2} \tag{8.10}$$

where I_x and I_y represent the Gaussian smoothed components of the image. The NLSD and NLTD restoration model is obtained from the Gauss gradient smoothed component.

The NLTD restoration model is represented in Equation 8.11.

$$\partial_t I = \nabla \cdot (TVI) \tag{8.11}$$

where T indicates the tensor matrix.

The tensor matrix is illustrated in Equation 8.12.

$$T = \begin{bmatrix} u & v \\ v & w \end{bmatrix}$$

(8.12)

where

$$u = \frac{c_1 G_X^2 + c_2 G_Y^2}{I_G^2 + \varepsilon}$$

$$v = \frac{(c_2 - c_1)G_X G_Y}{I_G^2 + \varepsilon}$$

$$w = \frac{c_1 G_Y^2 + c_2 G_X^2}{I_G^2 + \varepsilon}$$

The expression I_G is Gaussian filter variant of the input image, and G_X and G_Y are the components of I_G. The terms D_1 and D_2 are the diffusion constants, represented in Equations 8.13 and 8.14.

$$D_1 = exp\left(-\left(\frac{I_G}{K}\right)^2\right)$$

(8.13)

$$D_2 = \frac{1}{5} * D_1$$

(8.14)

The tensor matrix elements are the function of image features. In spatial form, Equation 8.15 is denoted as follows.

$$\partial_t I = [\partial_X \quad \partial_Y] \begin{bmatrix} u & v \\ v & w \end{bmatrix} \begin{bmatrix} \partial_X I \\ \partial_Y I \end{bmatrix}$$

(8.15)

$$\partial_t I = [\partial_X \quad \partial_Y]\begin{bmatrix} u\partial_X I + v\partial_Y I \\ v\partial_X I + w\partial_Y I \end{bmatrix} \tag{8.16}$$

$$\partial_t I = \partial_X(u\partial_X I + v\partial_Y I) + \partial_Y(v\partial_X I + w\partial_Y I) \tag{8.17}$$

$$\partial_t I = \partial_X(u\partial_X I) + \partial_X(v\partial_Y I) + \partial_Y(v\partial_X I) + \partial_Y(v\partial_Y I) \tag{8.18}$$

The two new terms arise; $\partial_X(v\partial_Y I)$ and $\partial_Y(v\partial_X I)$ in NLTD filtering, while comparing with NLSD filtering.

In discrete form, NLTD filtering algorithm is represented in Equation 8.19.

$$I_{p,q}^{t+1} = I_{p,q}^t + \lambda\Big[v_1 I_{p-1,q+1} + w_1 I_{p,q+1} + v_2 I_{p+1,q+1} + u_1 I_{p-1,q}$$

$$-\left(\frac{u_{p-1,q} + 2u_{p,q} + u_{p+1,q} + w_{p-1,q} + 2w_{p,q} + w_{p+1,q}}{2}\right) \tag{8.19}$$

$$I_{p,q} + u_2 I_{p+1,q} + v_3 I_{p-1,q-1}\Big]$$

where

$$u_1 = \frac{u_{p-1,q} + v_{p,q}}{4}$$

$$u_2 = \frac{u_{p+1,q} + u_{p,q}}{2}$$

$$v_1 = \frac{-v_{p-1,q} + v_{p,q+1}}{4}$$

$$v_2 = \frac{v_{p+1,q} + v_{p,q+1}}{4}$$

$$v_3 = \frac{v_{p-1,q} + v_{p,q+1}}{4}$$

$$w_1 = \frac{w_{p,q+1} + w_{p,q}}{2}$$

The expressions in the RHS of the above equation are linear for the values of $I_{i,j}$. A quasi-convolution kernel of dimension 3 x 3 is used to represent the discrete form of the restoration technique.

8.3 Improved FCM Based on Crow Search Optimization

Clustering algorithms are widely used in medical image processing in order to extract ROI. The classical FCM algorithm has local minima and it is liable to noise. Many variants of FCM algorithms are there [15]; however, optimization algorithm, when coupled with FCM, is gaining importance in case of centroid initialization. The framed crow search optimization (CSO) depends on the biological characteristics of crow and less parameter tuning makes it an attractive one when compared with the other optimization techniques [16].

FCM clustering principle is depicted in Figure 8.1.

The CSO principle is depicted in Figure 8.2.

The four phases of improved FCM-based CSO algorithm are (i) Initialization, (ii) Evaluation of fitness function, (iii) Updation of memory, and (iv) Segmentation. In the initial phase, initialize the flight length (fl) and Awareness Probability (AP) of CSO and FCM algorithm.

In the second phase, estimate the fitness value and crows new position. The third phase corresponds to updation of memory and in the final phase; initialization of cluster centroids takes place by CSO for segmentation of FCM.

The cluster center is indicated in Equation 8.20.

$$V_i = \frac{\sum_{i=1}^{N} U_{ij}^f y_i}{\sum_{i=1}^{N} U_{ij}^f} \tag{8.20}$$

where y_i symbolizes the crow's position.

The membership function is demonstrated in Equation 8.21.

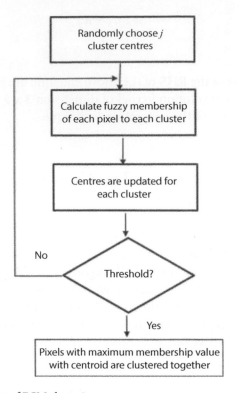

Figure 8.1 Flowchart of FCM clustering.

$$U_{ij} = \cfrac{1}{\sum_{c=1}^{C}\left(\cfrac{\left\|y_i - v_j\right\|^2}{\left\|y_j - v_c\right\|^2}\right)^{\frac{1}{f-1}}} \qquad (8.21)$$

The global solution is achieved, when the defined number of iteration is completed. Crows new position is estimated and phase ii, iii, and iv gets iterated until the minimization of objective function is achieved with global minima.

8.4   Prediction-Based Lossless Compression Model

Least square approach was incorporated in the prediction for the formulation of compression algorithm. The prediction coefficients are estimated

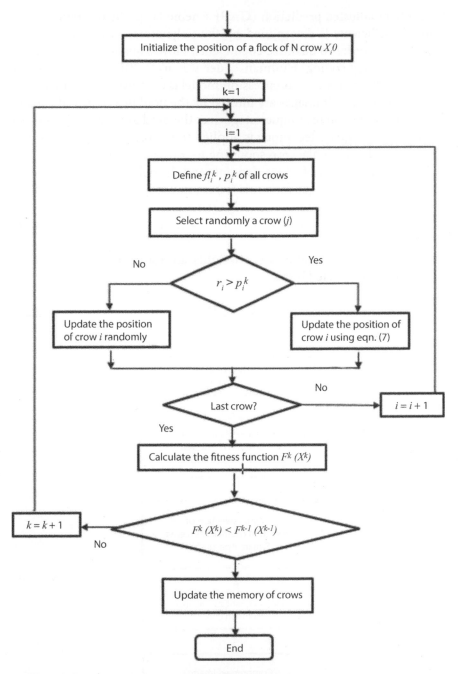

Figure 8.2 Flowchart of crow search optimization algorithm.

by gradient adjusted prediction (GAP) scheme [17]. The optimum selection of coefficients is determined by the polynomial least square fitting approach. In order to quantize coefficients, Lloyd's quantization was used and for entropy coding, Huffman coder was used. The flow diagram of prediction-based lossless compression model is portrayed in Figure 8.3.

The input CT/MR images are filtered by the nonlinear tensor diffusion filter. The prediction technique categorizes the pixel gray values into slope bins. The least square technique is applied to the predicted image for the generation of polynomial corresponding to row data as follows.

Image is a 2D array of image elements and the polynomial generated by the least square technique for a row (v_i) is represented as follows:

$$v_i = w_0 + w_1 u_1 + w_2 u_2 + \ldots + w_n u_n \tag{8.22}$$

From the linear equations, the weights are estimated. The system in matrix form is depicted below.

$$V = UW \tag{8.23}$$

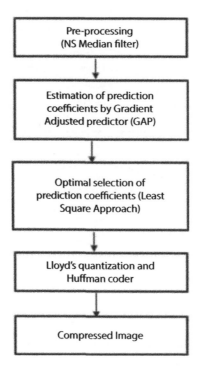

Figure 8.3 Flowchart of prediction-based lossless compression model.

$$
\begin{bmatrix} v(0,1) \\ . \\ . \\ v(0,p) \end{bmatrix} = \begin{bmatrix} u(1,1) & . & u(1,p) \\ & . & . & . \\ & . & . & . \\ u(p,1) & . & u(p,p) \end{bmatrix} \begin{bmatrix} w(1) \\ . \\ . \\ w(p) \end{bmatrix} \quad (8.24)
$$

where u(m,n) symbolizes the covariance matrix elements.
The elements of the covariance matrix are determined as follows.

$$
u(m, n) = \Sigma_{m,\,n\in W}x(n-s)x(n-T) \quad (8.25)
$$

The weight coefficients are estimated as follows.

$$
W = U^{-1}V \quad (8.26)
$$

In slope bins, each and every image element is estimated using least square–based predictor. The least square–based GAP compression scheme is portrayed in Figure 8.4.

The prediction image is represented below.

$$
\hat{Y}(p,q) = f(\varnothing(p,q)) \quad (8.27)
$$

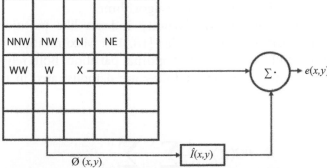

Figure 8.4 Image compression based on least square based prediction.

where $\emptyset(p, q)$ represents the casual context of neighbouring image elements.

The error image is expressed as follows.

$$e(p,q) = Y(p,q) - \hat{Y}(p,q) \qquad (8.28)$$

The Huffman coder is employed for entropy coding and in the receiver; the restoration of image is done.

8.5   Results and Discussion

The variants of diffusion filter are proficient in the filtering of CT/MR images. The role of preprocessing is vigorous since it improves the accuracy of the segmentation and compression algorithms. The performance metrics reveal that NLSD and NLTD provide promising results while comparing with classical anisotropic diffusion filter. Figure 8.5 depicts the segmentation results of different clustering algorithms corresponding to the MR input images from Brainweb database. The first, second, third and fourth row illustrates the input MR images and output of K-Means clustering, FCM, and Crow-FCM segmentation, respectively.

Figures 8.6 and 8.7 depict the segmentation results of various clustering techniques corresponding to real-time CT abdomen images and MR brain images. The first, second, third, and fourth row depicts the input images and results of K-Means clustering, FCM clustering, and Crow-FCM segmentation, respectively. Figures 8.8 to 8.10 depict the performance metrics of Crow-FCM segmentation results. The higher value of PC and lower value of PE is an indication of an efficient clustering algorithm. The lower value of Xie and Beni Index (XBI) and Fukuyama and Sugeno Index (FSI) indicates the proficiency of clustering algorithm.

Clustering is evaluated with validity indexes like partition coefficient (PC) and partition entropy (PE) [18, 19]. Maximization of PC (or Minimization of PE) yields best and optimal partition. Both rely on compactness and cluster variations and they are demonstrated in Equations 8.29 and 8.30.

$$PC(K) = \frac{1}{N} \sum_{k=1}^{K} \sum_{i=1}^{N} F_{ik}^2 \qquad (8.29)$$

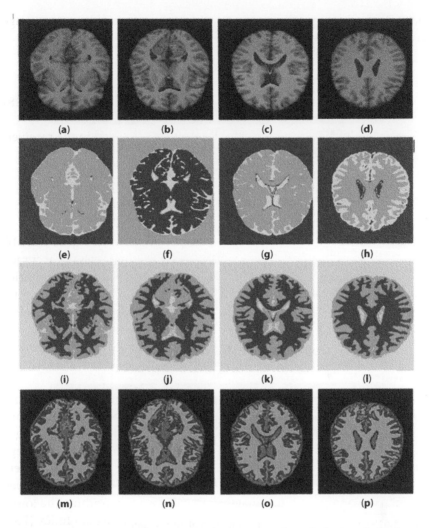

Figure 8.5 Segmentation results corresponding to images from the brain web database. (a–d) Input Image, (e–h) Output of K-Means clustering, (i–l) Output of FCM, (m–p) Output of Crow-FCM.

$$PE(K) = \frac{1}{N} \sum_{k=1}^{K} \sum_{i=1}^{N} F_{ik} log_2(F_{ik}) \qquad (8.30)$$

XBI is illustrated in [13]. Here, the optimal clustering result corresponds to minimum value of XBI and is described in Equation 8.31.

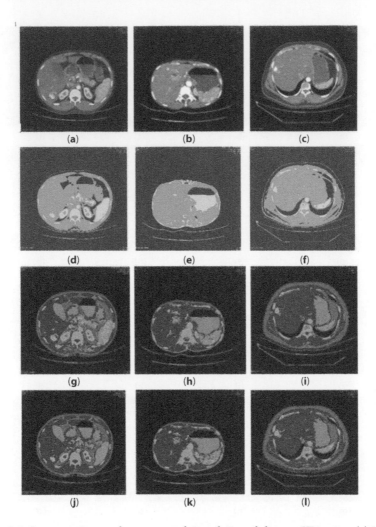

Figure 8.6 Segmentation results correspond to real-time abdomen CT images. (a) Input of ID1, (b) Input of ID2, (c) Input of ID3, (d) K-Means clustering output of ID1, (e) K-Means clustering output of ID2, (f) K-Means clustering output of ID3, (g) FCM output of ID1, (h) FCM output of ID2, (i) FCM output of ID3, (j) Crow-FCM output of ID1, (k) Crow-FCM output of ID2, (l) Crow-FCM output of ID3.

$$XBI(K) = \frac{\sum_{k=1}^{K} \sum_{i=1}^{N} F_{ik}^2 \|y_i - v_k\|^2}{N . \min_{i \neq j} \|y_i - v_j\|^2} \qquad (8.31)$$

In FSI equation, the first and second term denotes the compactness and degree of separation, respectively. The optimal output is achieved when FSI belongs to minimum value [20].

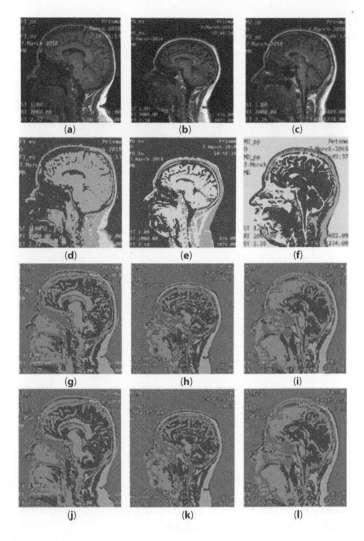

Figure 8.7 Segmentation results correspond to real-time MR brain images. (a) Input of ID4, (b) Input of ID5, (c) Input of ID6, (d) K-Means clustering output of ID4, (e) K-Means clustering output of ID5, (f) K-Means clustering output of ID6, (g) FCM output of ID4, (h) FCM output of ID5, (i) FCM output of ID6, (j) Crow-FCM output of ID4, (k) Crow-FCM output of ID5, (l) Crow-FCM output of ID6.

$$FSI(K) = \sum_{k=1}^{K} \sum_{i=1}^{N} F_{ik}^m \left\| y_i - v_k \right\|^2 - \sum_{k=1}^{K} \sum_{i=1}^{N} F_{ik}^m \left\| v_k - \hat{v} \right\|^2 \quad (8.32)$$

The compression results corresponding to real-time CT and MR images are depicted in Figures 8.11 and 8.12. The proposed compression model

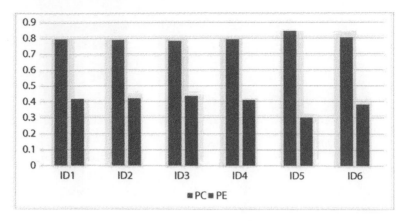

Figure 8.8 Performance plot of partition coefficient and entropy.

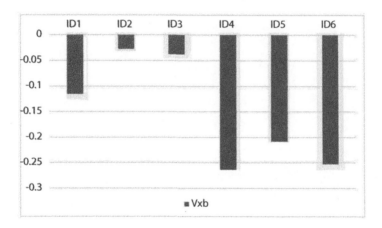

Figure 8.9 Performance plot of Xie and Beni Index.

was compared with the classical approaches and the validation metrics plots are depicted in Figures 8.13 to 8.20.

The validation metrics for the assessment of compression techniques relies on the input image and the reconstructed image. The expression for PSNR and MAE are represented as follows:

$$PSNR = 10 \, log\left(\frac{255^2 P(i,j) \times Q(i,j)}{\|P(i,j) - Q(i,j)\|^2} \right) dB \qquad (8.33)$$

$$MAE = \frac{\|P(i,j) - Q(i,j)\|}{P(i,j) \times Q(i,j)} \qquad (8.34)$$

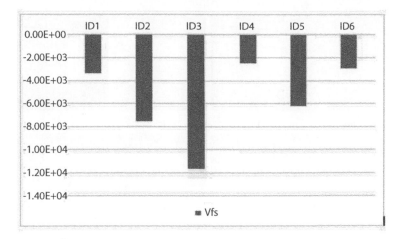

Figure 8.10 Performance plot of Fukuyama and Sugeno Index.

where $P(i,j)$ and $Q(i,j)$ depict the original image and the reconstructed image. For good compression algorithm, PSNR value is high and MSE value is low.

Normalized Cross-Correlation (NCC) represents the degree of closeness between input and decompressed image, closer the value to 1 represents the robustness of compression approach, which is represented below.

$$NCC = \sum_{i=1}^{m} \sum_{j=1}^{n} \frac{P(i,j) \times Q(i,j)}{P(i,j)^2} \tag{8.35}$$

Normalized Absolute Error (NAE) value should be low for proficient compression algorithm; the expression of NAE is represented below.

$$NAE = \frac{\sum_{i=1}^{m} \sum_{j=1}^{n} (P(i,j) - Q(i,j))}{\sum_{i=1}^{m} \sum_{j=1}^{n} P(i,j)} \tag{8.36}$$

The closer the value of Structural Content (SC) to 1, the better the proficiency of compression algorithm and the expression of SC is represented below.

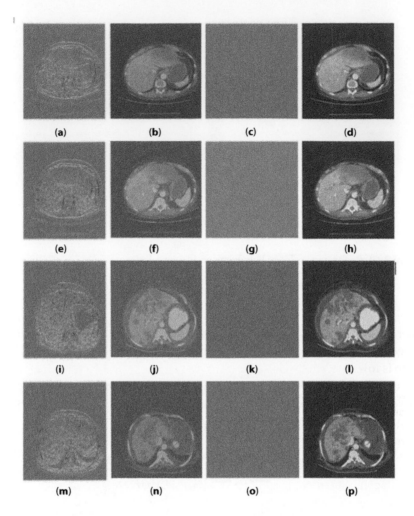

Figure 8.11 Compression results corresponding to real-time abdomen CT images.
(a) Gap classification of ID1, (b) Predicted output of ID1, (c) Error image of ID1,
(d) Reconstructed image of ID1, (e) Gap classification of ID2, (f) Predicted output of ID2,
(g) Error image of ID2, (h) Reconstructed image of ID2, (i) Gap classification of ID3,
(j) Predicted output of ID3, (k) Error image of ID3, (l) Reconstructed image of ID3,
(m) Gap classification of ID4, (n) Predicted output of ID4, (o) Error image of ID4,
(p) Reconstructed image of ID4.

$$SC = \frac{\sum_{i=1}^{m}\sum_{j=1}^{n}(P(i,j))^2}{\sum_{i=1}^{m}\sum_{j=1}^{n}(Q(i,j))^2} \qquad (8.37)$$

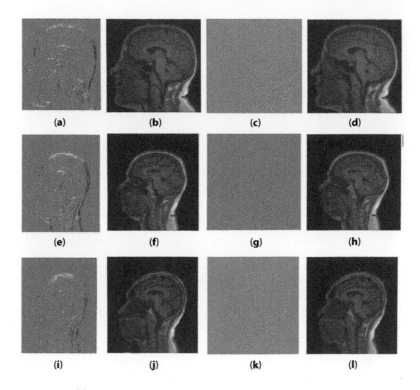

Figure 8.12 Compression results corresponding to real-time brain MR images.
(a) Gap classification of ID5, (b) Predicted output of ID5, (c) Error image of ID5,
(d) Reconstructed image of ID5, (e) Gap classification of ID6, (f) Predicted output of ID6,
(g) Error image of ID6, (h) Reconstructed image of ID6, (i) Gap classification of ID7,
(j) Predicted output of ID7, (k) Error image of ID7, (l) Reconstructed image of ID7.

Laplacian Mean Square Error (LMSE) represents the quality of the reconstructed image and for a good compression algorithm; LMSE value must be low.

$$LMSE = \frac{\sum_{i=1}^{m} \sum_{j=1}^{n} [L(P(i,j)) - L(Q(i,j))]^2}{\sum_{i=1}^{m} \sum_{j=1}^{n} [L(Q(i,j))]^2} \qquad (8.38)$$

Quality is designed by loss of correlation, luminance distortion, and contrast distortion

$$Q = \frac{\sigma_{xy}}{\sigma_x \sigma_y} \cdot \frac{2\overline{xy}}{(\overline{x})^2 + (\overline{y})^2} \cdot \frac{2\sigma_x \sigma_y}{\sigma_x^2 + \sigma_y^2} \qquad (8.39)$$

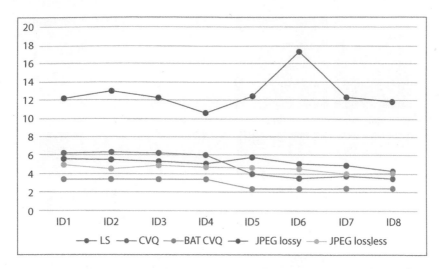

Figure 8.13 Performance plot of compression ratio.

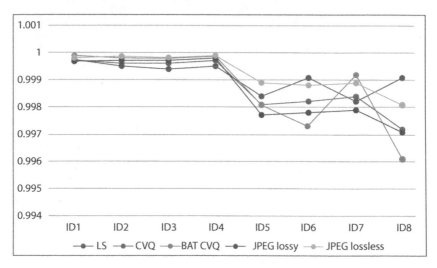

Figure 8.14 Performance plot of FSSIM.

Compression ratio defined as the ratio of uncompressed to compressed image size.

$$CR = \frac{Size\ of\ Uncompressed\ image}{Size\ of\ compressed\ image} \tag{8.40}$$

FSSIM similarity score is computed from the local and global similarity map.

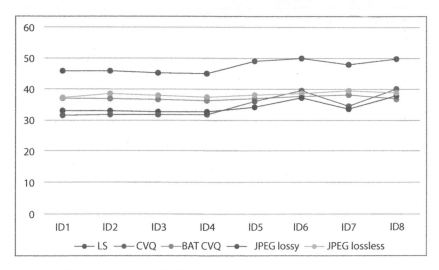

Figure 8.15 Performance plot of PSNR.

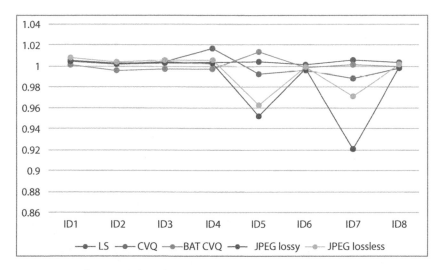

Figure 8.16 Performance plot of SC.

$$FSSIM = \frac{\sum_{x\in\Omega} S_L(x).PC_m(x)}{\sum_{x\in\Omega} PC_m(x)} \quad (8.41)$$

The propos ed lossless compression model, least square–based prediction is depicted in the plots as LS. For comparative analysis of the proposed

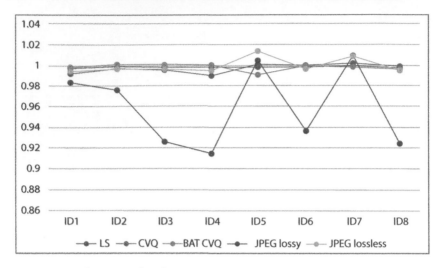

Figure 8.17 Performance plot of NK.

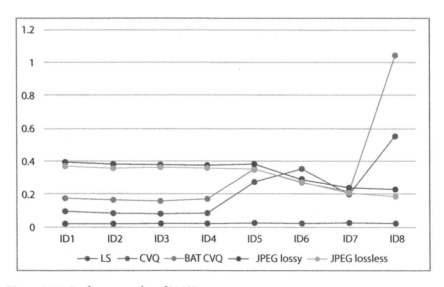

Figure 8.18 Performance plot of LMSE.

compression model, the contextual vector quantization (CVQ) [21], BAT-CVQ [22], JPEG lossy [23], and JPEG lossless [24] approaches are taken into account.

The implementation of hardware for the analysis of image processing algorithms is depicted in Figure 8.21.

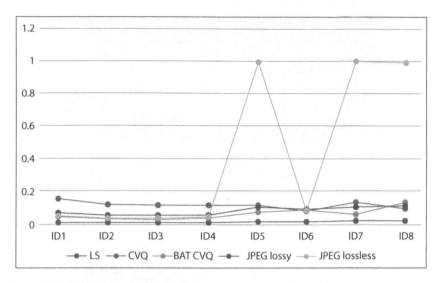

Figure 8.19 Performance plot of NAE.

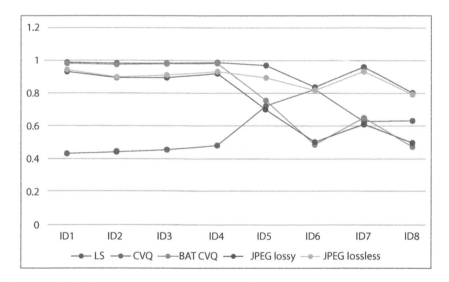

Figure 8.20 Performance plot of compression quality.

The GUI interface for the loading of the DICOM image is depicted in Figure 8.22. Figure 8.23 depicts the options available in the GUI interface. Figure 8.24 depicts the Crow-FCM segmentation result. Figure 8.25 depicts the compression and decompression with cloud facility for loading and retrieving the decompressed images.

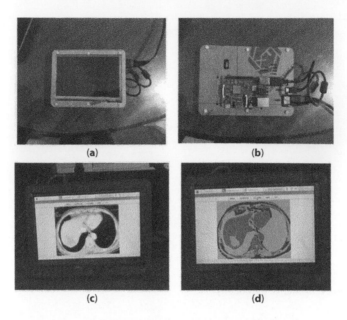

Figure 8.21 Hardware implementation of the image processing algorithms. (a) Front view of proposed system, (b) Back view of proposed system, (c) Filtering output, (d) Segmentation output.

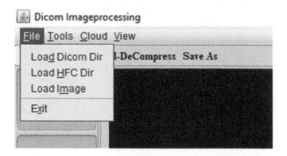

Figure 8.22 GUI interface for the loading of the DICOM image.

The various steps that a user can perform in the GUI are as follows:

Step 1: Initially load the DICOM directory or DICOM image.
Step 2: Choose the desired option Denoising, Segmentation, or Compression/Decompression.
Step 3: The denoising icon when clicked generates the denoised image.
Step 4: The segmentation icon when clicked generates the ROI extracted output.

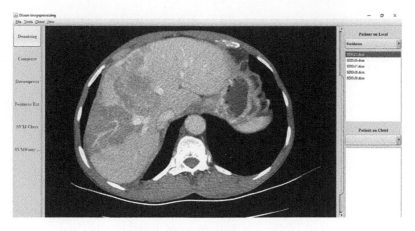

Figure 8.23 Options available in the GUI interface.

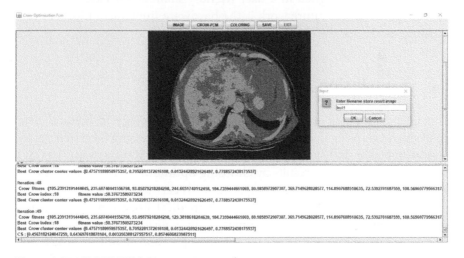

Figure 8.24 CROW-FCM segmentation result.

Step 5: The compression can be performed on a single image or a group of images in a folder. The user can choose any one of the options for compression. After compression, the data is stored in .hfc format and can be feed into cloud.

Step 6: The decompression also can be done on a single image or group of images in a folder and can be retrieved from the cloud.

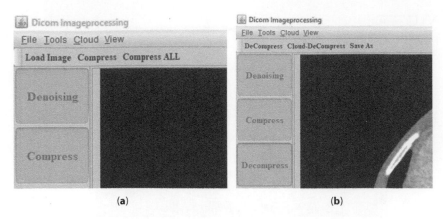

Figure 8.25 Stages of GUI for feeding the compressed images into the cloud.
(a) Compression GUI, (b) Decompression GUI.

The GUI was designed in a user friendly manner for ease in analysis of medical data. The future work is the hardware implementation of deep learning model for the classification of anomalies.

8.6   Conclusion

This chapter focuses on the applications of teleradiology in medical data analysis and transfer. In order to extract ROI, preprocessing is carried out by nonlinear tensor diffusion filter; FCM coupled with CSO was used. The CSO ensures good clustering results by choosing optimum centroids and results were found to be better, while comparing with classical K-means and FCM clustering algorithm. The compression of medical images was performed by prediction-based least square compression algorithm. The performance metric evaluation reveals the efficiency of compression algorithm. The hardware implementation uses Raspberry PI processor for data transfer and analysis for teleradiology applications. The low cost portable embedded system is an attractive solution in rural areas for teleradiology applications.

Acknowledgment

Authors Parasuraman Padmanabhan and BalazsGulyas acknowledge the support from Lee Kong Chian School of Medicine and Data Science and AI Research (DSAIR) Center of NTU (Project Number ADH-11/2017-DSAIR and the support from the Cognitive NeuroImaging Centre (CONIC) at

NTU. Author S.N. Kumar would also like to acknowledge the support provided by Schmitt Centre for Biomedical Instrumentation (SCBMI) of Amal Jyothi College of Engineering.

References

1. Gravel, P., Beaudoin, G., De Guise, J.A., A method for modeling noise in medical images. *IEEE Trans. Med. Imaging,* 23, 10, 1221–1232, 2004.
2. Buades, A., Coll, B., Morel, J.M., A review of image denoising algorithms, with a new one. *Multiscale Model. Simul.,* 4, 2, 490–530, 2005.
3. Pham, D.L., Xu, C., Prince, J.L., Current methods in medical image segmentation. *Ann. Rev. Biomed. Eng.,* 2, 1, 315–337, 2000.
4. Sonka, M., Hlavac, V., Boyle, R., *Image processing, analysis, and machine vision,* Cengage Learning, 2014.
5. Rahman, M.M., Bhattacharya, P., Desai, B.C., A framework for medical image retrieval using machine learning and statistical similarity matching techniques with relevance feedback. *IEEE Trans. Inf. Technol. Biomed.,* 11, 1, 58–69, Canada, 2007.
6. Wu, D., Tan, D.M., Baird, M., DeCampo, J., White, C., Wu, H.R., Perceptually lossless medical image coding. *IEEE Trans. Med. Imaging,* 25, 3, 335–344, 2006.
7. Rodrigues, J., Advances in Telemedicine for Health Monitoring: Technologies, design and applications. *Inst. Eng. Technol.,* June 2020.
8. Thanki, R. and Kothari, A., Multi-level security of medical images based on encryption and watermarking for telemedicine applications. *Multimedia Tools Appl.,* 80, 4307–4325, 2020.
9. Sommer, A.C. and Blumenthal, E.Z., Telemedicine in ophthalmology in view of the emerging COVID-19 outbreak. *Graefe's Arch. Clin. Exp. Ophthalmol.,* 258, 1–12, 2020.
10. Thanki, R. and Borra, S., *Medical imaging and its security in telemedicine applications,* Springer International Publishing, Heidelberg, Germany, 2019.
11. Wang, L. and Alexander, C.A., Big data analytics in medical engineering and healthcare: methods, advances and challenges. *J. Med. Eng. Technol.,* 44, 6, 1–17, 2020.
12. Bohr A, Memarzadeh K. The rise of artificial intelligence in healthcare applications. Artificial Intelligence in Healthcare. pp. 25–60, 2020.
13. Paul, Y., Hickok, E., Sinha, A., Tiwari, U., Mohandas, S., Ray, S., Bidare, P.M., Artificial intelligence in the healthcare industry in India, in: *The Centre for Internet and Society,* India, 2018.
14. Weickert, J., *Anisotropic diffusion in image processing.* Stuttgart: Teubner, vol. 1, pp. 59–60, ECMI Series, Teubner-Verlag, Stuttgart, Germany, 1998.

15. Forouzanfar, M., Forghani, N., Teshnehlab, M., Parameter optimization of improved fuzzy c-means clustering algorithm for brain MR image segmentation. *Eng. Appl. Artif. Intell.*, 23, 2, 160–168, 2010.
16. Parvathavarthini, S., Visalakshi, N.K., Shanthi, S., Mohan, J.M., Crow search optimization based fuzzy C-means clustering for optimal centroid initialization. *Taga J. Graphic Technol.*, 14, 3034–5, 2018.
17. Avramović, A. and Reljin, B., Gradient edge detection predictor for image lossless compression. *Proceedings ELMAR-2010*, IEEE, pp. 131–134, 2010, September.
18. Wu, K.L. and Yang, M.S., A cluster validity index for fuzzy clustering. *Pattern Recognit. Lett.*, 26, 9, 1275–1291, 2005.
19. Pal, N.R. and Bezdek, J.C., On cluster validity for the fuzzy c-means model. *IEEE Trans. Fuzzy Syst.*, 3, 3, 370–379, 1995.
20. Kim, D.W., Lee, K.H., Lee, D., Fuzzy cluster validation index based on inter-cluster proximity. *Pattern Recognit. Lett.*, 24, 15, 2561–2574, 2003.
21. Hosseini, S.M. and Naghsh-Nilchi, A.R., Medical ultrasound image compression using contextual vector quantization. *Comput. Biol. Med.*, 42, 7, 743–750, 2012.
22. Karri, C. and Jena, U., Fast vector quantization using a Bat algorithm for image compression. *Eng. Sci. Technol. Int. J.*, 19, 2, 769–781, 2016.
23. Skodras, A., Christopoulos, C., Ebrahimi, T., The jpeg 2000 still image compression standard. *IEEE Signal Process. Mag.*, 18, 5, 36–58, 2001.
24. Carpentieri, B., Weinberger, M.J., Seroussi, G., Lossless compression of continuous-tone images. *Proc. IEEE*, 88, 11, 1797–1809, 2000.

9

Innovative Ideas to Build Smart Cities with the Help of Machine and Deep Learning and IoT

Shylaja Vinaykumar Karatangi[1], Reshu Agarwal[2*],
Krishna Kant Singh[3] and Ivan Izonin[4]

[1]G L Bajaj Institute of Technology and Management, Greater Noida, India
[2]Amity Institute of Information Technology, Amity University, Noida, India
[3]Faculty of Engineering & Technology, Jain (Deemed-to-be University),
Bengaluru, India
[4]Lviv Polytechnic National University, Ukraine, Europe

Abstract

In today's modern world, with the advancement of technologies like Internet of Things (IoT) and machine learning (ML), applications have become smarter and connected devices give rise to their exploitations in all aspects of a smarter city. Fast urbanization has achieved incredible difficulties to our everyday lives, for example, traffic clog, natural contamination, vitality utilization, and open security. Research on shrewd urban areas expects to address these issues with different advancements produced for the IoT. Recently, the examination center has moved toward handling of gigantic measure of information consistently created inside a city situation, e.g., physical and participatory detecting information on traffic flow, air quality, and human services. Procedures from computational insight have been applied to process and examine such information and to remove valuable information that assists residents with bettering comprehend their environment and educates city specialists to give better and increasingly effective open administrations. Artificial intelligence (AI) is relied upon to fundamentally bolster practical improvement of future brilliant urban areas. This chapter proposes various smart city applications and its challenges with the help of ML and IoT. Finally, various research challenges and opportunities are proposed for implementing the proposed architecture.

Corresponding author: agarwal.reshu3@gmail.com

Krishna Kant Singh, Akansha Singh and Sanjay Sharma (eds.) Machine Learning Approaches for Convergence of IoT and Blockchain, (205–232) © 2021 Scrivener Publishing LLC

Keywords: Smart city, IoT, machine learning, deep learning, waste management, traffic management, smart policing

9.1   Introduction

In today's modern world, cities are hubs for monetary increase, process creation, new ideas, technological evolution, communication and networking, statistics, and social transformation. A smart city is a designation given to a city that incorporates information and communication technologies (ICTs) to enhance the quality and performance of urban services such as energy, transportation, and utilities in order to reduce resource consumption, wastage, and overall costs. The overall aim of a smart city is to enhance the quality of living for its citizens through smart technology. The combination of technologies such as the Internet of Things (IoT), machine learning (ML), and artificial intelligence (AI) will enable the transformation toward sustainable smart city.

According to the data circulated by the UN, the complete people will reach up to a farthest reaches of 9.7 billion preceding the completion of 2050. It is presumed that for all intents and purposes 70% of those masses will be an urban people with various urban networks obliging over 10m inhabitants. As the number creates, we will have to encounter troubles as for making a game plan for resources and essentialness to the whole of the tenants and at the same time, keeping up a vital good ways from condition rot. Another essential test is association and the administrators to thwart sanitation issues, calm traffic stop up, hinder bad behavior, etc. In any case, an extensive part of these issues can be repressed by the use of AI-engaged IoT. Using mechanical movement to empower the new experience for tenants can fill their heart with delight today living progressively pleasant and secure. This has offered ascend to the idea of shrewd urban communities. A smart city is a city that utilizes data and advancements to improve the quality, and execution of urban administrations (like energy and transportation), in this way, decreases the utilization of resources, forestalls wastage, and, by and large, expenses. Keen urban areas have ICT as well as utilize innovation in a manner that decidedly impacts the occupants.

AI joined with IoT can possibly address key difficulties presented by an over the top urban populace which incorporates traffic the executives, social insurance, energy emergencies, and numerous different issues as shown in Figure 9.1. It can improve the lives of the residents and organizations that occupy a smart city.

Figure 9.1 Impact of IT on top urban populace.

9.2   Related Work

Cognitive city is a term which expands the concept of the smart city with the aspect of virtual environment where goal-driven communities gather to share knowledge. A model was proposed for cognitive cities driven by human-technology interaction [1]. Further, a cognitive management framework was proposed using IoT [2]. In this framework, dynamically changing real world objects are represented in a virtualized environment. This framework is divided into three sections: service-level components, CVO-level components, and VO-level components. The service level derives the functionality of the requested service that is required by a stakeholder or a given application. These functionalities are delegated to CVOs to be carried out. The main contribution of this paper is that service execution time is decreased leading to lower operational expenditures. Further, this model was enhanced to empower the current IoT with a "brain" for high-level intelligence [3]. They proposed an operational framework which mainly characterizes the interactions among five fundamental cognitive tasks: perception-action cycle, massive data analytics, semantic derivation and knowledge discovery, intelligent decision-making, and on-demand service provisioning. Further, [4] extended the above model for building smart homes using cognitive dynamic system. The main contribution of this paper is the combination of cognitive dynamic system and IoT to form CIoT (Cognitive IoT). A model was proposed based on fog computing, which helps in location-awareness, latency-sensitive monitoring, and intelligent control [5]. This model helps to support quick response at neighborhood-wide, community-wide, and city-wide levels, providing high-computing performance and intelligence in future smart cities. Further, the relationship between the smart city and IoT was explained in [6], while in [7] explains the economic and pricing policies and their relationships in communication and data collection using IoT. Further, researchers survey the architecture for smart cities [8] and consider security perspectives of a smart city [9]. Further, in support of smart cities intelligent IOT gateway is required [10]. This model helps in overcoming the fragmentation problem and helps in enabling the efficient integration of horizontal IoT services.

Further, for making smart cities, smart parking lots should be planned properly [11]. Smart parking system provides the facility to trace arrival and departure times of various cars [12]. Thus, these parking plenty must be planned in the sort of way to take a number of cars in each location into consideration. Furthermore, new parking lots ought to be installation wherein there are extra cars [13]. This provider works based totally on street sensors and intelligent displays which lead drivers to the satisfactory direction for parking within the city [14]. Furthermore, healthcare system should also be well planned for a smart city. Various health-monitoring systems have been proposed for getting the location of the ambulance, blood product and different organs for transplantations [15]. A model was proposed for bio-signal monitoring system in which the patient condition is investigated through heterogeneous wireless access-based methods to enable for getting the patient data anywhere [16]. For a smart city, proper weather system should be properly planned. Several works have been done in the field of weather systems by using sensors for supplying data such as temperature, rain, solar irradiation, and wind speed [17].

9.3   What Makes Smart Cities Smart?

Before diving into the implantation part, it should research a segment of the portions of smart urban networks. A sharp city has stores of use cases for AI-controlled IoT-enabled advancement, from keeping up a progressively favorable condition to improving open vehicle and security as appeared in Figure 9.2.

9.3.1   Intense Traffic Management

AI and IoT can realize canny traffic answers for ensure that tenants of a savvy city get beginning with one point then onto the following in the city

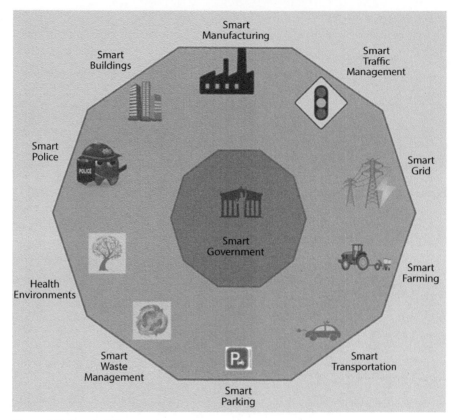

Figure 9.2 Smart cities overview.

as safely and profitably as could sensibly be normal. Los Angeles is one of the most blocked urban networks on earth to grasp shrewd traffic answer for control the movement of traffic as appeared in Figure 9.3. It has presented road surface sensors and shut circuit TV cameras that send constant updates about the traffic stream to a central traffic the board system. The data feed from cameras is poor down and advises the customers regarding the blockage and traffic signal glitches.

9.3.2   Smart Parking

Finding a halting opening especially during event time is a real fight. With road surface sensors embedded in the ground on parking spots, quick halting game plans can choose if the parking spots are free or included and make a progressing halting guide as appeared in Figure 9.4. This will in

Figure 9.3 Traffic management.

Figure 9.4 Smart parking.

like manner limit the time drivers expected to clutch find an empty space which would similarly help diminishing blockage and defilement.

9.3.3   Smart Waste Administration

Waste grouping and its real organization and move are a fundamental city organization. This development in the urban masses requires the apportionment of splendid techniques for waste the board. Getting AI for insightful reusing and waste the officials can give a legitimate waste organization structure. One such model could be of Barcelona's waste organization structure which has sensors and contraptions fitted on waste canisters that send notification to the pros to dispatch the waste variety trucks when they are full. They moreover keep discrete canisters for paper, plastic, glass, and waste sustenance things in every district.

9.3.4   Smart Policing

Since offense is certain, sharp urban networks moreover require astute policing where law approval workplaces use verification-based data driven philosophies that are convincing, gainful, and moderate. In Singapore, where this has quite recently been begun, an arrangement of cameras and sensors have been presented in essentially every corner which recognizes people who are smoking in confined zones or are faltering from a raised structure dwelling as appeared in Figure 9.5. The cameras engage the pros to screen swarm thickness, orderliness of open regions and moreover track the precise improvement of each enrolled vehicle.

9.3.5   Shrewd Lighting

Street lights are basic; anyway, they eat up a lot of imperativeness, which can be lessened with the use of smart lighting. Other than this, the light posts can, in like manner, be fitted with additional sensors or fill in as Wi-Fi mastermind hotspots. The lights can in like manner change the magnificence subject to the proximity of individuals by walking, cyclists, or vehicles as appeared in Figure 9.6. It uses a continuous cross-section framework to trigger neighboring lights and causes a protected to drift of light around a human occupant.

9.3.6   Smart Power

The principal manner of thinking of keen urban territories is to make a pleasing and supportive life for its tenants. Subsequently, canny city structure

Figure 9.5 Smart policing.

Figure 9.6 Shrewd lighting.

Figure 9.7 Smart power.

is not done without sharp organization. Splendid organization surmises the use of ICT keenly in order to improve fundamental administration through better planned exertion among different accomplices, remembering government and occupants as appeared for Figure 9.7. Insightful organization would have the alternative to use data, evidence, and various resources for improve essential administration and consistence toward the necessities of the occupants.

9.4   In Healthcare System

According to the CB Insights report of 2016, about 86% social insurance and life science associations including tech suppliers for human services are utilizing AI. A normal of $54 million will be expensed by these associations on AI by 2020. In medicinal services, man-made brainpower has a boundless degree. It is utilized in overseeing therapeutic records and patient history. Robots assemble, store, and redesign information to give simple access. Man-made intelligence is sent in planning a treatment framework for a specific patient. It examinations information, keeps beware of patient reports, clinical evaluation, and outside research and redoes the course of treatment.

Simulated intelligence–based applications are utilized in computerized conference. The clients can nourish their side effects into the application which prescribes suitable activity by investigating the client's restorative history. One such application is being utilized in the UK which is known as "Babylon". Another application utilized in Boston Children's Hospital gives fundamental well-being data to debilitated youngsters and answers prescription related inquiries and recommends whether the kid needs to see a specialist or not. Body checks that utilization AI can without much of a stretch pre analyze an individual thinking about the hereditary qualities and anticipates the conceivable outcomes of medical problems that may happen in future.

9.5   In Homes

Home computerization is only the ability displayed by man-made reasoning. Everything from keen meters to shrewd security in the house is overseen by AI.

9.6   In Aviation

Man-made reasoning is conveyed in plane test systems to process the information caught from recreated flights. Computer-based intelligence is likewise utilized in re-enacted airplane fighting. Utilization of AI autopilot is not new. Shockingly, utilization of autopilots in business flights returns to 1914 thinking about the crudest type of autopilot. As per reports from The New York Times, the Boeing plane records for 7 minutes of physically directed trip on a normal which commonly includes the activities for departure and landing.

9.7   In Solving Social Problems

Numerous U.S. scholastic establishments are misusing AI to beat probably the best social and monetary difficulties. Like the Center for Artificial

Intelligence in Society (built up by University of Southern California) is utilizing AI in fighting social issues, for example, vagrancy. Stanford analysts are utilizing AI in discovering the territories concentrated with most elevated levels of neediness through satellite pictures.

Ninety-seven percent of social insurance solicitations utilized in Netherlands are advanced. AI is utilized to neutralize shortcomings during medications, work process wasteful aspects, and forestalls persistent hospitalization if not required.

9.8   Uses of AI-People

9.8.1   Google Maps

As each Google client realizes, Google Maps helps in recognizing any mainstream or remote area just with a tap as shown in Figure 9.8. Moreover, maps can, without much of a stretch, examine traffic developments and report any sort of mishaps, developments, or any significant thing occurring along the street you drive. It helps workers in proposing the briefest course that sets aside time and cash both. This occurs through machine insight dealing with exponential measures of datasets at rocket speed.

9.8.2   Ridesharing

Uber and Ola use AI to foresee the rider request, decide cost, and decrease the holdup timing. The whole get to drop replacement is advanced. Danny Lange, Uber's Head of Machine Learning, says that Uber utilizes AI for

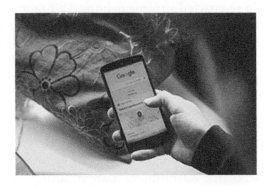

Figure 9.8 Google maps.

ETAs for rides. It assesses feast conveyance times on UberEATS and examines ideal get areas and misrepresentation discovery.

9.8.3 Voice-to-Text

The average element of the present cell phones is Google's voice-to-content. It causes you in changing over your recorded discourse into content while performing search capacities. This application is accessible coordinated with other versatile applications as well. This framework utilizes counterfeit neural systems for voice change. Microsoft avows to have made an all the more dominant discourse acknowledgment device that can decipher discourse with more exactness contrasted with people.

9.8.4 Individual Assistant

Smart frameworks like Google Now which is supplanted by a further developed framework called Google collaborator can act like your own colleague by utilizing AI. It can assist you with setting updates, make a plan for the day, and complete web searches and substantially more. Then again, an all the more dominant AI device, Alexa, tunes in to your voice direction and as needs be makes plan for the day, orders things on the web, and replies to your inquiries through a web search. Incorporated with keen speakers, for example, Echo, it can play music per your interest, request a pizza, book a taxi, and even connection with other savvy home gadgets. There are a lot progressively such AI applications that are being utilized by individuals and the savvy urban areas around the world. Be that as it may, the number is truly not significant. Significant is the way shrewdly you retain man-made consciousness into your way of life.

9.9 Difficulties and Profit

Machine-based knowledge is changing the way in which urban zones work, pass on, and keep up open accommodations, from lighting and transportation to network and prosperity organizations. Regardless, the gathering can be prevented by the decision of advancement that does not successfully participate or arrange with other city organizations. From this time forward, it is basic to consider retrofitted plans.

Another critical thing to manage while grasping AI is facilitated exertion. For urban networks to truly benefit by the potential that insightful urban regions offer, a change in mindset is required. The pros should plan and over various divisions. Despite the way that the fiscal remittance can be another issue to consider, the delayed consequences of the successful execution of insightful city portions over the world exhibit that at whatever point completed fittingly, sharp urban territories are generally moderate. Savvy city progress makes occupations, yet in addition helps spare the earth, lessen vitality consumption, and produce more income.

9.10 Innovations in Smart Cities

Innovation has gotten the supposed "backbone" for the brilliant urban communities. It is absolutely impossible that we can overlook the word "innovation" while discussing shrewd urban areas. The term has been rising wherever as urban areas contend to exhibit how information get to, mechanization, fiber systems can make them progressively associated, livable, and supportable.

Truly, the facts demonstrate that innovation is significant to create, upgrade, and continue the savvy city space as shown in Figure 9.9. Nonetheless, amidst this tumultuous environment where keen city innovation has become the focal point of activity for urban organizers, urban overseers, land organizations, and private innovation firms, human centricity has gone fluffy.

We do not deny the way that savvy urban communities around the globe are building up the space keeping livability one of the center motivations.

Figure 9.9 Innovation in urban communities.

Be that as it may, notwithstanding this methodology, occupants of brilliant urban communities are not ready to associate with their city well. There is something that as yet needs. In any case, what is going on here? We should discover it out from the realities talked about ahead.

9.11 Beyond Humans Focus

To get keen, a city must get human. Despite the fact that right, this really animates a dubious idea at the top of the priority list. What does it truly mean to get human? Let us comprehend this with greater lucidity. A city envelops a cover of framework that incorporates structures, green spaces, travel frameworks, roadways, pathways, and considerably more. Thinking about the present situation, each shrewd city framework is furnished with the trend setting innovation of 21st century. Be that as it may, the way every individual experience these frameworks are not general. Consistently, every individual uses and encounters the urban offices in various manners. So, it is coherent to state that savvy urban areas are not molded by the innovation, however, by the individuals who utilize the innovation.

Accordingly, it is significant for the keen urban communities to see how they can archive, organize, and bolster singular human experience through the sensible selection of arranged innovation and information. Grasping this sort of an individualistic methodology and structuring responsive frameworks, approaches, and administration around people is vital to turning out to be what we call it as "human".

9.12 Illustrative Arrangement

Congestion in certain pieces of the city represent a more noteworthy strain on a specific region prompting elevated levels of air contamination which thusly can affect human well-being adversely. For keen city pioneers, the inquiry that emerges here is which activities could bring about most prominent improvement in blockage just as general well-being.

Satirically, the cutting edge sensors introduced at street convergence can assemble enormous measures of information, yet they do not give all way to examine it. They can give a rich image of the physical city yet not the social city. Information researchers need instruments they have to comprehend various components that impact the manner in which urban areas work. Henceforth, to comprehend the equivalent another mechanical idea called specialist based demonstrating has become exposed.

Operator-based demonstrating is a sort of PC recreation which builds up a model of the conduct of people as they move around and associate in a virtual world. A city could have its very own operator-based model by including virtual workers, walkers, cabbies, customers, and so forth. This model can incorporate the qualities of the people that are later customized by analysts considering hypotheses and information about how individuals act. Going further, researchers could examine the congested driving conditions or social isolations by joining the urban datasets with the specialist based model of individuals followed by tweaking and re-running the model. In the long run, when they land at the correct model, they could think back on the conduct and attributes of their virtual residents to more readily comprehend why a traffic blockage develops at a specific spot (for instance) and help the city to determine the issue. Moreover, if the model functions admirably in the ongoing, it could be conceivable to perform transient estimates on a specific occasion in the city—simply like the traffic blockage.

9.13   Smart Cities with No Differentiation

We comprehended a piece of becoming "human" in keen urban areas. Another significant point of view that mirrors the genuine importance of being human is the means by which keen urban communities take care of urban issues while concentrating on each sex, each age, and each class of individuals. Since be it poor or rich, ladies or men, and old or youthful, everyone has various needs and encounters that connection with each part of a shrewd city as shown in Figure 9.10. Everyone's administration should be at the focal point of the origination and configuration procedure of a city.

Ladies have fewer than 20% of expert occupations in ICT to their name. This speaks to that ladies are not getting equivalent chances with the goal that they can feature their viewpoints, initiative characteristics, and inventiveness in the savvy city space. Nonetheless, this does not imply that ladies are not making extraordinary walks in making a brilliant and comprehensive future for urban locales. We have the case of Mayor Ann-Sofie Hermansson of Gothenburg who teamed up with Volvo to get ready for self-driving vehicles—demonstrating the centrality of open private organization. In Vienna, a conjunctive exertion to see how ladies utilize urban foundation leads to progress in lighting offices, person on foot development and open vehicle. This upgraded the livable benchmarks both for people.

Figure 9.10 Smart cities for all.

On the off chance that ladies are offered opportunity to feature their abilities, keen urban areas will have extra half of the human inventive insight tending to the issues of the urban space. Dr. Ayesha Khanna Co originator and CEO of ADDO AI, Singapore pushed the way that human centricity is vital to making effective shrewd urban areas at the Fujitsu World Tour in Stockholm this year. She said that shrewd city thought is not only for the rich urban areas yet in addition for the more unfortunate zones far and wide.

"There are a great many minimal ranchers on the planet that live between $1 and $4 per day and they are unimaginably powerless against a wide range of dangers, floods, bothers, and soil disintegration. No one discloses to them when to plant a specific seed. They use age-old strategies that they have been utilizing for a considerable length of time. No one lets them know there is a nuisance invasion coming and they need manure. In any case, with man-made consciousness, we can do only that. We are building another stage those utilizations remote detecting satellite symbolism and computerized reasoning to really illuminate ranchers early if there is an irritation pervasion in a neighboring town, or when they can anticipate downpour."

9.14   Smart City and AI

The Road and Transport Authority (RTA) has for some time been taking a shot at utilizing the intensity of man-made consciousness in all divisions of traffic the board. What is more, presently, it has effectively propelled its

"Raqeeb System" which helps in watching the prosperity of 300 transport drivers in Dubai. Organization of this AI-fueled framework has prompted a sensational decrease in the quantity of mishaps that are caused because of tired transport drivers on the streets of Dubai as shown in Figure 9.11. The framework discovered that five out of eight mishaps happen every day because of exhaustion or absence of mindfulness. Raqeeb System has had the option to lessen the quantity of fatigue related mishaps by 65%, according to RTA. Right now, the authority has brought the framework into two of its Dubai Trams on a preliminary premise. The framework is one among the 75 AI ventures which are set up as a feature of the Smart City and Artificial Intelligence Program over the emirate.

The AI-based activities include the establishment of observation cameras in more than 10,000 taxicabs. This progression has prompted 83% expansion in consumer loyalty, according to RTA. Another activity to screen transport paths has diminished the quantity of transport path infringement by 83% and improved the timeliness of transports by 20%. Moreover, a savvy walker flagging framework has been built up in 15 areas. This framework increments or diminishes the time required for the people on foot to go across a street relying upon the pedestrian activity present at a specific time. As it is realized that Dubai is one of the spots where breezing through a driving assessment is dubious, even the student's drivers' aptitudes are currently being tried utilizing AI innovation.

The RTA has led the keen yard for testing student drivers in 14 areas which was finished effectively. The keen city has changed driver testing

Figure 9.11 Smart cities to prevent road accidents.

vehicles into brilliant vehicles that are equipped in identifying the testing moves and estimating the driver's reaction to everyone. The brilliant yard is outfitted with modern cameras and sensors associated with a focal processor equipped for social affair data and consequently identifying mistakes. The framework can give the test outcomes naturally—regardless of whether the driver has fizzled or passed.

UAE intends to be one of the main AI-fueled nations on the planet and "The National Artificial Intelligence Strategy 2031" is moving quickly to satisfy the vision over each part of society including taxpayer supported organizations, human services, versatility, and training, and that is only the tip of the iceberg. Thus, will get return again with additionally fascinating headways with regard to the Middle East locale!

9.15 Further Associated Technologies

Various parts of AI and ML can add to development of smart cities [18].

9.15.1 Model Identification

City cooperative energy is maybe the most significant part of AI in shrewd urban communities. It helps in contemplating and examining data that is as of now present, to settle on better choices later on while managing some noteworthy changes in their activities. Because of the multifaceted nature of urban communities, numerous difficulties may emerge during the use of a reasonable model. Deciding the correct model for every city assumes a significant job in diminishing the money related danger of tremendous forthright capital expenses. AI characterization calculations like Bayes Network (BN), Naïve Bayesian (NB), J48, and Nearest Neighbor (NN) can be utilized to foresee climate information particularly temperature and downpour [19].

9.15.2 Picture Recognition

This can be an intriguing method to battle traffic and is as of now steady in the bustling avenues of New York City. IntelliScape.io has joined forces with the NYC Department of Transportation to comprehend and check significant traffic occasions in the city. This, when applied in all the traffic ridden urban areas on the planet, will have a constructive outcome toward lessening traffic and henceforth will spare a great deal of time. The wondrous blend of AI and picture acknowledgment empowers the framework to identify automobile overloads, leaving infringement, and climate projections and send continuous cautions to city authorities. The cameras fixed at the crossing points catch and procedure action, stream back discoveries, and significant information continuously, such as sending traffic alerts for vehicles abusing the principles. This innovation can be mixed with climate, segment, and area explicit information for ongoing investigation.

The procedure of item acknowledgment utilizing MF ArtMap classifier can be utilized in rush hour gridlock checking frameworks. In this procedure, we catch the picture of an obscure vehicle, set up its picture, remove nearby highlights, pass the neighborhood include descriptors to the MF ArtMap classifier, get the rundown comprising of classes and participation estimations of test to these classes, and apply heuristics to give results [20].

9.15.3   IoT

An IoT framework incorporates data from huge ranges of sensors. This data should be decreased with the goal that it very well may be taken care of by existing systems, screened to guarantee honesty and to guarantee it follows security strategies and handled and put away so it gets usable to the possible purchasers [21]. The three basic highlights of a brilliant city are being instrumented, interconnected, and smart. This is accomplished

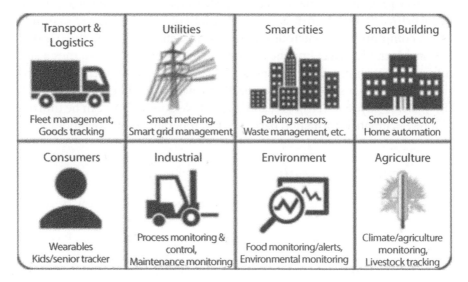

Figure 9.12 Applications of IoT.

through IoT. It serves to remotely screen, control and oversee gadgets, get to constant information, and dissect it by introducing sensors (RFID, IR, GPS, laser scanners, and so forth.), interface them to the web and accomplish canny acknowledgment, following, checking, area and the executives. Some significant uses of IoT are appeared in Figure 9.12. IoT can be executed for proficient stockpile and use of water, imaginative answer for traffic clog, progressively solid open vehicle, changing structures to be vitality effective and for open security. ICT has applications in the field of medication, transport, the travel industry, and administration; wrongdoing avoidance, fiasco the board, and the rundown go on. One of the applications is surrounding helped living for senior residents. This innovation empowers them to remain at home and get their body parameters distinguished time to time by wearing body sensors [22].

9.15.4   Big Data

RFID labels on vehicles will help in managing and estimating traffic. Another system of producing power from trash gathered in a city is being created by CISCO. This will help with dispensing with dump trucks from the city. Information can make life more verified—youngsters playing in the parks can wear a sensor-installed arm ornament, which tracks them on the off chance that they disappear. Keen Energy Grids are another development in this field. They can be utilized to distinguish the nearness of individuals in a specific region and modify the road lights appropriately, which permits sparsely populated zones to turn off their lights and spare vitality.

Huge information can likewise empower fiasco versatility for a brilliant city. Fiasco administrators can distinguish the potential hazard; make activities to forestall the hazard lastly empower city's flexibility [23]. Enormous information gathered from different medical clinics the nation over can decide basic manifestations about another ailment and work together in spreading mindfulness and finding the correct remedy for the sickness, in this way sparing the lives of a great many individuals. This idea can be taken to a worldwide level where specialists from various medical clinics from everywhere throughout the world meet up to totally annihilate such lethal sicknesses.

9.15.5   Deep Learning

This strategy has been broadly and adequately utilized for the examination of various types of information including pictures, recordings, discourse, and message. In keen urban communities, there is a great deal of time arrangement information which is transferred from the sensors. Luckily, profound learning has gained a ton of ground in the field of computerized reasoning in the ongoing years and loans itself to consecutive information investigation. It very well may be utilized for air quality expectation in brilliant urban areas. This model comprises of LSTM neural systems alongside SVR [24]. Profound learning stage encourages speedy structure of different applications utilizing succession learning models to take care of issues of fluctuated unpredictability including water dispersion and spillage identification, vitality preservation, squander transfer, and some more. At the point when the motors have been prepared utilizing profound learning systems, the actuators that take activities naturally can likewise be controlled.

9.16   Challenges and Issues

In what follows, we feature a few testing issues and challenges.

9.16.1   Profound Learning Models

Analysts have applied diverse essential profound learning designs in tackling numerous handy issues and accomplished promising outcomes. The basic concern in these examinations has been high exactness (e.g., for classification) or low bungle (e.g., for expectation). Computation unpredictability, e.g., preparing cost, has been to a great extent overlooked. It additionally appears that the specialists have not been completely mindful of some most recent advancement in profound learning. As system structures become further and more profound, learning will, in general, be amazingly hard and in proficient. A great part of the ongoing examination stresses of learn effectiveness, for instance, (ResNet) Deep Residual Network in [25] presented alternate way associations that permit convolution neural systems to have very profound structures without significantly expanding calculation intricacy. Transformer-based strategies [26] utilized just consideration instruments with position installing to take in portrayals from arrangement information. It not just improved the cutting edge in the zone of machine interpretation yet in addition accomplished signification improvement in preparing time. Similarly, trust that brilliant city analysts focus on the learning proficiency in planning profound models and incorporate calculation multifaceted nature as the extra assessment metric.

9.16.2 Deep Learning Paradigms

Unaided learning will become undeniably increasingly significant in the more extended term, as human and creature learning is to a great extent solo and they find the structure of the world for the most part by perception [27]. It is specific case meant for brilliant urban information, that is on perception and a large portion for which is unlabeled. Generative ill-disposed system is a promising solo worldview initially structured in the field of picture handling [28]. It is a powerful (unaided) generative system has two contending neural systems (i.e., discriminator and generator) prepared at the same time. It has been utilized to create photos that take a gander in any event superficially bona fide to individual onlookers. Likewise has extraordinary prospective in savvy city application to notify the issues, for example, lost sensor information estimation, peculiarity location for condition and shipping, motor vehicle identification and re-identification in open well-being, and numerous others.

Move knowledge is a learning engineering to increased expanding considerations as of late. In reasonable applications, regularly, the marked informational collections might be too specific or little to prepare successful models without any preparation. For this situation, move learning can be applied: first taking in a rough model from a pre-prepared system on an enormous related informational collection and afterward new-tune the system with the information for additional task. For instance, information picked up by figuring out how to perceive numerous classes with enormous informational index could apply to perceive specific classes. One might say, move learning energizes reuse of existing educated models and can possibly spare extensive calculation cost. Information in brilliant city is exceptionally circulated; for one application area, information gathered from various land areas shares a lot of shared characteristic. This trademark makes move adapting especially appealing for progressively productive information examination. Truth be told, that applied a set quantity of little level concentrates, for example, fire recognition [29] and parking garage location [30]. Later on, it would expect broad utilizations of move learning in numerous other shrewd city spaces. Creating powerful profound models requires considerable endeavors in design building which is tedious and costly procedure. Neural Architecture Search (NAS) is a developing profound learning worldview that means to naturally and additionally plan powerful profound structures for specific errands limiting human support. The fascinating exploration heading has immediately drawn impressive consideration of specialists from computational knowledge, specifically, developmental registering. As of late, transformative calculations (e.g., hereditary programming) [31, 32] and support learning–based strategies includes that utilized to structure latest neural models. Research has revealed that the profound models found by NAS can beat an enormous number of physically planned models. In spite of the fact that the present NAS strategies generally center around picture classification assignments, it accepts that worldview will apply to another profound model and utilized keen urban spaces sooner rather than later.

9.16.3   Confidentiality

Though brilliant metropolitan applications may guarantee our living condition more secure, greener, and progressively maintainable, as additionally brings difficulties with respect to residents' protection. With so much information gathered, put away, investigated, and utilized, regularly by obscure gatherings, residents truly stress over their own data being abused or mishandled by governments and organizations. As opposed to anticipating for the laws and guidelines to be made, the examination network has just begun formulating different systems in securing residents' secretive information, e.g., data allotment, records modification, information mining calculation, information covering up, and protection safeguarding [33]. As of late, for the most part, touchy information type, i.e., medicinal information, examines can apply to the Generative Adversarial Network to deliver great manufactured patient records [34] and area-based information to ensure individual delicate data and revealed promising outcomes on genuine information in numerous analyses [35]. In any case, here is no such procedure that protects residents' security in all circumstances. Otherwise, further developed methods for particular applications should be created, on different, laws and guidelines for ensuring security, e.g., the General Data Protection Regulation (GDPR) from EU, are required.

9.16.4   Information Synthesis

Up until now, shrewd city has showed up as an assortment of inexactly coupled applications in various spaces, and little connection can be identified from these applications. The ebb and flow inquire about is a lot of like applying profound figuring out how to recognize and remove superficial information. Information from various spaces might be corresponded and may influence one another, e.g., terrible climate may influence traffic conditions, traffic blockage may bring about additional fuel utilization, air and clamor contamination, and such contamination may cause cardiovascular and respiratory illness. Be that as it may, such relationships have been to a great extent ignored in the current research. Savvy urban is likewise a Cyber-Physical-Social framework (CPS) and the information from the digital, physical, and social universes has various qualities, for instance, reliability of the information gathered from the social world might be flawed; and information as of the objective world ordinarily have low-level semantics and cannot be effectively coordinated with social information. Be that as it may, information found from various universes can supplement and fortify each other so as to determine progressively significant bits of knowledge, e.g., traffic peculiarity can identified by both circle sensor introduced on streets and internet based life information distributed on the web. The data from the two unique sources changes in nature yet gives subtleties supplementing each other accept that increasingly wise information can be inferred in the event that it can find the relationships among information since the physical, digital, and community universes. This information combination procedure requires methods that can adequately deal with cross-area and multi-modular information. On the off chance that think a brilliant town as an integrative framework needs to interconnect the resulted information examination into every entity space and wire the scholarly information any place conceivable to make a framework that is really shrewd. Profound learning systems are considered as acceptable competitors for the information combination [36, 37].

9.16.5 Distributed Intelligence

A model was proposed based on "disseminated insight", which moves a significant part of the savvy computation (e.g., reasoning, smoothing, data aggregation, and investigation) as of server farms to the a lot littler even as independent unit at various level of urban environment, e.g., sensor nodes, gateways of smart phones, wireless sensor networks, or versatile edge systems [38]. In request to handle the difficulties brought next to the volume and speed of enormous urban information. Thus, it needs to mull over the capacity of these figuring gadgets as they are far less ground-breaking contrasted with servers in server farms. For profound learning, the need to grow all the more light weight models is conceived so they can be executed on the capacity obliged gadgets. Distributed knowledge additionally gives incredible potential to move realizing, where pre-prepared models are embedded into conveyed gadgets for fine-tuning.

9.16.6   Restrictions of Deep Learning

Albeit profound learning has exhibited extraordinary achievement and outflanked numerous other traditional AI techniques, it is anything but a flexible answer for each application in keen city. There are at any rate various confinements that brilliant city analysts need to consider: 1) profound learning models are famously costly to prepare, and it is not phenomenal for the preparation to take day 7 with top of the line processing gadgets. In the interim, it is likewise hard to configure the models; in some cases, numerous examinations should be directed so as to find legitimate or approach ideal configurations; 2) for regulated adapting, enormous measure of preparing information is required. Applications where, just information of little or middle range is accessible, execution of a profound knowledge representation might not be ensure; and 3) an adapted profound representation is generally difficult to decipher in natural manners. It generally mechanism like a "black box" directs a contribution to a yield and may not be a decent.

9.17   Conclusion and Future Scope

Brilliant city information examination is a mind-boggling research point because of a few reasons, for example, a wide range of errands in a wide range of use areas, the enormous measure of information of various kinds and modalities, and the spatial and fleeting conditions among the information. Along these lines, the current exploration on the meeting area with profound knowledge and on the shrewd urban is assessed and intended to draw an unmistakable scene for it. From the strategy arranged point of view, it hence introduced, in detail, extraordinary essential and broadened profound learning models and examined how these methods empower information revelation from city information; while from the application situated viewpoint, since, it showed how issues in specific applications can be tended to by different profound learning strategies. Consequently, further exploring various difficulties in this field, future research headings for this quickly advancing field can be suggested like developing profound learning standards, profound learning–based information combination, and security safeguarding. Savvy city analysts additionally investigate this energizing exploration point and grow increasingly imaginative and computationally down to earth profound learning models and AI utilizing IoT specifically intended for shrewd city applications.

References

1. Kaltenrieder, P., Portmann, E., Myrach, T., Fuzzy knowledge representation in cognitive cities. *Proceedings of IEEE International Conference on Fuzzy Systems*, Turkey, pp. 1–8, 2015.
2. Vlacheas, P., Giaffreda, R., Stavroulaki, V., Kelaidonis, D., Foteinos, V., Poulios, G., Demestichas, P., Somov, A., Biswas, A.R., Moessner, K., Enabling smart cities through a cognitive management framework for the internet of things. *IEEE Commun. Mag.*, 51, 6, 102–111, 2013.
3. Wu, Q., Ding, G., Xu, Y., Feng, S., Du, Z., Wang, J., Long, K., Cognitive Internet of Things: a new paradigm beyond connection. *IEEE Internet Things J.*, 1, 2, 129–143, 2014.
4. Feng, S., Setoodeh, P., Haykin, S., Smart Home: Cognitive Interactive People-Centric Internet of Things. *IEEE Commun. Mag.*, 55, 2, 34–39, 2017.
5. Tang, B., Chen, Z., Hefferman, G., Pei, S., Tao, W., He, H., Yang, Q., Incorporating Intelligence in Fog Computing for Big Data Analysis in Smart Cities. *IEEE Trans. Ind. Inf.*, 13, 5, 2140–2150, 2017.
6. Arasteh, H., Hosseinnezhad, V., Loia, V., Tommasetti, A., Troisi, O., Shafie-khah, M., Siano, P., IoT-Based Smart Cities: A Survey. *Proceedings of IEEE 16th International Conference on Environment and Electrical Engineering*, Florence, Italy, pp. 1–6, 2016.
7. Luong, N.C., Hoang, D.T., Wang, P., Niyato, D., Kim, D., II, Han, Z., Data collection and wireless communication in the Internet of Things (IoT) using economic analysis and pricing models: A survey. *IEEE Commun. Surv. Tutorials*, 18, 4, 2546–2590, 2016.
8. Silva, W.M., Alvaro, A., Tomas, G.H.R.P., Afsono, R.A., Dias, K.L., Garcia, V.C., Smart cities software architectures: A survey. *Proceedings of 28th Annual ACM Symposium on Applied Computing*, Coimbra, Portugal, pp. 1722–1727, 2013.
9. Ijaz, S., Shah, M.A., Khan, A., Ahmed, M., Smart cities: A survey on security concerns. *Int. J. Adv. Comput. Sci. Appl.*, 7, 2, 612–625, 2016.
10. Al-Fuqaha, A., Khreishah, A., Guizani, M., Rayes, A., Mohammadi, M., Toward better horizontal integration among IoT services. *IEEE Commun. Mag.*, 53, 9, 72–79, 2015.
11. Neyestani, N., Damavandi, M.Y., Shafie-Khah, M., Contreras, J., Catalão, J.P.S., Allocation of Plug-In Vehicles' Parking Lots in Distribution Systems

Considering Network-Constrained Objectives. *IEEE Trans. Power Syst.*, 30, 5, 2643–2656, 2015.

12. Yazdani-Damavandi, M., Moghaddam, M.P., Haghifam, M.R., Shafie-khah, M., Catalão, J.P.S., Modeling Operational Behavior of Plug-in Electric Vehicles' Parking Lot in Multienergy Systems. *Proceedings of IEEE Transmission and Distribution Conference and Exposition*, USA, pp. 124–135, 2016.

13. Neyestani, N., Damavandi, M.Y., Shafie-khah, M., Catalão, J.P.S., Modeling the PEV traffic pattern in an urban environment with parking lots and charging stations. *Proceedings of IEEE Eindhoven PowerTech*, Eindhoven, Netherlands, pp. 1–6, 2015.

14. Lee, S., Yoon, D., Ghosh, A., Intelligent parking lot application using wireless sensor networks. *Proceedings of the International Symposium on Collaborative Technologies and Systems*, Irvine, CA, USA, pp. 48–57, 2008.

15. Niyato, D., Hossain, E., Camorlinga, S., Remote patient monitoring service using heterogeneous wireless access networks: Architecture and optimization. *IEEE J. Sel. Areas Commun.*, 27, 4, 412–423, 2009.

16. Atzori, L., Lera, A., Morabito, G., The Internet of Things: A survey. *Comput. Networks*, 54, 15, 2787–2805, 2010.

17. Botta, A., De Donato, W., Persico, V., Pescapé, A., Integration of Cloud computing and Internet of Things: A survey. *Future Gen. Comput. Syst.*, 56, 684–700, 2016.

18. Navarathna, P.J. and Malagi, V.P., Artificial Intelligence in Smart City Analysis. *Proceedings of International Conference on Smart Systems and Inventive Technology*, Tirunelveli, India, pp. 44–47, 2018.

19. Chin, J., Callaghan, V., Lam, I., Understanding and personalizing smart city services using machine learning, The Internet-of-Things and Big Data. *Proceedings of IEEE 26th International Symposium on Industrial Electronics*, Edinburgh, UK, pp. 2050–2055, 2017.

20. Lorencik, D. and Zolotova, I., Object recognition in Traffic Monitoring Systems. *World Syposium on Digital Intelligence for Systems and Machines*, Kosice, Slovakia, pp. 277–281, 2018.

21. Harmon, R.R., Castro-Leon, E.G., Bhide, S., Smart cities and the internet of things. *Proceedings of International Conference on Management of Engineering and Technology*, Portland, USA, pp. 485–494, 2015.

22. Dlodlo, N., Gcaba, O., Smith, A., Internet of Things Technologies in Smart Cities. *Proceedings of IST-Africa Week Conference*, Durban, South Africa, pp. 1–7, 2016.

23. Yang, C., Su, G., Chen, J., Using big data to enhance crisis response and disaster resilience for a smart city. *Proceedings of IEEE 2nd International Conference on Big Data Analysis*, Beijing, China, pp. 504–507, 2017.

24. Kok, I., Simsek, M.U., Ozdemir, S., A deep learning model for air quality prediction in smart cities. *Proceedings of IEEE International Conference on Big Data*, Boston, MA, USA, pp. 1983–1990, 2017.

25. He, K., Zhang, X., Ren, S., Sun, J., Deep residual learning for image recognition. *Proceedings of IEEE Conference on Computer Vision and Pattern Recognition*, Las Vegas, NV, USA, pp. 770–778, 2016.

26. Verykios, V.S., Bertino, E., Fovino, I.N., Provenza, L.P., Saygin, Y., Theodoridis, Y., State-of-the-art in privacy preserving data mining. *ACM SIGMOD Record*, vol. 33, pp. 50–57, 2004.

27. LeCun, Y., Bengio, Y., Hinton, G., Deep learning. *Nature*, 521, 7553, 436–444, 2015.

28. Goodfellow, I., Abadie, J.P., Mirza, M., Xu, B., Farley, D.W., Ozair, S., Courville, A., Bengio, Y., Generative adversarial nets. *Proceedings of 27th International Conference on Neural Information Processing Systems*, pp. 2672–2680, 2014.

29. Muhammad, K., Ahmad, J., Baik, S.W., Early fire detection using convolutional neural networks during surveillance for effective disaster management. *Neurocomput.*, 288, 30–42, 2018.

30. Valipour, S., Siam, M., Stroulia, E., Jagersand, M., Parking-stall vacancy indicator system, based on deep convolutional neural networks. *Proceedings of IEEE 3rd World Forum on Internet of Things*, pp. 655–660, 2016.

31. Sun, Y., Yen, G.G., Yi, Z., Evolving unsupervised deep neural networks for learning meaningful representations. *IEEE Trans. Evol. Comput.*, 23, 1, 89–103, 2019.

32. Real, E., Moore, S., Selle, A., Saxena, S., Suematsu, Y.L., Le, Q., Kurakin, A., Large-scale evolution of image classifiers. *Proceedings of 34th International Conference on Machine Learning*, pp. 2902–2911, 2017.

33. Vaswani, A., Shazeer, N., Parmar, N., Uszkoreit, J., Jones, L., Gomez, A.N., Kaiser, L., Polosukhin, I., Attention is all you need. *Proceedings of 31st International Conference on Neural Information Processing Systems*, Long Beach, CA, USA, pp. 5998–6008, 2017.

34. Choi, E., Biswal, S., Malin, B., Duke, J., Stewart, W.F., Sun, J., Generating multi-label discrete patient records using generative adversarial networks. *Proceedings of 2nd Machine Learning for Healthcare Conference*, pp. 286–305, 2017.

35. Yin, D. and Yang, Q., GANs based density distribution privacy preservation on mobility data. *Secur. Commun. Network*, 2018, 2, 1–13, 2018.

36. Hou, J.-C., Wang, S.-S., Lai, Y.-H., Tsao, Y., Chang, H.-W., Wang, H.-M., Audio visual speech enhancement using multimodal deep convolutional neural networks. *IEEE Trans. Emerging Topics Comput. Intell.*, 2, 2, 117–128, 2018.

37. Wang, W., De, S., Zhou, Y., Huang, X., Moessner, K., Distributed sensor data computing in smart city applications. *Proceedings of IEEE 18th International Symposium on A World Wireless, Mobile and Multimedia Networks*, Macau, China, pp. 1–5, 2017.

38. Wang, W. and Zhang, M., Tensor deep learning model for heterogeneous data fusion in Internet of Things. *IEEE Trans. Emerging Topics Comput. Intell.*, To be published. 4, 1, 32–41, 2020.

Index